A CELTIC QUEST

SEXUALITY AND SOUL IN INDIVIDUATION

*A depth-psychology study of the
Mabinogion legend of Culhwch and Olwen*

by
JOHN LAYARD

Revised and Edited by Anne S. Bosch

1975

Spring Publications
c/o Postfach 190
8024 Zürich
Switzerland

ACKNOWLEDGEMENTS

This book was among several other full-length manuscripts that awaited publication when John Layard died in November 1974. It is the first work to be printed from his *Nachlass*. Fortunately, he had already appointed Anne S. Bosch to put the manuscript in order and see the book into print. Her devotion to this task in all its complexities and ramifications has made possible this substantial contribution to the psychology of individuation. She both collaborated on the text and supervised its production. Richard Layard generously contributed spiritually and materially to its publication. — J. H.

*

Kind permission has been received from the publishers to quote from the following works: *The Mabinogion* translated by T. P. Ellis and John Lloyd, Clarendon Press; *The Greek Myths* by Robert Graves, Penguin Books; *The Mabinogion* translated by Gwyn Jones and Thomas Jones, J. M. Dent and Sons; *The Gods of the Greeks* by Carl Kerényi, Thames and Hudson; *Celtic Heritage: Ancient Tradition in Ireland and Wales* by Alwyn Rees and Brinley Rees, Thames and Hudson.

John Layard acknowledged the kind assistance he received, with respect to matters concerning Welsh language and culture, from I. Ll. Foster, M.A., Professor of Celtic, Jesus College, Oxford. We are also indebted to the Department of Oral Tradition and Dialects, Welsh Folk Museum, St. Fagans, Glamorganshire, for invaluable assistance with meaning and location of place names and proper names, especially Robin Gwyndaf.

Linguistic notes are by Alexei Kondratiev, who has also made editorial contributions. (The modern Welsh spelling has been used throughout the text as much as possible, although this is sometimes at variance with quoted matter.)

The book was composed by Lynda Cowan and Daryl Sharp who also did the index. The cover is by Jan Luss. The illustrations are by Sarah Smith and Anne S. Bosch.

Spring Publications is a non-profit activity of
THE ANALYTICAL PSYCHOLOGY CLUB OF NEW YORK, INC.
28 East 39th Street, New York City 10016

ISBN 0-88214-110-4

Composed, Photo-offset and Manufactured in Switzerland
by Buchdruckerei Schrumpf, 8123 Ebmatingen Zürich
for Spring Publications, Postfach 190, 8024 Zürich

CONTENTS

FOREWORD

The Welsh word for meaning is simply *ystyr* — related to the Latin *historia*: story, history. The root of *ystyr* signifies "knowing, learned, wise man, judge".

Ancient Welsh storytellers have bequeathed us a precious key to their sense of meaning in *The Mabinogion*, which came to the attention of English-speaking readers when it was translated for the first time and published by Lady Charlotte Guest, in the middle of the nineteenth century. "Culhwch and Olwen" is one *cyfarwyddyd* — one story from the eleven in *The Mabinogion* collection. *Cyfarwyddyd*, however, implies more than does our word 'story' — as the ornateness of the word, strange to our 'English' eyes and tongues, suggests. The stem is *arwydd*, meaning "sign, symbol, manifestation, miracle"; and it comes from the root "to see". So *cyfarwyddyd* implies "guidance, direction, instruction, knowledge, skill, prescription".

The storyteller (*cyfarwydd*) himself "was originally a seer and a teacher who guided the souls of his hearers through the world of 'mystery' " (From A. and B. Rees: *Celtic Heritage: Ancient Tradition in Ireland and Wales.*)

A. S. B.

English-speaking readers are often intimidated by Welsh spelling: its outlandish appearance, they feel, must express correspondingly difficult sounds. This, however, is not the case. Welsh orthography is a logical phonetic system which can be mastered easily. Here are its essential rules:

Vowels have their "Continental" values, with the following exceptions:

u corresponds to French *u* and German *ü*, or (in modern Welsh) to the *ee* of English *deer*.

w corresponds to *oo* in English *moon*.

y has two sounds: 1) in the last syllable of a word, it is usually like *ee* in *deer*; 2) elsewhere it is pronounced like the *u* of English *but*, or German unaccented *e*.

The diphthongs *ae, oe, wy* are pronounced *ai, oi, ui*, while *ei* and *eu* are pronounced as in German.

Of the *consonants,* the following should be noted.

f corresponds to English *v*.

ff corresponds to English *f.*

th corresponds to *th* in English *thick*.

dd corresponds to *th* in English *then*.

ch is a guttural spirant, as in Scottish *loch* or German *Nacht*.

ll is a lateral spirant, related to *l* in the same way *th* is to *t* and *dd* is to *d*. It is pronounced by hissing with the tip of the tongue touching the palate.

c is always sounded like *k*, never like *s*.

r is trilled.

The other consonants are generally like their English counterparts.

Words are usually accented on the penultimate syllable.

Examples:

Culhwch — kil´ooch

Ysbaddaden Pencawr — isbatha´den pen ka´oor

Twrch Trwyth — toorch ´ troo´eth

A. K.

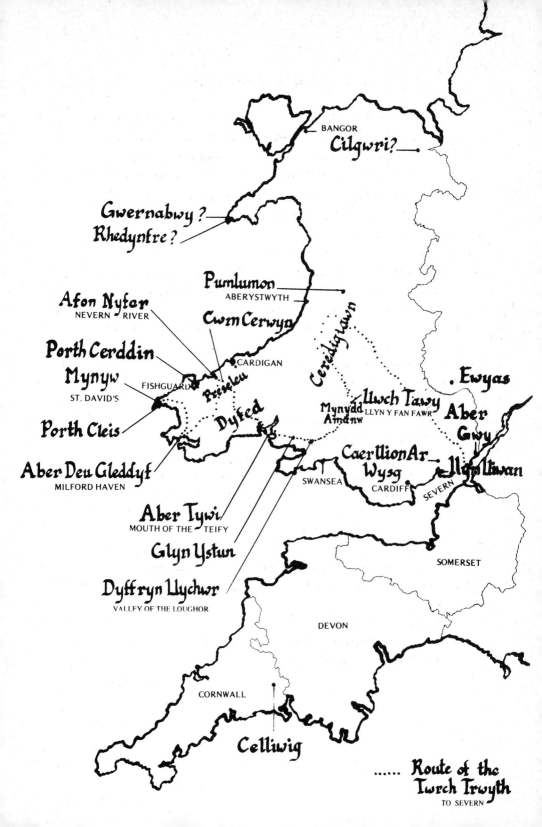

Cilgwri?

BANGOR

Gwernabwy ?
Rhedynfre ?

Pumlumon
ABERYSTWYTH

Cwm Cerwyn

Afon Nyfer
NEVERN RIVER

Ceredigiawn

Ewyas

Porth Cerddin

Mynyw
ST. DAVID'S

CARDIGAN

FISHGUARD

Preseleu

Dyfed

Llwch Tawy
LLYN Y FAN FAWR

Aber
Gwy

Mynydd
Amanw

Porth Cleis

Caerllion Ar
Wysg

Llan Lliwan

Aber Deu Gleddyf
MILFORD HAVEN

SWANSEA

CARDIFF

SEVERN

Aber Tywi
MOUTH OF THE TEIFY

SOMERSET

Glyn Ystun

Dyffryn Llychwr
VALLEY OF THE LOUGHOR

DEVON

CORNWALL

Celliwig

...... Route of the
Twrch Trwyth
TO SEVERN

CHAPTER 1

INTRODUCTORY: THE TWO MOTHERS

Of all mythological accounts of the boar hunt in Europe that have been recorded, that which touches most nearly the deepest levels of the human psyche is the remarkable tale called *Culhwch and Olwen,* appearing in that earliest written collection of Celtic bardic literature known since the days of Lady Charlotte Guest, its first translator into English, as *The Mabinogion.*

This term properly applies only to the four tales called "The Four Branches of the Mabinogi", from which she extended it to cover the eleven stories in the collection. The term *mabinogi* itself is of interest to us, being, according to G. and T. Jones, "by common consent of Welsh scholars to-day...derived from the word *mab* (youth), and is equated in meaning with the Latin *infantia* and the French *enfance.* It meant first 'youth', then a 'tale of a youth', then a 'tale of a hero', and finally little more than 'tale' or 'story'." (*The Mabinogion,* p. xii.)

The stories are a mixture of vivid fantasy and semi-historical or pseudo-historical fact, but their "matter is primarily mythology in decline and folk-lore, though it is unlikely that the story-tellers were themselves often, if ever, aware of this". (P. x.) But that many of the personages involved "are in both the literary and mythological sense of divine origin, is so conclusively to be proved from the Mabinogion itself...and from our knowledge of the myth-making and myth-degrading habits of our remote world-ancestors, that the theme needs no development at our hands." (P. x.) To take one example, as quoted from G. and T. Jones, it has been shown by Professor W. J. Gruffydd (*Math vab Mathonwy,* Cardiff: University of Wales Press Board, 1928) that, despite accretions and misunderstandings, the Four Branches of the Mabinogi are basically concerned with the birth, exploits, imprisonment and death of the mythological hero Pryderi.

These seem to have been written down early in the second half of the eleventh century. But *Culhwch and Olwen* appears, from the orthography and other evidence, to have been committed to writing in the tenth century.

It is of course agreed by all authorities that the tales must be much older than their transcription. Thus G. and T. Jones say "no one doubts that much of the subject matter of these stories is very old indeed, coeval maybe with the dawn of the Celtic world" (p. ix) and the oldest of them all, "the incomparable and unclassifiable *Culhwch and Olwen*", is described as "the earliest Arthurian tale in Welsh" (p. x). Ellis and Lloyd had previously said "It is the first of the five stories in the Mabinogion dealing with Arthur, and, unlike three of them, displays no foreign influence. It is purely Welsh." (Vol. I, p. 162.) Referring to the tasks set to the hero, they say "It is impossible to speculate as to the meaning if any of the tasks, or even as to the time when the stories originated. It may be noted, however, that the hunt of the *Twrch Trwyth* [the mythical man-boar, whom G. and T. Jones refer to as the Otherworld beast] which occupies so large a space in *Kulhwch and Olwen,* was known to Nennius in the eighth century; and it is referred to by him as if it were, even then, a story invested with the hoariest antiquity," which "carries us back frequently to the very dawn of history, in fact far back into pre-history". (Vol. I, p. 168.)

A still earlier reference than the eighth century is to be found in Lady Charlotte Guest's note (1877 edition, p. 260) on the alleged family connection of Culhwch's mother's father, Prince Anlawdd, another of whose daughters was the mother of a certain saint who flourished in the sixth century, while yet another of his daughters was Eigr, the fair Ygraine of romance and mother of King Arthur. This also explains the frequent references to Culhwch as being Arthur's cousin, each thus being the other's mother's sister's son. A further point of interest is the purely matrilineal nature of this 'cousinship'. Such matrilateral relationships are of frequent occurrence in this tale, and, as 'mythological' elements, are in strong contrast to the pronounced patrilineal or patrilateral nature of its more superficial 'historical' elements, in which the kinship between father and son is stressed, as over against that between mother and son in the mythology.

The references to Arthur may puzzle some who only see in him the King of the Round Table of later romance. As G. and T. Jones put it, in mentioning the historical and pseudo-historical references elsewhere, "it would be an omission not to stress that *Culhwch and Olwen* is a document of the first importance for a study of the sources of the Arthurian legend. The Arthur it portrays is, of course, remarkably unlike the gracious, glorious emperor of later tradition, whether exemplified in the literatures of France, Germany or England, or for that matter in the concluding romances of the present volume, subject as they have been to Norman-French influences" (p. xxii). The Arthur here seen is a British King "which in this connexion means Welsh" and is here "uncontaminated by the Cycles of Romance, though necessarily affected by the vast complex of Celtic myth and legend" (p. xxii). As will be seen in the following account, he is very far from holding himself aloof from the struggle, but himself does battle with elemental forces in the form not only of the 'boar' but also of the dread 'hag' herself, the 'Black Witch' who, as elsewhere invariably in all these mythological boar-tales, lurks behind and actually occasions the boar's devastating activities. Arthur plays the role of the superordinate hero to Culhwch's lesser but more individual one, killing the hag himself, despite the protestations of his non-understanding counsellors who, not recognising this as the supreme task needing the utmost and indeed 'superhuman' courage, think this beneath the dignity of so great a man. The fulfilling of this task is in fact the foundation of Arthur's greatness, as it is that ultimately of any 'hero'.

The tale of *Culhwch and Olwen* is, however, quite astonishing in the clarity with which it demonstrates from the very outset the existence in the hero-story (as in that of every individual life) of the problem of the 'two mothers': 'Mother Nature' on the one hand, and the 'Cultural or Initiating and apparently Bad Mother' (here, as so often, figuring as the stepmother) on the other, and how they interrelate. Here is the barest possible outline of the story. The 'natural mother' gives birth to the hero among the swine. She is in this respect to be equated as Great Mother with both Isis and Demeter, both of whom may have been, in their original symbolic manifestations, sows. Her son the hero himself is called *Culhwch* meaning "pig-run". The 'cultural mother' causes the hero to seek an unknown and far distant bride (Olwen) who shows certain indications of being a moon-maiden and, reading between the lines, is her own daughter, but not his father's; in other words a sister-bride of a peculiar kind, whose nature will be discussed later. The search for her involves mortal combat with the girl's father who is a fearsome giant, and the hunting of a boar-man named Twrch Trwyth of terrible power, capable of laying waste huge stretches of country and

4

slaying innumerable knights — a hunt conducted by Arthur himself on Culhwch's behalf. When the boar is at last conquered (though never killed — he is immortal and lives on for other heroes to fight), the 'hag' (Black Witch) appears, and it is here that Arthur does the terrible deed of slaying her. It turns out in the end, if once more we may read between the lines, that Boar-Hag-Witch-and-at-least-one-of-the-mothers, not to speak of the mother-nature-bound part of Culhwch himself, are all one; in other words the boar, like the giant, is the emissary of the Terrible Mother who is at the same time the Initiating One. When he and the hag have both been overcome by Arthur, Culhwch himself at last comes into his own and marries the moon maiden, who becomes his 'only wife', a sure sign that she is his sister-anima.

The name *Culhwch* has caused some difficulty to the translators, it having been rendered variously as 'swine's burrow' by Lady Charlotte Guest, and 'pig-run' by G. and T. Jones. These latter refer to it as "a fanciful explanation, from hwch: pig" (p. 95, note), while Ellis and Lloyd (p. 171, note 6) had previously described it as "a fanciful medieval philological derivation as if Kulhwch came from 'cil' a retreat, 'hwch' a sow". This view about 'fanciful explanations', on the part of the early chroniclers, of names otherwise appearing meaningless even in their time, is widespread among scholars, and doubtless this process has been at work at various times. But that it should be considered so widespread in Celtic literature as to include vast numbers of names at a time when men still thought and expressed themselves in symbols seems unlikely, and is possibly owing to a curious rationalistic misunderstanding of what myth is about. The characters in mythology are not people, any more than the images of persons seen in dreams are actual people. They do and are all sorts of things that no real 'person' would ever do or be, but appear as symbols for psychic attributes, or attitudes of the dreamer himself. Why else should dreams need to be 'interpreted'?

5

The basic factor is the dreamer's own psychic contents, which are mirrored in the dream images. So also in myth, the person — 'hero', 'villain', 'helper', 'mother', 'son', 'father' or whoever he or she may be, even if it be an animal, tree, plant, or sun or moon — is symbol for some kind of psychic factor operative in the general (collective) psyche of a given race or society at the time when the myth took shape. It is not the man (hero or what not) who is given a symbolic or chance name. It is the symbolic content which, since the psyche has no language except that of visual (and therefore symbolic) imagery, is clothed in the form of a man, woman, animal or whatever form the psyche chooses to express itself in, as most nearly symbolising what it wishes to convey.

Once this is understood, many names in Celtic mythological literature (as in other literatures, including most religious, mystical, and even imaginative satirical literature, not to speak of most fairy tales) can cease to be regarded as merely 'fanciful', and may be seen to express hidden truths by means of the very symbols that have appeared so childish or apparently meaningless. I would suggest here that Culhwch is one of these, the meaning of which is clear when we consider it in the context of the alleged (i.e. symbolic) birth of the hero among the swine from a mother who is herself symbolically a sow. *Hwch* does not mean simply 'pig' but specifically 'sow', and *kil* or *cil,* which Lady Charlotte Guest translates as 'burrow', and Ellis and Lloyd as 'a retreat', also has the meaning of something more like a 'ditch' or 'furrow', a crevice made or appearing in the earth. It needs little imagination (or rather an imagination tuned in to dream-imagery and mythological imagery in general, in which the earth is a woman made pregnant by the 'husbandman' who digs and sows the seed) to see in this an archetypal image of the entrance into the womb of the Earth Mother, in this case the sow, an entrance which is also an exit; so that the word Culhwch, translated hitherto as 'found in a swine's burrow' or 'found in a pig-run' may equally well mean 'found in a sow's vagina', or issuing from it, or even 'delivered from it' (in both senses, physiologically and spiritually), and so 'born of a sow'. This is in fact, according to the myth, precisely what he was.

This kind of symbolic thinking can be carried a step further when we come to consider the name of the mother herself, who, though symbolically a sow, is called Goleuddydd meaning something equivalent to 'the light of day' (*goleu,* light; *dydd,* day). Why should a sow be called 'the light of day' — which is in fact the sun? One of the answers to this apparent paradox is to be seen in the name of the distant bride whom Culhwch seeks out and finally weds as greatest possible antithesis to his own mother: Olwen, meaning literally 'white track' and which (as shown later) equates her with the moon. She is the moon-bride, the sister-anima representing the soul, and therefore symbolises an inward experience — that of the *hieros gamos* within the psyche (that is to say consummated symbolically at night time). Such an experience is therefore always connected with the 'moon' which symbolises inner consciousness, or introversion, as opposed to the sun representing extraversion or anything that happens openly in the full light of day.

Animal life is extravert, that is to say straight-forwardly instinctive and untransformed, and therefore connected with the day ('the woman clothed with the sun' who is anathema to the spiritually-minded writer of the Apocalypse, who wants all instinct changed into spirituality or 'inner' value). Demeter (in her 'sow' nature) is a typical extravert, in contrast to her daughter Persephone, queen of the underworld, who is equated, through transformation of her pig nature, with the moon.

In this way 'sow' and 'sun' or 'light of day' are psychologically equivalent, both being symbols of extraversion untransformed, on the most primitive matriarchal level. The sun, being the provider of all things and the life-giver at a time before the generative function of men was known, was thought to be female, a concept reversed in later patriarchal civilisations in which the sun is usually considered as male and the moon female.

Though there are one or two Christian references in the text, such as Culhwch being baptised (the transcribers were presumably monks), these are extremely rare and the whole story is obviously pre-Christian. The archetypal role of Culhwch himself can be seen not only from the name 'pig-run' he bears from having been born in one, thus demonstrating his place in pig mythology, but also from the fact that, in all this extensive literature with its innumerable repetitions of personal names, his own name is unique and nothing is known of him. As Lady Charlotte Guest tells, "beyond the adventures here ascribed to him, no particulars of the hero...have come down to us" (1877 edition, p. 259). He bears all the marks of a 'hero' in the psychological sense. He is of royal birth, but at the same time he is born like an animal. He has to seek an unknown bride. In order to win her, he has to overcome apparently invincible monsters, both 'male' and 'female', though not, as we have seen, without the help of Arthur who here appears as a kind of superordinate self. He is thus not one of the greatest heroes, accomplishing his tasks alone, but he is nevertheless a hero, and follows a hero's path.

Quotations to give the story itself are taken from G. and T. Jones's translation (pp. 95-136):

> Cilydd son of Cyleddon Wledig[1] wished for a wife as well born as himself. The wife that he took was Goleuddydd[2] daughter of Anlawdd Wledig.[3] After his stay with her the country went to prayers whether they might have offspring, and they got a son through the prayers of the country. But from the time she grew with child, she went mad [Lady Charlotte says, "became wild, and wandered about"] without coming near a dwelling. When her time came upon her,

her right sense came back to her; it came in a place where a swineherd was keeping a herd of swine, and through terror of the swine the queen was delivered. And the swineherd took the boy until he came to the court. And the boy was baptized, and the name Culhwch given to him because he was found in a pig-run. Nonetheless the boy was of gentle lineage: he was first cousin to Arthur. And the boy was put out to nurse.

And after that the boy's mother, Goleuddydd daughter of Anlawdd Wledig, grew sick. She called her husband to her, and quoth she to him, "I am going to die of this sickness, and thou wilt wish for another wife. And these days wives are the dispensers of gifts, but it is wrong for thee to despoil thy son. I ask of thee that thou take no wife till thou see a two-headed briar on my grave." That he promised her. She summoned her preceptor to her and bade him strip the grave each year, so that nothing might grow on it. The queen died. The king would send an attendant every morning to see whether anything was growing on the grave. At the end of seven years the preceptor neglected that which he had promised the queen. One day when the king was hunting, he drew near the graveyard; he wanted to see the grave whereby he was to take a wife. He saw the briar. And when he saw it the king took counsel where he might get a wife. Quoth one of his counsellors, "I could tell of a woman would suit thee well. She is the wife of king Doged."[4] They decided to seek her out. And they slew the king, and his wife they brought home with them, and an only daughter she had along with her; and they took possession of the king's lands.

It seems clear that in this opening scene of the two wives of Cilydd, who are to become the 'two mothers' (mother and stepmother) of the hero, his son Culhwch, we have, on the level of social anthropology, the extremes of matrilineal and patrilineal concepts. On the one hand we have the 'matrilineal mother' Goleuddydd, the natural or biological mother who does not live with her husband but lives her natural life 'in the country'. She has no use for a man except as a fertilising agent for the production of her hero-son. Below the anthropological level — that is to say on the level of the psyche — she is not even human. She is Nature itself. Her marriage even, and consequent conception of a human child, both send her 'mad' in the human sense and in the eyes of society. She cannot brook even a human habitation, much less the civilisation which it entails. Only by understanding this can we perceive the depth of meaning conveyed in the statement that "when her right sense came back to her" (that is to say her sense as a child of nature rather than as a product of human culture) she went, not to her husband but among the swine, to be delivered of her son. She thus saw to it that he also, despite his kingly lineage, was produced as a child of nature among the animals. It emphasises that if full spiritual life is to be attained "nature must come first", as the necessary foundation for any sound future development.

Added to this is the particular form taken by her 'naturality', that of, quite clearly, a sow. With all that we have learnt regarding the mythological role of sows, boars, and pigs in general as symbols of cultural and psychological transformation due to their fierce nature, their early domestication, and subsequent sacrifice, this by itself should give us a hint of what the story will be about. Swineherds abound in ancient literature all over Europe as guardians of animality domesticated for the use of man. It is to a swineherd that she entrusts her son whose father is unknown to him, or rather, to whom the myth-making archetypal wisdom which gave rise to the story entrusts him, as fitting foster-father of the child. The 'terror' of the swine that caused the mother to be delivered is characteristic of all transformation symbols, and represents the terror experienced by all natural phenomena at prospect of change. This terror is repeated later in the story in the descriptions of the mighty ravaging 'boar' that has to be overcome by every generation in turn, by every hero. He never dies since he appears again in every new life, and he is the image himself of nature outraged at having to be transformed, female in origin but in male guise to indicate its wild destructiveness.

Like mother, like child. The hero Culhwch has also a pig nature as indicated by his name. 'Born in a pig-run' is equivalent to being 'born of a sow'. Culhwch starts life equipped with all the powers of nature derived from his mother, who shares with other earth goddesses such as Isis and Demeter, the high distinction of bringing uncontaminated femininity (the productivity of nature) into the service of man. "Nonetheless the boy was of gentle lineage: he was first cousin to Arthur". We have seen how this cousinship to Arthur was also on a matrilateral basis. And Arthur was a bear, another of the great maternal symbols.

If Goleuddydd, Culhwch's natural mother, was 'matrilineal', existing in her own right independently of men, no greater contrast could be thought of than that with Cilydd's second wife, the hero's stepmother. Nothing could be more violently and absolutely 'patrilineal' than the way in which she was acquired, by Cilydd's men slaying her former husband, and by her meekness in acquiescing to her change of overlord. She is not even named. She is the 'patrilineal mother' in the sense that she was subservient to the father in a way that the natural mother most certainly was not, but in fact dominated him even to the extent of trying to prevent him, by a trick of which we shall have more to say later, from marrying again after her death. If he had not done so, there would have been no hero and no story. For this second mother was also the spiritual one, pointing the way by which

11

Culhwch should win his hero-hood by marrying her daughter.

This daughter is important. For it will be noted that, whereas the hero's natural, biological mother has an only son — the hero himself, by his own father — his spiritual mother has an only daughter who is not his father's and who is no blood relation to him at all. The spiritual mother thus has her individual being, apart from the father. But it is of a different kind from that of the natural mother. The mother-daughter relationship means something quite other than that between mother and son. We can, for example, postulate that the latter ('Every mother wants a son') is heterosexual. The former, however, has difficulties (possible sexual rivalries and other conflicts) and spiritual development of the daughter away from the mother is from the 'natural' to the 'unnatural'.

The 'patrilineal' (Erich Neumann — "a general psychological state") or 'spiritual' mother is, moreover, in terms of the story, the stepmother, who is traditionally bitter and hostile to the child. In this case, however, she is not so. For the figure of the stepmother is a very complex one. She is the 'bad mother' of innumerable fairy tales, but as these tales equally invariably end up with her defeat and with the counter-image of the fairy godmother who turns the child's misfortunes to good advantage, it becomes evident that she, as archetypal figure, cannot be wholly bad. The fairy godmother usually operates, if the child is a girl, by providing a king's son or fairy prince for her bed, which she would never have had but for the influence of the 'bad' stepmother. If the child is a boy, it is, with or without the intervention of the fairy godmother, his very misfortune, due to the wicked stepmother, that drives him out from home security into the hard world. Thence he returns a wealthy and self-made independent man apparently in spite of (but really because of) her apparent cruelty. Stepmother and fairy godmother are thus seen to represent two aspects of the same female spiritual principle, at first appearing to be 'bad' but turning into the 'good'. Such will be seen to be the nature of the stepmother in the present tale, who in fact causes the hero to undertake all sorts of fearsome tasks so as, in the end, to win the prize most worth having, the spiritual bride, or soul.

Let us examine first of all the relation between the 'two mothers' of our tale, the 'matrilineal' nature-mother and the 'patrilineal' spiritual one, both good and necessary, but the one static and the other dynamic. The 'static mother' is the 'matrilineal' or 'nature' one, who always wishes everything to remain just as it was, to reproduce her kind without change or transformation. Such was Goleuddydd, our hero's mother, who shunned human habitations and clung to her 'animal' nature despite the human son who had been begotten on her. We have already seen the positive side of her as Mother Nature bestowing the blessings of uncontaminated instinctive life on her progeny. But, like all archetypes, she is ambivalent. She also wishes to prevent any change, in the form of preventing the king her husband from marrying again — that is to say from adding to Mother Nature the spiritual principle, both for his own sake and for her son's.

She is, however, thwarted in this design. And here we meet with another archetypal symbol of wonderful simplicity but infinitely subtle meaning. This is the 'two-headed briar' which seems so insignificant if not absurd, but represents in fact the link, in this case, between nature and spirituality. As Mother Nature, she has to die and knows it. Death is her role in so far as this means 'unchangeability'. Like flowers in the field, her one purpose in life is to reproduce herself. There is no more in life for her to do. But as she dies the dreadful thought comes to her that her husband will wish for another wife. She knows in her deepest nature that this is inevitable, as nature knows, to its despair, that one day it will have to suffer change, and give way to some higher principle by means of which 'death' or immutability

13

will be reversed or overcome. So, with all the ambivalence inherent in every living thing and well known to the psychologist in his consulting room, she with one and the same gesture points the way to the future and at the same time tries to prevent it from coming about. She begs him to 'take no wife' till he see a 'two-headed briar' on her grave, which in fact means *growing out of herself.* But on the sly "she summoned her preceptor to her and bade him strip the grave each year, so that nothing might grow on it". Her husband is so nature-bound that he submits, and for seven years remains a widower.

Plants growing out of a grave are commonly supposed by folklorists to symbolise a future extension of the personality. We have to consider what this particular form of it means. Such symbols as the 'two-headed briar' are so frequent in dreams that we may pause for a moment to consider what this means. The symbol may appear as the letter Y, or as forked roads, or as a two-headed Janus, all symbolising two things sprouting from one. This is no place to go into the symbolism of twins, of two sexes, of sun and moon, light and darkness or any other dualities. The symbolism of two growing out of one, or out of a common matrix, is too world-wide and capable of too many interpretations to be discussed here. In this case, however, it clearly symbolises the two wives, that is to say two aspects of womanhood, or of the feminine principle, the matrilineal and the patrilineal, the natural and the spiritual, and on a deeper level still incest *versus* the incest taboo. 'Incest' is here taken psychologically as indicating a closed system impervious to change, the 'incest taboo' as that which breaks this closed circle and allows of expansion into something larger and more worth while, but at the risk of losing the original value without attaining the other goal which has been set. Change always involves risk, which it is the role of the hero to undertake. Mother Nature, however, has no interest in heroes. She wants to conserve. But she cannot conserve indefinitely. Forces which grow out of her herself push on to new endeavour. These are 'male' forces, symbolised by the 'man child', which feel constrained by too great safety. But they are rare — as rare as the dynamic element which frees itself from the matrix to forge ahead. They draw their strength from her, in order to escape from her and prove their manhood independently from her. The fact, however, that they draw it from her (whence else can man born out of woman derive his strength?) is shown in the symbolism of the 'two mothers', one of whom is nature-bound and matrilineal, the other of freer spirituality and patrilineal. The contrast may, in mythology, be represented in many ways. Nor is it confined to women. The best known example with regard to men is that of Jacob and Esau who 'struggled together' in their mother's womb. And God said "Two nations are in thy womb, and two manner of people shall be separated from thy bowels; and the one people shall be stronger than the other people; and the elder shall serve the younger... And the first came out red, all over like an hairy garment; and they called his name Esau. And after that came his brother out, and his hand took hold on Esau's heel; and his name was called Jacob... " (Gen. XXV:22-26.) It is generally supposed that on one level Esau represents instinct (the earthy element) and Jacob the spiritual one. Earth values came first, followed by spiritual ones, but "Jacob's hand took hold on Esau's heel" is taken on this level to mean that there can be no spiritual values which are not rooted in earthy ones.

So also, in our story, the two kinds of feminine values, the earthy, animal, matrilineal kind, and the more spiritual, patrilineal kind, are both rooted in the earthy-animal, which is the primary of the two. Both 'grow out of' the matrilineal mother's grave. So she need not really be so frightened. But she is. It will be remembered, however, how the conflict between Esau and

Jacob for the birthright was solved by trickery, in which the trickster Jacob was nevertheless regarded as the more holy and spiritual one. This is a typical kind of ruse undertaken by the autonomous psyche, which seems to ego to be mere trickery, or a "slip of the tongue", or in dreams an unaccountable mistake running completely counter to all ego's wishes and assumed ideals, but nevertheless is willed by the autonomous psyche which turns out in the end to be right and to hold in it the germ of future development. So here, as an *apparent* mistake, "at the end of seven years the preceptor neglected that which he had promised the queen". In other words, the 'superego' tired of its task of everlasting destructful watchfulness, and the autonomous psyche took over. At last the 'two-headed briar' was allowed to grow out of the grave of the dead natural mother.

How far away from civilisation this grave was is seen by the fact that the king only chanced on it when he was out hunting. As the whole epic ends in a hunt to slay — on behalf of the hero — the negative mother-image, this preliminary hunt may be taken as a prefiguration on the part of the father to free himself from his. "One day when the king was hunting, he drew near the graveyard; he wanted to see the grave whereby he was to take a wife." His long period of waiting on the clogging will of his first wife (the boundness to untransformed nature) was now over. "He saw the briar", and all was well. He married again, this time 'patrilineally' and spiritually.

There follows a most interesting scene, incomprehensible unless we take it psychologically. "Upon a day as the good lady went walking abroad, she came to the house of an old crone who was in the town, without a tooth in her head." Note that, unlike the matrilineal mother, she did not shun human habitation, but lived in it. "Quoth the queen: 'Crone, wilt thou for God's sake tell me what I ask of thee? Where are the children of the man

16

who has carried me off by force? ' Quoth the crone: 'He has no children.'
Quoth the queen: 'Woe is me that I should have come to a childless man!'
Said the crone: 'Thou needst not say that. It is prophesied that he shall
have offspring. 'Tis by thee he shall have it, since he has not had it by another. Besides, be not unhappy, he has one son.' "

This extraordinary dialogue with the old crone, who plays with double-
meanings, saying at one moment 'he has no children' and a few seconds later
'he has one son', can only mean that this son is no ordinary one. The father
has had no offspring by any other, but is a kind of soul-child proving his
manhood not in a biological way but in a spiritual one befitting his new
spiritual bride. The account goes on: "The good lady returned home joy-
fully, and quoth she to her husband, 'What reason hast thou to hide thy
child from me? ' Quoth the king, 'I will hide him no longer.' "

Note here the conflict on the conscious level with the 'spiritual' wife,
whereas there was no conflict with the 'natural' wife except after her death;
that is to say unconsciously. This represents an advance in consciousness.
One revelation follows another. Once he has produced or acknowledged
his son, revealing to her his potentially spiritual manhood, she then proceeds
to reveal her potentially spiritual womanhood by introducing her daughter.
In neither case is the 'child' born out of their union, but in both cases from
a previous and presumably much more unconscious one. This is a real marriage for him, on the conscious level, whereas the other was not. His first
marriage appears now to have been a 'mother' one, and hers a 'father' one.
He has now freed himself from the mother by killing the father in the form
of his new wife's husband, and thereby also has freed her from her father-
substitute. By this action, each is now fully adult, he in possession, independently of her, of a 'soul-son', and she, similarly independent of him, of
a 'soul-daughter'. In this way they become fit parental figures (natural

father and spiritual mother) for the hero, who is now sent for, and the spiritual mother begins to exert her influence on him: "Messengers were sent after the boy, and he came to court. His stepmother said to him, 'It were well for thee to take a wife, son, and I have a daughter meet for any nobleman in the world.' "

This would seem to be a bold statement, were it not for the fact that these figures are mythological. The hero is now initiated into his destiny, in moving terms and with moving result: "Quoth the boy, 'I am not yet of an age to take a wife.' " The dialogue is very subtle. According to old Welsh custom, the age at which a boy was permitted to marry was fourteen. This is the age of puberty, but the reference is almost certainly to psychological maturity — at any age, from seven or earlier — to seventy. "Said she in reply: 'I will swear a destiny upon thee, that thy side shall never strike against woman, till thou win Olwen, daughter of Ysbaddaden Chief Giant [Pencawr].[5] The boy coloured, and love of the maiden entered into every limb of him, although he had never seen her. Quoth his father to him, 'How, son, why dost thou colour? What ails thee? ' 'My stepmother has sworn on me that I shall never win a wife until I win Olwen daughter of Ysbaddaden Chief Giant.' 'It is easy for thee to achieve that, son,' said his father to him. 'Arthur is thy first cousin. Go then to Arthur to trim thy hair, and ask that of him as his gift to thee.' " This is the end of the introduction to the story. Culhwch then sets off on his quest.

In the above passage the stepmother emerges in her true role of godmother pointing the way. The dialogue about the daughter has been interpreted as Culhwch refusing her and suffering as a consequence from his stepmother's wrath. But surely this is a very superficial interpretation. Reading between the lines, it seems on the one hand that Olwen is certainly an anima figure, known only, at this stage, to the stepmother. It transpires later in the story that even Arthur had never heard of her. She is moreover, like Culhwch himself, unknown to history, and does not appear in any other tale. This unknownness calls to mind, by way of contrast, extreme familiarity such as that existing between brother and sister, whose very familiarity, as being 'part of one another', is the cause of unconscious mutual projections of an extreme nature, the girl projecting her animus on the brother, and he projecting his anima on her. It may therefore be taken to be significant that the unnamed daughter (Culhwch's half-sister, and not necessarily the daughter she at first 'brought along with her') and Olwen are coupled together in almost the same breath by the stepmother, by way of contrast yet indicating their oneness. She obviously has in mind that he should marry her daughter, but when he says that he is "not yet of an age to take a wife", meaning that he is not yet mature, her answer is, in agreement, to "swear a destiny" upon him that his "side shall never strike against woman" till he shall win Olwen daughter of Ysbaddaden Pencawr. I here suggest that the 'daughters' are identical in the sense of being aspects of a psychological whole: on one level the stepmother's flesh-and-blood daughter(s), and Olwen, on another level, Culhwch's own sister-anima — the hero's goal, his contrasexual self. The boy blushes for love of this maiden whom he 'had never seen' (for she has been, to him, wholly unconscious). His father says "What ails thee? " thinking that he is ill. It is indeed a moment of deep emotional affect, corresponding to any breakdown leading to search for oneself.

If this interpretation is correct, we are now in a position to guess the identity of the father of this maiden, the dread Ysbaddaden Pencawr, the slaying of whom occupies part of the ensuing heroic struggle; he has to be killed before his daughter can be obtained. He can on the one hand be an aspect of the stepmother herself, the possessive animus part of her as the wicked stepmother that she herself in her other role of fairy godmother knows has to be killed. She thus shows the ambivalence of her own archetypal nature which (unlike that of the 'natural mother' who first gives birth and then destroys that which she had given birth to) first sets tasks (reversing that process) which seem destructive in order to bring about rebirth. On the other hand, Ysbaddaden Pencawr is the natural mother's negative animus, the matriarchal mother seeking to castrate the hero (but in fact ending by being castrated himself). He can be identified as a repressive father figure — the castrating father, but more precisely a guise for the *vagina dentata* of the mother figure: in sum, a mother's negative animus.

This giant is afraid of the moon, after being wounded in the eye, in that he is liable to "giddiness each new moon" (Jones, p. 113). His daughter Olwen on the other hand shows signs of being a moon-woman, in the description of her "whiteness" (p. 110-11). A poet refers to her, as legendary beauty, as "Olwen of the slender eyebrow, pure of heart" (Guest, 1877 edition, p. 260), both moon symbols. Her name means 'white track', or 'white traces' (*ol,* 'track'; *wen,* 'white'). The white track is the moon's reflection in the water. "Four white trefoils sprang up behind her wherever she went; and for that reason was she called Olwen" (Jones, p. 111). The moon, with its changes, is a transforming symbol. It would seem that, on the pig-moon level the whole stepmother-complex including the stepmother, her 'daughter', Ysbaddaden Pencawr and his daughter Olwen, were 'moon-folk', as opposed to the natural mother who was a sow. Culhwch, 'born in a pig-run' but actively engaged in getting out of it, is himself, as most heroes are, the uniter of opposites: his own pig nature with Olwen's moon one.

But first the hero has to encounter the giant. He quails at the task. But his father tells him " 'It is easy for thee to achieve that, son. Arthur is thy first cousin. Go then to Arthur to trim thy hair, and ask that [the

20

winning of Olwen] of him as his gift to thee.' " The trimming of the hair
implied, in ancient Wales as elsewhere, "subordination to, and, therefore,
protection by the trimmer" (Ellis & Lloyd, p. 173, note 19): the secular
tonsure. "In the eighth century, it was the custom of people of consideration to have their children's hair cut the first time by persons for whom they
had a particular honour and esteem, who in virtue of this ceremony were
reputed a sort of spiritual parents, or godfathers to them" (Guest, 1877 edition, p. 260). It is a complex symbol involving the imaginative substitution
of the whole body for the phallus in such a way that it fulfills a role not unlike that of circumcision in respect to part of the body being offered for
the whole. In this way Culhwch is told to subordinate himself to Arthur
(as ego to a superordinate figure representing the Self). But this symbol
attains infinitely greater importance as the tale proceeds, for it is in the end
Ysbaddaden Pencawr who is himself shaved with the razor, the shears and
the comb taken from between the ears of the great boar Twrch Trwyth, for
which the whole hunt was waged. This operation finally brought about the
giant's defeat, thus releasing Olwen for Culhwch's embrace.

With this advice to seek out Arthur, the introduction to the story
ends. Culhwch then sets off on his quest. I would, however, suggest to
those engaged in psychotherapy and particularly in dream analysis, how
very like the preamble to a dream this is. The introductory text so far discussed takes up only two pages out of a total of forty, the rest being all in
the form of active adventure. They have, so far as I know, not been noticed
by any of the commentators, or editors of the story in shorter form. Yet
they provide the basis of understanding without which the story itself is
well-nigh incomprehensible. So many dreams of 'action' have a similar preamble — some vague or fleeting scene — that has apparently little or nothing
to do with what follows, but which in fact provides the clue.

CHAPTER 2

CULHWCH AND ARTHUR: EGO AND SELF

From the moment our young hero sets out, he is every inch the 'hero' in his external aspect. "Off went the boy [note how youthful he is] on a steed with light-grey head, four winters old, with well-knit fork, shell-hoofed, and a gold tubular bridle-bit in his mouth." But though so young this does not minimise his superhuman strength. "A battle-axe in his hand, the fore-arm's length of a full grown man from ridge to edge." And he is out after no ordinary foe. "It would draw blood from the wind; it would be swifter than the swiftest dewdrop from the stalk to the ground, when the dew would be heaviest in the month of June." What he is after is intangible, but nevertheless all-pervading. These are symbols of spiritual power, which comes from possessing a dual nature, female as well as male. Descriptions of the accoutrements of chivalry may seem banal, but looked at with an eye familiar with symbolic imagery they reveal more. "A gold-hilted sword on his thigh, and the blade of it gold" is phallic enough, but what of what follows: "and a gold-chased buckler upon him, with the hue of heaven's lightening therein, and an ivory boss therein"? These are ordinary descriptions of matter-of-fact weapons, but one is for attack, the other for defence. The buckler is breast-shaped and has an 'ivory' boss. Is ivory of such great use in battle? A buckler with such a boss is symbolic of the strong earth-mother protecting her man-child.

Should this symbolic duality be doubted, the next item on the list of the hero's attributes does but emphasise it. It is an image taken from the hunt but has deeper significance. "And two greyhounds, whitebreasted, brindled, in front of him...The one that was on the left side would be on the right, and the one that was on the right side would be on the left, like two sea-swallows sporting around him." Such behaviour would hardly be conducive to good hunting in the external world, but it seizes the imagination, and as an echo of the two-headed briar, an image of the dynamic interplay of ego and non-ego, or of the male and female elements in a supremely well-organised psyche, it is on a par with the caduceus of Mercury (two snakes intertwined about a staff); or of the *ida* and *pengali* of Kundalini yoga, those psychic nerve-substances which intertwine, alternate-siddly, about the vertebral column. This marks the archetypal nature of the hero as archetypal figure. The same form of imagery is doubled and so made fourfold (symbol of completion) in the next item in the list of his attributes: "Four clods the four hoofs of his steed would cut, like four swallows in the air over his head, now before him, now behind him." Right and left are here doubled by up and down — clods flying in the air to show his mastery of earth and air, himself in the centre of this complex curving and counter-curving of psychic elements, female earth and male air. Each image is tacked on to a symbol of instinct transformed for the use of man, in the form of the two kinds of domesticated animal, the horse for riding, symbol of feminine libido, the underlying dynamic force which 'carries' a man, and greyhounds (masculine libido) for the hunt.

The fourfold imagery is carried a step further and has added to yet another attribute in the form of "a four-cornered mantle of purple upon him, and an apple of red gold in each of its corners". Purple is a well known colour representing transformation through suffering. It is the colour of wine pressed from the bruised grape. It is the colour of Good Friday and 'passion' (repentance) in the Christian tradition. It represents, in Goethe's sense, the 'passing-over' of blue into red, the 'blue' of introverted innocence into the 'red' of fullest experience. As all of these it is the colour of royalty, derived from times when the royal personages were spiritual heroes, and so is worn by bishops in our own ecclesiastical hierarchy. Such heroes were originally those who were made holy (whole) through suffering and conquest over the regressive powers of darkness and possessive femininity which psychologically are the Devouring Mother, called by the Church 'evil'. The apples were heroes' passports to paradise (cf. the Hesperides, Avalon).

These are the attributes with which our hero Culhwch is now endowed. His 'horse' is the female aspect of his instinctive nature, as borne out in Celtic as well as Norse and Greek mythology, and also in dream psychology: that which is stronger and swifter than individual man but which he nevertheless controls, and whose instinct is better than that of his own ego. It bears him along: they are at one. "Never a hair-tip stirred upon him, so exceeding light his steed's canter under him on his way to the gate of Arthur's court."

There is no account of his journey thither. There are no obstacles until he comes to the gate, where he behaves in the most arrogant manner conceivable, assured of his welcome in spite of the opposition of the gatekeeper. "Quoth the youth, 'Is there a porter? ' 'There is. And thou, may thy head not be thine, that thou dost ask! I am porter to Arthur each first day of January.' " Psychologically this is equivalent to dawn, birth, and an opening. Januarius (Janus, the doorkeeper) has two faces, one looking back, the other forward. There is no doubt which way our hero looks — forward.

24

Nor is there any doubt which way the porter does, in his present mood —
backwards, in trying to oppose his entry. The porter's name is Glewlwyd
Gafaelfawr.[6] He is a male form of the mother principle, here trying to prevent the boy from finding himself in a process not of birth out of the mother (Culhwch has had no difficulty in this, his mother being a good nature-
mother), but of the beginning of rebirth through entering into the father
world of Arthur's court. This is at the same time the world of the stepmother or patrilineal mother as we have called her, since it was she who
set him on this quest.

The 'godfather', in this case Arthur, is a 'male mother'. Though male,
his kingdom has to be 'entered' as though it were a woman. This entry into
the male world which is a 'second mother' is what all initiation rites are concerned with, a subject which, however, there is no space to dwell on here.
It is man's 'third estate', which frees him from the earlier two, his boundness to his own mother, (the first) and to his own father (the second). The
third state is hermaphrodite, and is achieved in union with the sister-anima,
which is the goal of this quest. In his role of godfather, Arthur adumbrates
this union and helps him to it later by standing in his stead. He is thus, as
'male mother', an image of the *bisexual* Self.

It is a remarkable feature of this story that Culhwch had no hesitation
whatever about his right and ability to enter into this citadel, to seek the
help of one who has trodden the hero-path before. It is as if, having been
born as a child of nature, he knows his way in and out of all doors. " 'Open
the gate'," he says. " 'I will not.' 'Why wilt thou not open it? ' " The porter (or gatekeeper) replies in a set phrase which is again repeated later,
" 'Knife has gone into meat and drink into horn [dynamic sex symbols],
and a thronging in Arthur's hall. Save the son of a king of a rightful dominion, or a craftsman who brings his craft, none may enter.' " He will not open

the gate for Culhwch alone. So he procrastinates, testing the hero's importunity by offering to let him in next day when a new throng will arrive. But
Culhwch will have none of this being reduced to the level of an ordinary
guest. He is an individualist bent on individuation, and does not flinch from
threatening even Arthur himself if he is not let in immediately. " 'If thou
open the gate, it is well. If thou open it not, I will bring dishonour upon
thy lord and ill report upon thee... And every woman with child that is in
this court shall miscarry, and such of them as are not with child their wombs
shall turn to a burden within them, so that they may never bear child from
this day forth.' " Culhwch, despite his tender years, is no ninny. The curse
on women supports the view that we have all through this epic to do with
the ultimate overcoming of the mother, for which entry into the father
world is but a preliminary step.

The dialogue with the gatekeeper proceeds on terms of extreme familiarity — for are not all these figures ultimately one, aspects of Culhwch
himself? Glewlwyd Gafaelfawr shows his annoyance at the lad's imperti-
nence by bawling " 'Shout as thou wilt about the laws of Arthur's court,
thou shalt not be let in till first I go and have a word with Arthur.' " The
gatekeeper, as intermediary looking both ways, has to connect ego with his
own Self. And incidentally, like all these archetypes, he shows his ambivalence. He goes in to Arthur, and identifies with him as archetype of the past
combined with the present, that is to say the Old Wise Man, by saying, in
reply to Arthur's question as to his news, " 'Two-thirds of my life are past,
and two-thirds of thine own.' " The third third will be Culhwch, the hero,
who holds the future in his hands and is now knocking at the door, seeking
to rouse the immemorial Self to action on his behalf. The gatekeeper goes
on to emphasise his and Arthur's antiquity and Arthur's exploits in the dim
past and in all parts of the known universe. " 'I was of old,' " he goes on,

enumerating places in pairs where he had served Arthur, such as India the Great and India the Lesser, and 'I was there of old when thou didst slay... [and] conquer' including 'Greece unto the east'. Having thus established his hoary antiquity, he then returns to the present and shows his real mind by saying " 'Fair kingly men saw we there, but never saw I a man so comely as this who is even now at the entrance to the gate.' "

Then comes Arthur's surprising reply. Far from resenting his guest's reported importunity, he says " 'If thou didst enter walking go thou out running. And he that looks upon the light, and opens his eye and shuts it, an injunction upon him... A shameful thing it is to leave in wind and rain a man such as thou tellest of.' " Cei,[7] Arthur's senechal, objects to this open-handedness, regarding it as surrender of rights: " 'If my counsel were acted upon, the laws of court would not be broken for his sake.' " But Arthur insists. The gate is opened, and Culhwch, disdaining to dismount as every other man would do, did not, "but on his steed he came inside".

Arthur made no demur. "Quoth Culhwch, 'Hail, sovereign, prince of this Island. Be it no worse unto the lower half of the house than unto the upper...' " To this double-statement, Arthur replied " 'God's truth, so be it, chieftain.' " He bids him take his place among his warriors, and says " 'When I dispense my gifts to guests and men from afar, it shall be at thy hand that I so begin in this court.' " The youth, however, far from expressing gratitude, only proceeds with threats: " 'If I obtain my boon, I will repay it, and I will praise it. If I obtain it not, I will bear hence thine honour...' " in words not unlike those used to the gatekeeper. Arthur still does not object: " 'Though thou bide not here, chieftain, thou shalt obtain the boon thy head and thy tongue shall name..., save only' [and here he names his ship and his mantle, his sword, his spear, his shield, his dagger, and then significantly] 'and Gwenhwyfar[8] [Guinevere] my wife.' " He thus reserves his personal anima, for all his three 'wives' had been called Guinevere. Culhwch queries " 'God's truth thereon? ' " Arthur replies " 'Name what thou wilt.' " Culhwch does not immediately ask for what he really wants, but says " 'I will. I would have my hair trimmed.' " Then "Arthur took a golden comb and shears with loops of silver, and he combed his head."

Thus the great Arthur is, it would appear, hectored and bullied by this unknown hero into accepting his offering, giving him his blessing, and adopting and protecting him. It is a remarkable relationship. The Self, after its initial defence by means of the gatekeeper, seems to be as eager to give as ego is to demand even by means of threats. We are reminded of the mystics' sayings about 'storming the citadels of God'. "Knock and it shall be opened to you" does not imply meekness. It implies insistence to the point of importunity. Culhwch as hero does not behave like a well regulated adult. He behaves like an imperious babe, sure that its mother will yield and give what is wanted. To continue the psychological analogy: the action has therapeutic significance. It is useless for an analyst to say that a patient is 'too demanding'. Of course he is demanding. It is his right, since what is sick in him is the unsatisfied needs of the child deprived by its mother at an age too young to stand thwarting. The analyst must give — as far as in him lies — the love and service withheld at infancy, including even admiration of the 'demands' that in an ordinary relationship would be intolerable and often quite impossible to fulfil. The analyst who cannot fulfil enough of these demands has failed, but he who can reaps a reward as great almost as the benefit which he bestows. It is a two-way relationship on two levels. The analyst is a Self figure for the patient, and, in so far as he responds, the patient's own Self responds. Ego and Self, which have been estranged, experience, both of them, intense relief at having this estrangement bridged, and can love one another to the extent that before they were at loggerheads.

This mutual movement of love through recognition of psychological 'kinship' between first patient and analyst, and through this then between the patient's ego and his own Self, is beautifully illustrated in this tale. Culhwch demands imperiously and without fear of censure. Arthur accepts this without demur, not standing upon his dignity, but giving through knowledge of his own worth. Each trusts the other, to the extent that Culhwch now submits, bowing to his authority. And this in turn produces such an effect on Arthur that he says " 'My heart grows tender towards thee: I know thou art sprung from my blood.' " Then comes the declaration, the hero's (or the patient's) baring of himself. Arthur now makes his own demand, saying " 'Declare who thou art.' " Culhwch replies " 'I will,' " revealing his mother's name, she being sister to Arthur's own mother. Note that the kinship is a matriarchal one, that is to say on the side of feeling, not intellect. "Quoth Arthur: 'True it is. Thou art then my first cousin. Name what thou wilt, and thou shalt have it, whatever thy mouth and thy tongue shall name.' "

Very important is this, that kinship is established not before, but after their mutual recognition as having a soul affinity and common destiny. It is Culhwch's insistence *in his own right* as an individual that won the day for him in Arthur's heart. The recognition of kinship came later, as a result of this and not a cause. As happens in dreams, which are a narrative of cause and effect on the psychic level, what comes after is due to what comes before. Culhwch's 'kinship' with Arthur is basically a psychological one, arising from Arthur's admiration of his fearless attack and Arthur's acceptance of it as a compliment rather than the reverse. This has a bearing on the willing acceptance of negative transference on the part of the analyst, who recognises it as an expression of love and longing on the part of the patient to be recognised himself. The 'fact' of physiological kinship is used only as confirmation of this, and, I would suggest, would not have been established had not the affinity on the psychic level preceded it.

The factor of faith in the 'patient', here faith in the hero's most unlikely desire, comes into this. Having declared who he is, Culhwch at last names his desire, accompanied as usual by the demand that it shall be fulfilled. He says to Arthur " 'My claim on thee is that thou get me Olwen daughter of Ysbaddaden Chief Giant. And I invoke her in the name of thy warriors.' " Then follows Culhwch's boon-list of warriors and other valorous people and animals. Our story consists of 42 pages in all: of this, seven are taken up by the boon-list. Arthur replies " 'Ah, chieftain, I have never heard tell of the maiden thou tellest of, nor of her parents. I will gladly send messengers to seek her.' " And so he did, but without avail. She and her father were discovered only after hazardous search. The sister-anima is indeed an unknown quantity. But Arthur undertakes without hesitation or any kind of condition, and with complete self-giving, to help him in his search. It will be noted moreover that Arthur's own tender emotion towards Culhwch after the trimming of his hair had been preceded by the only other tender emotion so far recorded in this tale, which was that felt by Culhwch after first hearing of Olwen, when "love of the maiden entered into every limb of him, although he had never seen her". Arthur's emotion towards him, as first step towards finding her, was the first response to this. From thenceforth the two are one in their search for her.

We have spoken of the 'feminine' or emotional and completely accepting side of Arthur's attitude towards Culhwch, and have compared this to the accepting attitude of the good analyst towards his patient's demands. This does not however, if understood dynamically, lead in the latter case to softness on the part of the patient. On the contrary, it gives him the basic confidence that leads to action. So also in our story, Culhwch now, in preparation for his search, invokes Olwen in the name of Arthur's warriors, and does this to the extent of invoking some 250 of them, beginning with well known ones but bringing in innumerable other names, many probably of local fame but tapering off into punned names and attributes and, actually, twenty women beginning with Gwenhwyfar, Arthur's own wife or anima.

Thus ends the second section of our story, dealing with the acquisition of Arthur as guide, protector, and friend. We have described him as male mother or godfather or, psychologically speaking, an aspect of the non-ego or Self, on which Culhwch is to rely for the attainment of his goal, the sister-anima or figurative image of the soul.

Arthur is, moreover, here no king in the romantic sense, or in the sense of Norman chivalry as we have been accustomed to think of him. Although, as befits so important a figure, he lives in a heavily guarded stronghold, this is no Christian court of King Arthur of mediaeval romance. Nowhere is he referred to as 'King'. He is throughout plain 'Arthur'. And though he entertains innumerable guests who feed at his willing expense, his kingdom is 'deep', not 'high'. It is an underworld kingdom representing the unconscious, into which the hero now enters, assisted by 'Arthur', who knows his way in and out of it and who later becomes the leader of the great hunt of the mythical wild boar referred to by other commentators as the Otherworld beast. He is easily identifiable as the emissary of the Devouring Mother, the overcoming of which is the main task necessary for the winning of the soul-bride.

CHAPTER 3

THE QUEST:

CUSTENNIN, HIS WIFE AND SON

Thus far we have dealt with the birth of the hero and the problem of the 'two mothers', and set out the nature of his quest for the moon-maiden, the sister-anima, in the first chapter. It led up to the transition stage of puberty and his first experience of inner desire. The second chapter saw him adolescent and, advised thereto by his biological father, seeking his spiritual father, godfather, or second self in the form of Arthur, and imperiously demanding his help. The price is that he shall submit to Arthur trimming his hair. Taking this as a symbolic phallic offering (every sacrifice being a form of exchange), the hero thereby sacrifices part of his manhood to Arthur. In exchange he receives something much more valuable: the spiritual force that Arthur puts at his service in acceding to his request, and promising to prosecute the youth's interests with all the resources at his command.

By forcing an entrance into Arthur's stronghold, the hero has already got into touch with his own psychic powers. The world of the psyche is, however, full of ambivalence. If he has found a powerful 'good' spirit-father and ally in Arthur, this is only to balance and outweigh the almost equally powerful hostile father-figure of Ysbaddaden Pencawr, Olwen's progenitor. This giant is in complete contrast to Arthur. Arthur, sure of his strength, never boasts once throughout the whole narrative, whereas the giant (with one vital exception) vaunts himself throughout many pages. But there is a yet more important difference. Although the giant should know his own daughter if anybody did, he actually knows her so little that he tries to keep her to himself and so frustrate her destiny. He is the possessive 'natural' father, corresponding to Culhwch's 'natural' mother, who wished to maintain the *status quo* and prevent development. Arthur, on the other hand, has never even heard of her, yet, through his support of Culhwch, is the instrument which delivers her from her 'natural' bondage. He, in contrast to the giant, is to be classed with the stepmother who, with the help of his own father, causes Culhwch to seek out Arthur to help him find his soul-mate.

The giant is thus an archetype of unbending and unyielding nature, incapable of transformation as ever Culhwch's mother was. As he is a giant, this indicates his psychic powers of superhuman proportions. Just as Culhwch's mother gave birth to the hero, so the giant gave birth to the hero's own other side, his anima. But neither can yield their grip, and so both have to die. But, with the ambivalence of all archetypes, they know that they are doomed and to be superseded by some other principle — although they do their utmost to prevent it. In the Oedipus situation in which the giant finds himself, he also pathetically knows he has to die the moment his daughter finds her rightful mate. But there is yet another point of resemblance between the giant and Culhwch's mother. If she was a 'sow', the giant's own death is intimately bound up with the elimination of the 'otherworld boar' to which the story leads up and with which it ends. Indeed, the two happenings are almost one. Is he then, as corresponding to the sow, in that she gives birth to the hero and he begets the hero's sister-anima, himself an aspect of the boar?

A word is needed now to explain the method which will be followed in dealing with the very complex remainder of the tale. In Chapter One, every word of the text was quoted, this being highly condensed. In Chapter Two, most of the text was quoted but not all, and the long list of Arthur's warriors and others invoked by Culhwch was left out. Henceforth this close following of the text will not be possible, since so many motifs are 'doubled' by the insertion of parallel stories and the author embroiders the tale in many ways. In this mass of poetic and mythological imagery certain main lines can all the same be traced. The lines I have selected will be those bearing primarily on boar mythology such as is dealt with throughout this book. This does not mean that the lines on it which will emerge are in any way foregone conclusions such as have been arrived at through study of boar mythology in other parts. True, these give certain hints; but there is so much new material in this story, not found elsewhere, that it repays study for its own sake and will of itself enlarge our view of what this complex imagery is all about, and of its psychological significance.

This third section begins with Arthur's remark to Culhwch: " 'Ah, chieftain, I have never heard tell of the maiden thou tellest of, nor of her parents. I will gladly send messengers to seek her.' " But this is of no avail. At the end of a year, Arthur's messengers still had no news of her. Culhwch complains " 'Every one has obtained his boon, yet am I still lacking.' " He even resumes his threats: " 'I will away and take thin honour with me,' " meaning that he will tarnish it wherever he goes. It is worth noting that, if anyone in real life made such a threat, particularly after having arrived unknown and yet been welcomed with honour and given lavish hospitality for a year, his action would hardly be considered 'noble'. Yet Culhwch *is* noble.

34

He is a hero, though he does precious little to achieve his object, the really hazardous dangers connected with the boar and the even more dread Black Witch, handled by Arthur and his men without Culhwch lifting a hand in them, or even appearing when they are done. A 'hero' of this type who has to have his battles fought for him, is hero only in so far as he is a babe demanding rightly what is his due, but is not old or mature enough to get it by his own efforts. All heroes are apt to be arrogant, but fully-fledged heroes can justify this by their deeds — such as Marduk or Hercules. Culhwch cannot. He does tackle the giant and thus faces his problem in so far as it is a straightforward Oedipus one. But when it comes to the deeper layers of the psyche represented by the boar and the witch, that is to say the problem of the devouring mother in all its intensity (cf. Neumann: "she is the sow that farrows and the boar that kills"), he leaves all that to Arthur. So much for Culhwch's arrogance and even contemplated treachery to his obliging host, a typical infantile characteristic indicating in himself a Devouring Mother attitude that he has not yet overcome. (Child and mother, in an undifferentiated state, are one.)

In seeking out the giant, Arthur himself takes no part — presumably because Culhwch himself is up to this task. He sends six of his chieftains, beginning with Cei and Bedwyr. Cei now says, " 'Ah, chieftain, overmuch dost thou asperse Arthur. Come thou with us. Till thou shalt say she exists not in the world, or till we find her, we will not be parted from thee.' " He is the worldly-wise one, now with a kindly heart. "Cei had this peculiarity, nine nights and nine days his breath lasted under water, nine nights and nine days would he be without sleep..." The number nine occurs very frequently in the account, nine indicating the period of pregnancy, that is to say of preparation for creation, or perhaps more specifically here, of search. For searching is basically a female attribute, if we are to believe or understand

35

the myths of Isis and Demeter in that they search for the respective objects of their desire — in each case the recovery of that which had been lost. It is also in another aspect an odd or male number. 'Breathing under water' is a frequent symbol of familiarity with unconscious elements which do not 'drown' the conscious ones but rather add to them. Further, one of the six is Guide, Cynddylig, and another Interpreter, Gwrhyr Gwalstawt Ieithoedd. The number six may possibly be taken in this context in one of its frequent connotations as being on the one hand connected with sex (in English: word similarity) and on the other with spirituality: that is to say with sex as an image of spirituality.

"Away they went till they came to a wide open plain and saw a fort, the greatest of forts in the world." The wide open plain is suggestive of the father-world, in contrast to the mother-world which is more likely to be symbolised by a wood, thicket, or valley. In fact, the fort turns out to be that of Ysbaddaden Pencawr, the jealous father guarding his daughter Olwen against all comers. "That day they journeyed. When they thought they were near to the fort they were no nearer than at first. And the second and the third day they journeyed, and with difficulty did they get thereto." This is descriptive of an emotional state, a typical accompaniment of every search with its varying moments of hope and disappointment, vision and blindness. It is not only figurative: it happens on a psychic level in dissociated states. A man may walk towards a house while it appears ever to be receding from him, till suddenly he finds himself inside. This is due to the fact that the house in question contains something or someone which one desires but is at the same time afraid of.

This is the frame of mind of those approaching the giant's castle containing the longed-for maiden, but also the father who will do everything in his power to prevent access to her. It will be remembered how Culhwch's heart momentarily failed him when told of the task he had to perform. What now would appear as 'magic' is on the one hand Culhwch's own reaction, but is also the first sign of Ysbaddaden's power over him to make him 'forget' or lose grip on his resolve. Magic is always 'female'. What seems to come from Ysbaddaden, and is indeed exercised through him as intermediary, is in fact the power of the devouring Earth Mother lurking behind the image of the 'bad father'.

There now occurs a curious scene which may or may not be an interpolation or 'doubling'. Culhwch, it will be realised, is now on the threshold of his 'rebirth', a 'second birth' which, as always, is out of the 'mother-world' of ordinary experience into the 'father-world' of the spirit. It is thus in a sense a repetition of his own biological birth on a different level. On the first occasion, of his actual birth, his mother met with a swineherd and gave birth to him among the swine. As we are now approaching the giant's castle who is himself associated with the terrifying 'otherworld boar' we might expect a swineherd to be his janitor. Instead we read that "as they were coming to the same plain as it [the fort was in], they could see a great flock of sheep without limit or end to it, and a shepherd tending the sheep on top of a mound..." The shepherd was clothed in skins and had a huge mastiff bigger than a nine-year old stallion. "It was the way of him that never a lamb had he lost, much less a grown beast." He was therefore a 'nature' man, good with domesticated instincts, but with regard to people "no company had ever fared past him that he did not do it harm or deadly hurt; every dead tree and bush that was on the plain, his breath would burn them to the very ground".

This shepherd's name was Custennin, a Welsh rendering of Constantine. Why he should be a shepherd and not a swineherd does not appear, but he is one of the many giant shepherds in Celtic literature. There may

37

be some hidden meaning in it, or it may simply be that this part of the story is of late date when sheep had replaced swine as chief domesticated animal. He here acts as a sort of guardian of the giant's castle, and in the most unwilling way. He and his wife are both extremely ambivalent figures. Our first impression of him is, however, that he is on the side of Ysbaddaden, and moreover that he is a man in the service of the Devouring Mother, since, in dream and mythological imagery, the mound he stands on would seem to symbolise the breast. From there he protects the 'lambs' (helpless creatures obedient to the Earth Mother), and blasts not only the countryside but also all humans trying to release the human soul (Olwen) imprisoned by the Earth Mother in the guise of the male giant.

In this respect, the giant's stronghold is the antithesis of Arthur's. He represents consciousness looking forward towards the future — the hero's progress. Ysbaddaden, on the contrary, is a giant, that is to say an inhuman monster bent on preventing progress and imprisoning the soul, which is also a female attribute, like that of the *Devouring* Mother. He is the male form of the Earth Mother resisting change, what Jung calls the mother's destructive animus, which indeed sears and destroys without mercy and without reason. Custennin shares this aspect with the giant. He will preserve the 'lambs', but will destroy all humans approaching his master's court. In this respect he does exactly what his master does in keeping Olwen inviolate from all suitors, whom he regards not as what the Germans call *Freier* ('suitor' meaning 'liberator') but as his deadliest enemies. That Custennin the shepherd (itself a mothering protective occupation) should be cast in the role of the 'bad breast' will come as no surprise to the psychologist, who knows the breast to be the first citadel which a child storms, an 'outpost' of the mother (as Custennin is in the position of 'outpost' to the giant's fort).

His own unwillingness to be cast for this role is immediately stated.

The six companions are at first overawed and terrified, but one of them promises to cast a spell over the shepherd's huge mastiff, whose nature and size show it to be akin to the giant himself and therefore to represent the hostile aspect of the shepherd's character. The man who promised this was Menw, son of Teirgwaedd, whom Arthur had chosen for the reason that "should they come to a heathen land he might cast a spell over them, so that none might see them and they see every one". What he saw was Custennin's enforced side-taking with the giant, and his real soul thus laid bare. So the giant says " 'There is no affliction to do me harm save my wife.' " This was a confession of his subservience to a female principle which he abhorred. They ask him " 'Whose are the sheep thou tendest, or whose is the fort? ' " He answers " 'Fools of men that you are! Throughout the world it is known that this is the fort of Ysbaddaden Chief Giant.' " They follow up: " 'And thou, who art thou? ' 'Custennin son of Mynwyedig am I, and because of my wife Ysbaddaden Chief Giant has wrought my ruin.' " This may also be rendered " 'Custennin the Exile [Mynwyedig] am I, and of my rightful possession has my brother Ysbaddaden Pencawr deprived me.' " It turns out that this same wife is sister to Culhwch's mother, and is therefore of the same blood as the devouring Earth Mother, who gives birth and then destroys that which she has produced. Thus Custennin's position outside Ysbaddaden's stronghold reflects his ambivalence, emphasised by his ultimate betrayal of Ysbaddaden's interests.

He now asks who they are. " 'Messengers of Arthur are here, to seek Olwen.' " He cries out aghast " 'Whew, men! God protect you! For all the world, do not that. Never a one has come to make that request that went away with his life.' " This scene leads up to Culhwch's first meeting with his sister-anima, though this is only to be a fleeting one.

Meanwhile, a most mysterious scene occurs. "The shepherd arose.

As he arose Culhwch [who has so far been passive and not even been mentioned here] gave him a ring of gold. He sought to put on the ring, but it would not go on him, and he placed it in the finger of his glove and went home and gave the glove to his wife. And she took the ring from the glove. 'Whence came this ring to thee, husband? 'Twas not often that thou hast had treasure-trove.' " He said " 'I went to the sea, to find sea-food. Lo! I saw a body coming in on the tide. Never saw I body so beautiful as that, and on its finger I found this ring.' " Then comes her significant reply: " 'Alas, husband, since sea does not tolerate a dead man's jewel therein, show me that body.' 'Wife, the one whose body that is, thou shalt see him here presently.' 'Who is that? ' the woman asked. 'Culhwch son of Cilydd son of Cylleddon Wledig, by Goleuddydd daughter of Anlawdd Wledig, his mother, who is come to seek Olwen.' Two feelings possessed her: she was glad that her nephew, her sister's son, was coming to her; and she was sad because she had never seen any depart with his life that had come to make that request."

This passage can be understood by the problem of the 'two mothers' in the opening passages, concerning the hero's birth and puberty, and the nature of his quest. The shepherd's wife combines in herself the feeling of both 'mothers'. "Two feelings possessed her." In the first place "she was glad that her nephew, her sister's son, was coming to her". She acknowledges her kinship with him as being his mother's sister, and thus profoundly and personally interested in his fate. She thus declares herself as, according to all primitive kinship systems, another 'mother' to him. This might on the surface be taken either way round, as meaning either that she was another natural matriarchal mother, or else another stepmother or patriarchal spiritual mother. The whole context, however, points to the latter. For one thing, she actually refers to Culhwch, whom she knows as 'come to seek Olwen' as 'coming to her' herself, thus obviously supporting his quest, the quest set him by the stepmother or 'spiritual mother'; she actually brings about their first meeting, Olwen apparently being at her beck and call. But she still has lingering on in her the natural feelings of the 'natural' mother; she was sad because the situation was dangerous.

She is the real 'wise woman' of the whole story, for does she not make the profoundest remark in saying "the sea does not tolerate a dead man's jewel therein"? This might be taken as a key to the whole hero myth. For it is the Sea herself who is the *natural* mother, who does *not* tolerate her son's (nor her husband's) defection to another woman, which seems to her like death. She will revenge herself for it, as she implicitly attempts to do in all this story by placing endless difficulties in her son's way: raising the giant Ysbaddaden against him, and the boar and the 'black witch'. She herself 'dies' quite early on, and is eventually supplanted by her very opposite, Olwen the sister-anima, the moon-maiden of inner self-realisation who finally ousts the matriarchal mother represented by the 'day-light' or 'sun' of untransformed instinct.

This gives us a clue: Culhwch produces the 'ring of gold' and offers it to the shepherd. Gold is the colour of the sun, and, in possession of a man, masculine. It represents the winning of his masculinity from the clutches of the possessive mother who covets it for herself. The ring is a symbol of in-dividuality and of union. Why then should he give it to Custennin, and why should the latter find that it does not fit him but hand it on to his wife? Ostensibly, if this were an extravert story, the proffering of the ring would simply be by way of enlisting Custennin's support to overcome the giant. But in its deeper, introverted meaning there may be a subtle reference to psychic experience on two levels. On the more manifest of these, it may symbolise the fact that men need men's society before they can satisfactorily

41

win women. But on a deeper level it probably has reference to the homosexual layer in every man's psyche based on the father-relationship, which
in psychic development supersedes that with the mother. ("I and the Father are one.") But Culhwch has not reached this stage. So Custennin,
most subtly, indicates Culhwch's need for a woman by placing it in his
glove, symbolising the 'son' within the 'mother', or phallic symbol contained in the female element, and hands it to his wife, who does assist Culhwch (as the shepherd does not) to meet his anima. She knows its value
immediately, and asks him where he had obtained it. He then makes his
mystic statement: " 'I went to the sea to find sea-food. Lo! I saw a body
coming in on the tide. Never saw I body so beautiful as that, and on its
finger I found this ring.' " The body from which the ring actually came
was Culhwch's, and coming in on the tide referred to Culhwch's approach.
But more deeply the sea, once more, is mother, the great inexhaustible life-
giver and reservoir of psychic contents. "I went to the sea to find sea-food"
can have a thousand meanings, and on one level refers to Custennin's own
search, as eventual minor hero, or helper of the hero. Culhwch possessed
new life and carried on his finger phallically the symbol of everlastingness.
Custennin only knew, however, its value. It was his wife, with deeper wisdom and knowledge of the opposites, who knew also its danger, and that
the mother "does not tolerate a dead man's jewel therein". She knows
that, for Culhwch, the dye is cast. He has 'died' to the past. The past will
catch him again if he is not helped on towards his future.

But first, she still displays her ambivalence. The party approaches
Custennin's 'court'. "She ran with joy to meet them". "Cei snatched a
log out of the wood-pile, and she came to meet them, to try and throw her
arms about their necks. Cei thrust a stake between her two hands. She
squeezed the stake so that it became a twisted withe [branch]. Quoth Cei,

'Woman, had it been I thou didst squeeze in this wise, there were no need for another to love me ever. An ill love, that!' "

It is not clear who started this misunderstanding, who was the 'traitor'; whether she in her godmother aspect really welcomed the visitors and Cei was unduly suspicious, or whether his fear was well-founded and he narrowly escaped being crushed to death by her as Devouring Mother. Taking the story as a whole it would seem that Cei knew what he was about; he knew the danger that, in her fear of siding with the progressive forces represented by the hero's party, she might suddenly turn traitor and strangle or break him under the guise of loving him. As extravert, he demonstrates that consciousness must use its own principles when dealing with the unconscious; he would have been defeated had he used the same principle that the unconscious uses to approach *him* (cf. Theseus's encounter with Cercyon).

The cause of her fear was soon to be revealed. The party enters her house, and "the woman opened a coffer alongside the hearth, and out of it arose a lad with curly yellow hair. Quoth Gwrhyr [Interpreter of Tongues], 'Twere pity to hide a lad like this. I know that it is no fault of his own that is visited upon him.' Quoth the woman, 'He is all that is left. Three-and-twenty sons of mine has Ysbaddaden Chief Giant slain, and I have no more hope of this one than of the others.' "

This last of twenty-four sons (representing possibly the last hour of the day — the last chance of overcoming the devouring giant) is another potential hero, his yellow hair being a sun-symbol representing masculine consciousness. The speaker knows that "it is no fault of his own that is visited upon him". It is ostensibly of course the giant's. But more intimately it is his mother's fear of the giant, her fear of recognising her own kernel of resistance to the giant who represents the Devouring Mother principle, and of developing her own consciousness as forward-looking woman of initiating

43

type. Cei understands the dilemma which the shepherd's wife is in, and takes the boy with him. "Quoth Cei, 'Let him keep company with me, and we shall not be slain save together.' "

This subsidiary hero is another aspect of the 'hidden treasure', of which we have now seen other examples: the birth of Culhwch among the swine and brought to court out of the body of a sow by a swineherd; the 'sea-food' which Custennin sought and which he found in the form of 'a body coming in on the tide...so beautiful...and on its finger...this ring.' His wife refers to it as 'treasure-trove'. Now her own 'treasure', her golden-haired son, youngest of twenty-four and all that she has left, is found hidden in a coffer. The mystical or psychological equivalence of coffer, coffin and womb are too well known to have to be emphasised here. He represents Custennin's wife's last, forlorn hope, though not quite dead and kept warm by being 'alongside the hearth'.

The inference is that Culhwch's party had arrived just in time to prevent the extinguishing of this last hope. This is always the moment when the 'hero' appears — he who is born often of despair, as Culhwch was when his mother had gone mad, and was 'delivered' of him (delivery being associated both with giving birth and with being rescued or saved).

That this boy indeed turns out to be a hero is evident if we examine the only three other references made to him in this tale (keeping in mind our analysis of his parents' characters and their double-faced situation). The first reference concerns the killing of another giant, called Wrnach, a kind of 'double' of Ysbaddaden. He is known to Ysbaddaden, who, as the last task which he commands Culhwch to perform, orders the obtaining of the sword of Wrnach the Giant and slaying him with it. In point of fact none of the forty tasks is fulfilled by Culhwch himself. Many also are simply forgotten by the narrator in his concentration on the supreme fight

with the 'otherworld boar'. But some of them are fulfilled by his companions, and among these it is Cei, the leader of the party, who also slays this
other giant. The tales of the two giants are thus closely parallel, and the
fate of this boy comes into both. But whereas in the case of Ysbaddaden
he is hidden, passive, and primarily connected with his mother, when it
comes to facing this other giant he is introduced as his father's son and is
in a position of trust.

The casual manner of his re-introduction into the story after this in-
terval is typical of myth telling, as such re-introduction of forgotten contents is often also in dreams. He would indeed be hardly recognisable as
the same boy without the analytical procedure which has been adopted
here with regard to this mythology, and which also applies to dream analysis. The account simply says that as Cei (with another special companion
of his called Bedwyr) was debating whether to risk entering the giant's
stronghold or not, they were joined by "a young lad who came inside with
them, the shepherd Custennin's only son". He is not yet named, as he was
not named in the first place, but it is to be noted that he is Custennin's
only son, which is also one of the marks of the hero and of his feminine
counterparts, just as Culhwch was the only son of his mother; the stepmother had an only daughter, and Olwen was also the only daughter of her
father. If we pair these out, we find that there are in this story four of
them, and that they form a superior or composite 'couple'. Culhwch and
Olwen, and a subsidiary couple, the stepmother's daughter and the shepherd's son. These latter two may be regarded as shadow figures to the
main hero and heroine, and it is interesting to note that, whereas the stepmother's daughter appears only at the very beginning and is never heard of
again, the shepherd's son makes his chief appearance at the very end, in a
surprising role. His change from being a mother's boy to his father's active

45

son is significant. This indicates his hero nature.

This second or shadow hero, who so casually appears among Cei's party, now in spite of his youth and lowly birth becomes for one incident the leader of it — the seventh element. "He and his comrades. . . crossed the three baileys as though this were a thing less than naught to them, until they came inside the fort. Quoth his comrades of Custennin's son, 'Best of men is he.' From then on he was called Goreu son of Custennin. [Goreu means 'best'.] They dispersed to their lodgings that they might slay those who lodged with them, without the Giant knowing." This is a typical act of treachery common to heroes not quite of the first order. They slay the enemy, but still cannot do it quite openly. In point of fact, the boy does not slay the giant himself, but his helpers. The giant is slain, by means of another trick, by Cei.

But the boy does slay the real giant in the end, though not before he has put in a preliminary appearance during the hunting of the boar, when he is one of the three minor heroes who for the first time drive him into the water in the river Severn. Here once more, however, at his second appearance as Goreu, he does not achieve, himself, but once more fades out of the story. His third appearance is at the very end, when Ysbaddaden having had his beard shaved off by Cadw, "Goreu son of Custennin caught him by the hair of his head and dragged him behind him to the mound, and cut off his head, and set it on the bailey-stake. And he took possession of his fort and his dominions."

The first scene with the subsidiary giant evidently partook of the character of an initiation rite, when he was named definitely as 'best' man and son of his father. His easy entrance into the giant's stronghold displayed the same confidence as that which characterised Culhwch's entry into Arthur's. It was in each case as 'mother's boy' in its positive aspect —

that is to say with undamaged instinctual fearlessness and knowledge of the instinctual world derived from the positive aspect of the Earth Mother — that the hero made his way into the father-world. He was familiar with all 'entrances' (female symbols), and also even the father-world itself once the way thereto has been pointed out. In the case of Goreu as Culhwch's shadow-figure and representative, his initiating-father figure was Cei, who was himself, as Arthur's right hand man, a shadow figure to Arthur, so that we have once more two pairs: Arthur-Culhwch and Cei-Goreu. In each case the former, at first superior and acting as initiator to the younger, in the end yields up his superiority and disappears out of the tale. The younger generation succeeds the older, the son the father, the hero enters into his own right, and ego absorbs the Self by first submitting to it without any feeling of inferiority, and finally becoming one with it and acting as its executive. "I and the Father are one," but "I am me." "I am."

In the same way the shadow hero, while doing the work, does this not for himself but for his master. Goreu slays Ysbaddaden for Culhwch, but does not claim the prize. It is Culhwch, and not he, who sleeps with Olwen that night. Not only is Culhwch an only son and she an only daughter, but she is his 'only wife'. The other characters in the story are all absorbed into these two. They are all 'characters', traits, or personality facets of the hero himself. Even his bride and he are one, in the mutual embrace of the *hieros gamos*. Inner and outer, male and female, brother and stepsister, ego and anima are one, through the intermediary of the Self. This was originally one, then became split first into two sexes and subsequently into a thousand other parts. Now all are finally absorbed into one another and united again in this symbol of brother-sister marriage, the 'incestuous' union consummated with the sister-anima.

CHAPTER 4

OLWEN: THE ANIMA

We have discussed the character of the shepherd's wife as being 'on the turn' from matriarchal Earth Mother, a victim to the natural process of death and decay, to becoming the helper of the hero in his search for inner value — for psychological integration of the personality. There is a further significance, too, of the twenty-four sons: she is basically a sun-woman, aware more of the twelve diurnal hours as expressed in the name of her sister, "the light of day". The two-headed briar of the introductory episode to our myth expressed this same duality, of which the 'day-time' mother represented only the extravert side and had to die in order to make way for the 'night-time' mother, the stepmother, who opened up the way for Culhwch to seek his 'moon' ('night-time', inner) bride Olwen.

One item of inner knowledge was indeed alive (had recently been born — he was the youngest), though as yet hidden in the psyche of the shepherd's wife. But twenty-three parts of her had not survived. With the fear associated with these, she tried to dissuade our hero from his quest. She asked Culhwch and his companions why they had come; they replied " 'We are come to seek Olwen.' " She cried " 'For God's sake, since none from the fort has yet seen you, get you back.' " But they reply " 'God knows we will not get us back till we have seen the maiden.' [It is, be it noted, a common search, of which the hero is but the chief representative.] 'Will she come to where she may be seen? ' " Though hardly daring as yet to face the inner world (so dangerous to the purely extravert earth-bound side of her), she is just able to introduce these people to it. She says " 'She comes hither every Saturday to wash her head; and in the bowl where she washes she leaves all her rings. Neither she nor her messenger ever comes for them.' " They say " 'Will she come hither if she is sent for? ' " The shepherd's wife displays her ambivalence and fear of what might come of this, but nevertheless opens the way (with that twenty-fourth part of her that *is* open) by saying " 'God knows I will not slay my soul. I will not betray the one who trusts in me. But if you pledge your word you will do her no harm, I will send for her.' 'We pledge it,' said they."

And thus she opens the gates that will eventually let in the flood which will sweep away the forces that have restricted 'her', and bring about the betrayal of former inhibiting values in favour of new and more expansive ones. Her conflict is at its height. But she comes down on the side of progressiveness, and of the liberation of the imprisoned anima. She does it with the utmost caution. She has clung to 'past attitudes', however disastrous such attitudes may be (and hers have cost her all her sons but one). But she has performed the task allotted to her, and now disappears. Her son goes on, as we have seen, to fulfil in consciousness what she has only dared to adumbrate.

Saturday is the last day of the week and so, like the shepherd's wife herself, marks a new turning point. Olwen's poor hopes have been poured out week after week, but up to now her riches, the rings she brings, she leaves and never takes back. She washes her head to make her beauty more

49

desirable — or possibly to cleanse her thoughts which never come to anything. She has not one ring, but many. For she is *anima,* undifferentiated,
which offers itself to any man, so long as someone may free her from her
loneliness. This is in striking contrast to the one golden ring which Culhwch
has, and corresponds to the psychological tendency that woman has a plur-
ality of *animi* (male figures in the unconscious), while man has generally
only one *anima.*

"She was sent for. And she came..." Remarkable — heavily guarded
as she was, and father-bound. She displays no will-power, quite possibly because of this. Her will is not her own, in contrast to Culhwch, who is the
very epitome of striving towards a goal. This is in order, however, as it is
on the deep level of purely instinctive life, in which the female element is
acquiescing in contrast to the dynamic male. For we must remember that
the figures in this tale are mainly not people, but archetypes representing
psychic functions rather than personalities.

And when she comes, we see the anima with all its attributes: "with
a robe of flame-red silk about her, and around the maiden's neck a torque
of red gold, and precious pearls thereon and rubies. Yellower was her head
than the flower of the broom, whiter was her flesh than the foam of the
wave; whiter were her palms and her fingers than the shoots of the marsh
trefoil from amidst the fine gravel of a welling spring. Neither the eye of
the mewed hawk, nor the eye of the thrice-mewed falcon, not an eye was
there fairer than hers. Whiter were her breasts than the breast of the white
swan, redder were her cheeks than the reddest foxgloves. Whoso beheld
her would be filled with love of her. Four white trefoils sprang up behind
her wherever she went; and for that reason was she called Olwen."

The dominant colours are red and white, red outwardly (the dress,
red gold, rubies), white inwardly (all parts of her body, as well as the track

she leaves). Moon symbolism is a very wide-spread attribute of the sister-anima in many parts of the world, indicating an inward and spiritual, not outward and physical relationship. Red and white are a familiar contrast in the world of femininity, red indicating on the one hand passion, and white on the other, a great number of subtle meanings ranging from creative 'virginity' (not to be confused with 'chastity', on the level of the 'virgin mothers', meaning mothers whose lover-instinct is not impaired) to destructive frigidity. What is clearly indicated here is not frigidity but unviolated femininity ready to be plucked by anyone bold and skilful enough to approach her. In her relationship to a suitor hoping to rescue her out of the clutches of a jealous father, we might think of the colour scheme as being in reverse: that is to say of her as the red object of passion surrounded by an impenetrable sheet of ice, or, conversely again, of her as the cool haven of delight surrounded by the father's red jealousy. The clue to such play with concepts is given by the contrasting colours, which invite not logical thinking but psychological play-thinking, or imaginative creativeness.

Pearls are an indication of preciousness, and also have moon-connotation both as to their colour and as to their being found inside the dark womb of an unprepossessing shell. Her yellow (golden) hair is like that of the hidden son. In the psychology of most moderns, the most powerful sister-anima figure is dark haired or black (compare Shaw's 'black woman in search of a soul'). This is because men nowadays are so largely divorced from real instinctive life. Therefore the anima is inclined to be black, in order to supply this lack. But Culhwch was 'born of a sow' and had no such lack of instinctive background, so could afford to have a light-haired anima, indeed needed one to complete himself. There is much coming together of 'pig' and 'moon' in primitive pig mythology.

"She entered the house and sat between Culhwch and the high seat, and even as he saw her he knew her. Said Culhwch to her, 'Ah maiden, 'tis thou I have loved. And come thou with me.' " This is no ordinary 'love at first sight', which sometimes brings happiness but as often leads to disaster precisely because emotions properly belonging to the anima-relationship get projected on to a real woman with dire results. He 'knows' this sister-anima because she is his own internal contrasexual partner, she of whom it was said at the beginning that "love of the maiden entered into every limb of him, although he had never seen her", and of whom his stepmother had said " 'thy side shall never strike against woman till thou win Olwen daughter of Ysbaddaden Chief Giant' ". This proves conclusively (together with the fact that she became "his only wife so long as he lived") that there is no question of her dying first or outliving him, because they are one (or does anyone suppose that a man of that period would never sleep with another woman?). Olwen is no fleshly woman, but a spiritual essence without contacting which he could not make a successful marriage at all. A man so earthy as to have been 'born of a sow', and so arrogant withal, cannot be successfully civilised unless he go very deep into his own soul and take the hero's part to find the anima, without which he would become an outlaw or go mad like his mother.

There is no wooing. She is 'his' without question — because she always has been; though, till now, he has 'never seen her'. This is a meeting with his soul. And with it comes his first realisation of guilt, the beginning of human consciousness, and of the tremendous difficulties that still lie in the way of their union. This first meeting with Olwen is like a dream adumbrating what is to come. At one and the same time it indicates the nature of the battle necessary in order to achieve it, while giving courage by affording a preview of the prize. When he says " 'Come thou with me,' " she answers " 'Lest sin be charged to thee and me, that may I not do at all...' "

He has thought 'now I have her', just as he might possibly have had his mother alone in the mother-world excluding the father principle. But Olwen
is a father-world soul-image born of the incest taboo which interposes the
father (and the mother's refusing animus) between the boy and the primary
object of his desire, thus creating an emotional vacuum which can only be
filled by an anima figure representing an object of spiritual or internal union.
The external object, the mother, just is not there for this purpose. Mother-
blocked thoughts then turn to the sister as to an even more fitting mate,
being more of an age with him and still not 'owned' by another man. But
union with her is blocked also by the incest taboo. In the introductory
stage of our story the incest taboo is represented by the stepmother, who
is the cultural mother in the father-world, who has herself submitted to a
husband's authority, who knows its advantages, and knows also that this is
the way to develop true femininity of a kind that will not devour that which
it brings forth. She looks forward to the future, and understands the boy's
problem in a way that, being 'not yet of an age' to understand, he cannot
without her help. She points to her own daughter, who would be a legitimate bride, being of no blood relation to Culhwch. But she knows that
Culhwch, with his immense natural strength, will, failing very special mea-
sures which that same strength will help him to undertake, surely run amok
if these are not imposed on him. So she swears a 'destiny' upon him to undertake the hero task of seeking his anima. This means, however, fighting
his own possessiveness, the possessiveness of a natural animal to whom all
females of its species are legitimate mates. It means fighting the assumption
that he can have absolute dominion over any object of his desire.

Till now, he has met with no such check on the anima level. True, he
has submitted to Arthur by making the symbolic phallic offering of having
his hair trimmed, but that was with the ulterior motive of obtaining a

'godfather' to help him to find 'the girl'. Now he has found her, and she herself withholds. He has to prove his manhood. It would be 'sin' not to do so, for, were he to have her otherwise and without a fight, that would indeed be 'incest' on the spiritual level. It would give him what he wanted 'naturally', and therefore without advancing him one iota towards self-knowledge, the knowledge of his own overweening negatively possessive side. This is precisely what the 'initiating mother' planned to prevent by sending him upon this arduous quest to meet his 'destiny'. Now he has met it. And it is Olwen herself, that 'destiny', who sees to it that he shall not escape this confrontation with himself.

There are two 'other selves' within a man. One is his contrasexual self, his anima. The other is the uncontrolled part of his 'natural' masculinity. This is technically known to analytical psychologists as the shadow. This can have more than one aspect. A man can be ignorant of his own 'good' (superior) shadow, or of his 'bad' (inferior) one. Both can be of great strength. We have already referred to figures like the great Arthur and the lesser companion-hero Goreu as partaking of the nature of shadow figures. These are on the superior side. They actually help him against his inferior shadow figure, which is the first major obstacle that he now meets. Strangely and horrifyingly enough, this is tacked on inseparably to his most highly desired anima, as her father. This is the chief giant Ysbaddaden, who has been inseparable from her from birth up. He is her progenitor *without a wife*. That is to say, no wife is mentioned. She is a father's daughter, as he is a mother's son. The two are complete opposites. Each brings with it its own obstacle. She brings her father's possessiveness. He brings his mother's. Her father-boundness shows itself in her subservience. His boundness to a mother-nature image shows itself in a supreme confidence that amounts to arrogance and in fact ignores the obstacle, which is the negative

54

side of this very two-sided quality. Possessive arrogance will be his downfall if he cannot control and get the better of it. It is composed of two elements, his 'fatherlessness' leading to arrogance, and his mother-boundness
leading to the extremity of his desire for a woman, or alternatively an anima,
to replace the all-giving mother whom he has lost. Of these the first to be
tackled, because most on the surface, is the arrogance masquerading under
the guise of over-masculinity. This is precisely also the character of Olwen's
father Ysbaddaden. This he can tackle to some extent alone, and does so,
as we shall see. But deeper by far is the problem of the 'natural' mother,
which can only be symbolised by something utterly strange and sub-human
of still greater power than the lack of adequate father-image. This will later
be symbolised by the ravaging boar.

The mother problem is, however, ignored by Olwen, who, as very
consciously a father's daughter, immediately calls his attention to the father
problem, and, with wisdom superior to his, cuts off all further truck with
him till he has tackled and overcome it. In her speech to him which now
follows — which is her only and hardly encouraging reply to his love-declar-
ation and imperious demand that she shall immediately come to him — it
must now be born in mind that we shall be operating all the time on two
levels. Olwen will be speaking of her father, as if she were a woman and he
her actual father. But we shall be thinking also psychologically in terms of
Olwen being Culhwch's anima, and Olwen's father the chief giant representing Culhwch's own monstrous overvaluation of his own one-sided masculinity, to which all female beings including his own anima should submit
without question. The anima, however, never does. If this is demanded of
her, she disappears, as indeed Olwen now does till he has won his self-battle
and conquered both parental images, the arrogant because non-contacted
father-image, and the yet more deeply ravaging mother one. She does not

55

mention the mother problem, being herself female and therefore probably too close to it. She only mentions the father, but does so in no uncertain terms.

Having refused point blank to go with Culhwch then and there 'Lest sin be charged to thee and me', here thought of as the 'sin' of spiritual incest bypassing the problem of the incest taboo, she goes on " 'My father has sought a pledge of me that I go not without his counsel, for he shall live only until I go with a husband. There is, however, counsel I will give thee, if thou wilt take it. Go ask me of my father. And however much he demand of thee, do thou promise to get it, and me too shalt thou get. But if he have cause to doubt at all, get me thou shalt not, and 'tis well for thee if thou escape with thy life.' 'I promise all that, and will obtain it,' said he."

This is on the surface a simple Oedipus problem, but on a deeper level we have here a subtle repetition of the two-headed briar motif. It is the nature of the anima to deal in subtleties and turn things upside down. She is the very opposite to the Earth Mother. The Earth Mother is a mother's daughter, since men as cultural entities leading to transformation of instinct do not enter into her purview. The anima, however, as father's daughter, is the prime factor in a man's life mediating such change. Like Athene, born out of her father Zeus's head, she mediates the wishes of the archetype of the cultural or spiritual father (the 'god-father' in the extremest sense), the father who 'frees', as over against the wishes of the personal 'natural' father who wishes only to possess. She represents the 'full moon' of inner patrilineally-orientated wisdom fully lit up by the sun, as opposed to the purely matrilineal mother who, as the 'black sow' represents the 'black moon' (the period of the moon's invisibility) whose union with the sun is on a totally unconscious level and therefore quite undifferentiated and unaware of her own destiny. She dies (the old moon wanes) and dwindles to nothingness, so that the new moon may rise, and wax, and fi-. nally, as full moon and fully developed anima, may inwardly rule over the hearts of men.

Everything is now in reverse. In this case, the two-headed briar motif is represented by two male figures, 'father' and 'son', of which the second (as with the 'two mothers') is the progressive one. The giant represents the 'nature' side of Culhwch himself, who wants a woman but does not want self-knowledge. This side of him wants to be the eternal matrilineal son-lover enjoying all women without the responsibility of facing the implications of this very demand, which is that he shall remain a lover without a child, since matrilineally children belong to their mothers and not to their fathers. The father fertilizes, but remains unattached and without marital rights. That is to say, psychologically, that he has no future. He is ephemeral, and dies 'without issue' — without a soul. For souls grow through inhibition of direct desire, and (if this is accomplished knowingly) consequent development of inner, as opposed to outer, value. The primary factor beginning the growth of souls is the incest taboo. This, in a patrilineal society, is overtly expressed in conflict with the patriarchal father. But in a matrilineal society — and on the matriarchal level of the psyche — there is no such father. Yet the incest taboo is there, enforced by the mother's brother and the mother herself and the whole ethos of the matrilineal society. The impact of it comes to the son through the mother, from cradle upwards, not through the father who has no power over either him or her.

And so it does to Culhwch now, through the female figure of Olwen, the anima, who fills up the gap caused by the withdrawal of the natural mother-image owing to the incest taboo. Whereas the 'natural' mother, however, fell victim by dying to the growing patrilineal influence, since she could not submit to it, the stepmother accepted it. Olwen, the father's daughter and sister-anima, proceeding from the father and therefore knowledgeable of the father world, far from falling victim to it, is master of it. What the 'natural' mother brought about unconsciously but consciously tried to oppose, the anima (who is 'beyond' nature and on a level of greater awareness of ultimate values and of the change brought about by the father principle) does consciously, reversing the order. She, like the 'natural' mother, is aware of the duality in human life, but agrees with it instead of opposing it. So, in referring to this duality, she does not use a nature symbol such as that of the two-headed briar (which, on account of its primitivity, possibly reveals to the initiated but withholds from common men). She speaks quite openly of the matter in intelligible human terms, in terms of two 'counsels' with regard to the father-image. " 'My father has sought a pledge of me that I go not without his counsel, for he shall live only until I go with a husband. There is, however, counsel I will give thee...' " The emphasis here is, first on the father's counsel, and then on hers. The father's counsel is of a very primitive and personal nature, giving voice to his personal jealousy, possessiveness, and fear that this might have to yield to a younger rival. In that case he would just 'die' as the 'natural mother' had 'died'. In both cases the fear was the same — that some change might occur which would rob each of his or her omnipotence and release each offspring from his or her grasp as 'natural parents'. This would let them grow up into another and a wider (or deeper) world, that is to say to realise themselves and their individual destinies.

So far as the father knows himself, behaving only as a personal father, he is therefore, from the point of view of human development, a purely negative figure. But the anima, having come out of him, and therefore knowing the inner truth concealed behind this purely personal exterior, sees in him an archetypal patriarchal figure carrying within itself its own

58

opposite, namely the function of initiator into the new life which in his consciousness he dreads but with his unconscious he furthers. Olwen's counsel to Culhwch appears conciliatory and even humiliating, but is as subtle with double meaning as is the father's patriarchal nature itself. It is in fact *her* nature as patriarchal woman that she now expounds to the still matriarchal youth. She represents the inner consciousness and forward-looking initiating nature of the father principle alive in her. She tells Culhwch what he must do, without, however, telling him why. It is the nature of the anima that she just has to be obeyed (and here we have a 'good' one), blindly trusting that she knows what she is about. " 'And however much he demand of thee, do thou promise to get it, and me too shalt thou get...' " The father's doubt would be, of course, Culhwch's own doubt: the two are one. Son and father represent ego consciousness (the son) and his own non-ego in its masculine aspect (the father). In this respect shadow (father) and anima (Olwen) are allied, and represent the non-ego in its bisexual totality. But whereas the masculine element does not know what it is about and acts blindly, and, as the sequel shows, causes its own destruction, the anima does know, and advises ego accordingly. Ego, frustrated in its immediate demands, has to obey without question, being urged on only by the dynamics of desire which eventually carry him through.

CHAPTER 5

YSBADDADEN PENCAWR: AND ARTHUR

The dynamics immediately operate. In the service of love there is immediate battle and destruction through killing, the first of many killings that will take place before the goal of union with the anima is reached.

"She [Olwen] went to her chamber." This is the last that we shall see of her till, after orgies of destruction, she is finally won. She draws on Culhwch and his party by herself simply personificating desire, which has to be followed at all costs (and without 'doubt') if the result is to be achieved. "Then they arose to go after her to the fort" and immediately without any further comment "slew nine gatemen who were at nine gates without a man crying out, and nine mastiffs without one squealing". Here we have the number nine again (combining both the female period of gestation and extreme masculinity) and also the mastiffs which we met with before (cf. the giant mastiff owned by Custennin).

"And they went forward to the hall." Culhwch has penetrated with ease first Arthur's, now this stronghold. They find themselves immediately in the presence of Olwen's father Ysbaddaden Pencawr (*her* contrasexual 'other self'; *Culhwch's* homosexual 'shadow'). They greet him, and when he hears that they are seeking Olwen for Culhwch, he first complains about the absence of his gatekeepers, and then utters a phrase which has often been taken as just a kind of amusing description of what a giant might be supposed to be like. He says (and later repeats): " 'Raise up the forks under my two eyelids that I may see my future son-in-law.' " This indicates two things. Firstly, that he had been asleep, a common figure of speech for a state of unconsciousness. Secondly that he already knew his fate was sealed, that Culhwch would win his daughter, and that he would die: that the future would triumph over the past, that the free-thinking anima would supersede the possessive parent-image of the father. This constitutes 'seeing': " 'that I may *see* my future son-in-law.' " This phrase reminds us of the old order passing into the new in the words of the Nunc Dimittis: "Lord, now lettest thou thy servant depart in peace, according to thy word: for mine eyes have seen thy salvation." Simeon accepted his fate with gratitude, while Ysbaddaden, however, strove to avert it. He is the 'Old King' who dies, to make way for the New. But he is a matrilineal king (possessive and clinging to what he has) not a patrilineal one. He is the hero's mother's negative animus. If, in this paradox of initiation, he did not know, Olwen his daughter did. But she needed the hero to implement her knowledge, and through fighting for her, to create his manliness, thereby fructifying her hitherto-imprisoned forward-looking femininity.

As the story unfolds itself, the figure of this old doomed giant of a mother's animus destroying itself is a pathetic one. He knows he cannot survive, yet does his utmost to this spurring on the 'hero' to assert his manliness over against the ever-departing but ever-returning past. He says: " 'Come hither tomorrow. I will give you some answer.' " This was but a trick, presumably to gain time or put them off their guard. "They rose and Ysbaddaden Chief Giant snatched at one of the three poisoned stone-spears which were by his hand and hurled it after them." There follows a three-fold scene. On each of three consecutive days they visit him and after a parley as they arose to go, he hurled a poisoned stone-spear at them, but missed. One of the party snatched it up and hurled it back at him, but in their hands it turned to iron, and as iron it pierced him as it returned. Ellis and Lloyd (p. 198, note 134) says "The episode is reminiscent of the change of material for weapons brought about as the Stone Age passed into the Iron Age." This may be so, but iron is well-known alchemically as representing soul-substance harder and more durable and effective than stone. It is in this sense that we may take it here, as indicating the greater soul-power of Culhwch and his company, as possessors of metal artefacts — power of warriors. The first time the spear pierced Ysbaddaden through the ball of his knee and he cries " 'Like the sting of a gadfly the poisoned iron has pained me.' " The second time it pierced him in the middle of his breast, and he cries " 'Like the bite of a big-headed leech the hard iron has pained me.' " The third time Culhwch himself hurled it back and it pierced him through the ball of the eye, and he cries " 'Like the bite of a mad dog to me the way the poisoned iron has pierced me.' " Each time the wound is higher up and the beast to which its attack is likened is fiercer, till it is finally a mad dog, the kind of animal used later to hunt the terrible boar.

Each time the giant is pierced, no matter who has thrown the iron weapon into him, he cries out " 'Thou cursed savage son-in-law!' " and curses the "smith who fashioned it", or "the forge wherein it was heated". The source of power worries him. The smith and forge are symbols of the greater toughness of soul, which he fears rightly will prevail against his failing one. In ancient times, the smith and the shaman (or as here, the sorcerer) often competed, both knowers of magical things, as interpreters of people's problems.

62

Culhwch and his party have meanwhile been lodging in the house of
Custennin, who now therefore has clearly sided with them, and whose house
thus becomes the vantage point from which to launch their offensive against
his erstwhile oppressive lord. On the second day they enter the giant's hall
"with pomp and with brave combs set in their hair. . ." Doubtless such head
decoration may have been usual under such circumstances, but in view of
Arthur's having taken "a golden comb and shears with loops of silver, and
. . . combed [Culhwch's] hair", and of the very important part which comb
and shears are shortly to assume in bringing about Ysbaddaden's own death,
this detail of their head-dress may not be a chance one, but also a kind of
vaunting prophecy, the import of which Ysbaddaden will dimly perceive.
Thus vaunting, they say " 'Give us thy daughter in return for her portion
and her maiden fee to thee and her two kinswomen. And unless thou give
her, thou shalt meet thy death because of her.' " His death and Olwen's
nuptials were two aspects of one and the same happening, as marriage and
dowry commonly are. And note that there is no question of bride-price.
The bride-price was the hero's steadfastness, the dowry was her father's
death which he paid for having tried to imprison her.

Ysbaddaden replies equivocally. It is to be noted that he never dares
to refuse her outright, but always equivocates, knowing in truth he cannot
help himself. What he does now is to appeal to the past: " 'She and her
four great-grandmothers and her four great-grandfathers are yet alive. I
must needs take counsel with them.' " Four is an archetypal number, here
doubled to eight, a mandala-formation in kinship terms. We hear no more
of them after this stalling.

On the third day, after the iron had pierced him through the ball of
the eye (a female receptive symbol: the knee is phallic and male), he complains bitterly " 'So long as I am left alive, the sight of my eyes will be the

worse. When I go against the wind they will water, a headache I shall have, and a giddiness each new moon.' " The moon, as we have seen, is associated as a symbol with Olwen in her capacity as sister-anima. This 'giddiness each new moon' may be another sign that he knows he will lose her.

After this three-days' altercation (the preparatory, initiatory period), the fourth day arrives. This brings matters to a point. "Quoth they, 'Shoot not at us. Seek not the harm and deadly hurt and martyrdom that are upon thee, or what may be worse, if such be thy wish. Give us thy daughter.' " 'Martyrdom' is an interesting word, as though it is a true sacrifice that will be imposed on him. In any case, giants are traditionally stupid. Their size is in itself an inhumanity, and can but hamper them in ordinary life. Though he has now thrice cursed his 'savage son-in-law', he does not yet seem to know which of the company his future son-in-law is. The giant asks " 'Where is he who is told to seek my daughter? ' " This is an extraordinary touch — 'he who is told'! How does he know he has 'been told' unless he is aware of a superior power? We know that the superior power was the step-mother. And we know also this: that the giant himself is dual. In his nega-tive aspect, he is the agent of the regressive matriarchal mother; but in his hidden positive aspect, as architect of his own death and actual creator of the situation which makes the 'hero', whom in the conscious he considers to be his rival, he is the male initiating agent of the 'initiating' patriarchal mother. It seems this is a subtle acknowledgement of that fact, expressed almost as though it were a slip of the tongue, a well-known way that the unconscious has of forcing itself through against the conscious will. Cul-hwch answers indeed " ' 'Tis I who seek her, Culhwch son of Cilydd.' " Then comes the momentous confrontation between these rival opposites. The giant says " 'Come hither where I may see thee.' A chair was placed under him, face to face with him."

There are two keys to this: 'where I may see thee' and 'face to face'.
He has in fact already seen this rival, but then was new to the sight, and was
in doubt what he should do. By now he may have consulted the 'four great-
grandmothers' and 'four great-grandfathers' — the ancestral shades, that is
to say the deepest recesses of his own nature, who may have put him wise
as to his real function. This may be one aspect of the revelation that he received in order to face him at last with seeing eyes. The prospect was one
awesome enough to rob him temporarily of strength. This strong man had
to sit. (Or was his seat a throne, the martyr's throne?)

In any case, the enemies now meet, and each knows that the other is
out for his life. This is a typical scene of what is known in terms of analytical psychology as "confrontation with the shadow". Neither flinches.
The old man knows that he has met his fate. So does the hero. Or rather,
they are both heroes now, the one about to die, the other to live, the one
to renounce, the other to take. But, as in all initiation rites, the task of
taking is made as difficult as may be. If Culhwch does not fail, the old
man dies. He is, incidentally, 'old' only archetypally — being for each new
generation of heroes a giant with almost superhuman strength. It will need
greater strength on the part of the hero to overcome these obstacles.

The old man now first makes quite sure whom he is talking to. For
the third time the question is put and answered. He asks him " 'Is it thou
that seekest my daughter? ' " Culhwch replies " ' 'Tis I who seek her.' "
Ysbaddaden then speaks in the mysterious way typical of all initiating figures: " 'Thy pledge would I have that thou wilt not do worse by me than
is just.'." This dark saying of the doomed man probably means that he
knows inwardly that he is providing the means for Culhwch's hero-dom
while outwardly trying to destroy him. It is a Judas-like situation. The betrayal leads to the salvation of the apparently betrayed one. Culhwch,

whether at this point he understands or not — probably not, but he follows the archetypal pattern of honouring an enemy whom one is going to butcher — pledges his word, saying " 'Thou shalt have it.' " To which Ysbaddaden replies " 'When I have myself gotten that which I shall name to thee, then thou shalt get my daughter.' " Culhwch submits: " 'Name what thou wouldest name.' "

What Ysbaddaden in fact gets, in manner typical of the trickster aspect of fateful happenings, is to him the most desirable object — the shining boar's tusk with which to 'shave' himself. That same object is used by the hero for his utter humiliation and death. This consummation is only achieved, however, after many vicissitudes and dangers are overcome on the hero's behalf, arising from the tasks the giant now sets him.

The tasks are many, forty of them (thirty-nine in one version), but they all have for their ultimate object the hunting and destruction of the terrible **Ravaging Boar**, and getting from its head the wherewithal whereby Ysbaddaden may wash his own head, and comb and shave his beard. The meaning of all this would be obscure but for the analysis of the whole myth which we have undertaken. We here content ourselves with pointing out that Culhwch's own quest started by having his hair trimmed by Arthur as an act of subservience to him: the whole myth ends by Ysbaddaden being forcibly shaved "beard, flesh and skin to the bone, and his two ears outright" and then being caught up by the hair of his head and having his head cut off.

The tasks set are recited in a kind of litany in the form of a long list of things which Culhwch must do. These all are centered ultimately round the successful hunting of the boar (or boars, for there are two, representing two aspects of the problem), with the sole object of obtaining from them the razor, shears and comb. Ostensibly this is so dangerous that Culhwch will perish in the attempt, and Ysbaddaden will then not have to part with his daughter. His psychological ambivalence, however, is shown by the fact that all along he is aware of the agonising fact that he will lose his daughter, and that all this boar-hunt is actually in preparation for her wedding feast. In this way, he actually instructs his rival how to accomplish this. Culhwch does not in his own ego-personality accomplish any of these tasks but relies on a higher power, Arthur, to do so for him.

He does, however, take all the credit for the possession of this higher power. In what I have called the 'litany' of demand and answer between Ysbaddaden and Culhwch, each item is followed by a set refrain, in which Culhwch answers " 'It is easy for me to get that, though thou think it is not easy,' " to which the giant rejoins " 'Though thou get that, there is that thou wilt not get.' " He then goes on to name the next task, which follows logically on the one preceeding it. The 'shadow', however, in the form of Ysbaddaden, continually tries to discourage him (though it has the result of only spurring him on) by a whole series of devaluations. Thus in many cases the giant, having named some auxiliary hero whose help Culhwch must seek in the great fight against the boar, adds menacingly that he will not go with Culhwch, nor will he comply in any way with fulfilling the tasks, 'of his own free will, nor canst thou compel him'.

This last phrase is the more remarkable in the light of the phrase used by Ysbaddaden about himself at the end, when he has lost his beard and Olwen too: he exclaims bitterly " 'Of my own free will thou shouldst never have had her. And it is high time to take away my life.' " For the present the giant himself has been compelled, and the agent of this is Arthur. He says to Culhwch at the end, " 'Thank Arthur who has secured her for thee.' " Indeed, a great number, if not all, of the auxiliary heroes whose help Ysbaddaden has conjured Culhwch to secure are Arthur's men, and are among those whom Culhwch invoked to help him at the beginning, naming some 250 of Arthur's associates. As Arthur acts for Culhwch this is in itself not so remarkable. It suddenly assumes the proportions of an immense paradox, however, when, in imposing the thirty-seventh task, Ysbaddaden tells Culhwch to seek out " 'Arthur and his huntsmen to hunt Twrch Trwyth' ", and adds " 'a man of might is he, and he will not come with thee — the reason is that he is a man of mine' ".

Arthur, who hunts the boar and brings about Ysbaddaden's own downfall and death, thus turns out to be Ysbaddaden's 'own man'. This demonstrates the ambivalence and duality of all archetypes. Just as, according to the imagery of the 'two-headed briar' which introduces the whole theme of ambivalence, the 'natural' mother and the stepmother are seen to be two aspects of the same archetype of basic womanhood, so also Arthur and Ysbaddaden are one and the same, two aspects of the initiating process in its masculine aspect. The 'giant', corresponding to the 'natural' mother, represents the huge, culturally and spiritually blind, force of unconscious nature upon which life is founded but which always resists change. Arthur, on the other hand, in ordinary human form, represents that other half of the same archetype which has the intelligence to understand that the same force has in it the seeds of overcoming itself, and that its very destructiveness can be used in order to 'destroy destruction' and build anew on the devastated ground thus cleared. Arthur is the spiritual aspect of Ysbaddaden, therefore his successor in historical, human development.

This is what Olwen, the anima, meant by telling Culhwch " 'And however much [my father] demand of thee, do thou promise to get it, and me too shalt thou get.' " In saying this she was overtly meaning her own father. But the man whom Culhwch had already asked was Arthur: " 'My claim on thee is that thou get me Olwen daughter of Ysbaddaden Chief

Giant. And I invoke her in the name of thy warriors' " — those very warriors whose help against himself Ysbaddaden now tells him to get. Thus Arthur, the mortal enemy of Ysbaddaden, in his capacity as Ysbaddaden's own 'man', does Ysbaddaden's bidding in destroying him.

This paradox concerns one of the deepest revelations of psychology, namely that the shadow is always split, having two aspects, a positive and a negative one, both of great power and almost, but not quite, equally matched. This is the direct result of the incest taboo and of the problem of the 'two mothers', now appearing under male guise. The matriarchal one often appears passive and at first innocuous since, being in possession, it has no need for activity and therefore at first sight appears good and desirable. It does not kick up a fuss since it has all that it desires. Its children belong to it and they are content till stirred by some vague longing for 'otherness' which, anthropologically, is represented by the father whose right and influence over his children has not yet been recognised. Thus Ysbaddaden sits in his fort and does not move till, forced by Arthur, the patriarchal father ('godfather' in the matriarchal system) he bestirs himself till his desires are satisfied and his own anima released. It is the releaser thus who first appears as the attacker, while the real villain of the piece often appears as the innocent victim, harming no one.

If Ysbaddaden represents the mother's animus in its negative aspect, Arthur his psychic 'twin' represents it in its positive aspect. Each is the other's 'man'. Without Ysbaddaden, Arthur would not, in terms of this myth, exist, since there would be no energy of destructively possessive inertia for him to fight against. Nor would there be any incentive to fight, since there would be no Olwen to fight for. The two half-archetypes (or the twin archetypes) are inseparable.

Apart from being empirically deducible from this myth, and, indeed,

69

providing the only key by which it can be understood as a psychological document, this concept is of the utmost importance in psychotherapy. Only by understanding this kind of paradox can the psychotherapist range himself alongside the apparently destructive forces in a patient's psyche at the moment of breakdown, knowing, as the patient does not know, that these are healing forces bent not on destroying the patient's ego, which he always fears, but on destroying that which needs to be destroyed in the way of false constructs based on identification with the omnipotent earth-mother image. Ego is lost if it thinks that the destruction is levelled against itself, which pride leads it to think. But it is saved once it realises that the power of destruction is a measure devised by the autonomous psyche for destroying the patient's own self-destructiveness, and can willingly submit to having it destroyed, even assisting in its work.

This concept is relevant to our story as it explains why Olwen advised Culhwch to accept all the dangers which Ysbaddaden chose to confront him with. This is not a matter of 'bravery', but a matter of self-knowledge. The patient coming into analysis in a state of breakdown has not got this self-knowledge, but the helper or psychotherapist should have it, for without it little of lasting value can be done. With it, the whole psychic scene can be transformed. Culhwch himself, who is only a 'half-hero' in the psychological sense, did not have it. He thought he could get Olwen without facing his own destructive side as represented by Ysbaddaden Pencawr. Encouraged by Olwen, however, he accepts the tasks. But still he does not accomplish them himself. He leaves this to Arthur. In the sequel, Arthur indeed gets them. Together with his warriors, Arthur does all the fighting, of which Culhwch reaps the reward. He is an adolescent figure dealing with adolescent problems, the deeper, more adult and mature aspects of which are coped with by Arthur.

CHAPTER 6

THE TASKS:

INTRODUCTORY AND YSGITHYRWYN

We have elaborated on the nature of the relationship between the twin figures of Ysbaddaden and Arthur, but we have not yet examined *why* these two opposite figures should be in such subtle alliance. Let us look at the tasks and the orgy of fighting to which they led.

By no means all of these tasks are fulfilled as the story proceeds. Many of the minor ones are not mentioned again. These mostly refer to obtaining the help of lesser heroes notable for this or that skill in hunting, which are not always important to the main lines of the story. The meaning of the minor tasks is easily understandable, as they form a consecutive series. The first seven tasks are of a general nature, and, if we think of the list of tasks as a kind of summary of what has to be achieved, form a kind of preamble. They deal with the fertility problem along fairly familiar lines, in terms of primitive agriculture, with particular reference to Culhwch's approaching marriage — the final consummation of which is never in question. In order for a true union to develop, proof of fertile grounds for it must first be obtained.

In proposing the first task, Ysbaddaden says to Culhwch " 'Dost see the great thicket yonder? ...I must have it uprooted out of the earth and burnt on the face of the ground so that the cinders and ashes thereof be its manure; and that it be ploughed and sown so that it be ripe in the morning against the drying of the dew, in order that it be made into meat and drink for thy wedding guests and my daughter's...' " The thicket is a Great Mother symbol, particularly in connexion with the boar hunt; there the boar turns at bay for its last self-defence before its death, and as such is commonly met with in classical literature. It is a tangled growth of almost impenetrable complexity which can be a refuge for wild animals, but can also be a last stronghold from which they attack their pursuers. Symbolising in this way the most withdrawn and labyrinthinely hostile defence mechanism of Mother Nature in her terrible aspect (its thorns are like Medusa's snaky hair), it may be regarded as the first task of a hero to uproot and burn it, and used (note the eternal paradox that what was most dangerous can become what is most valuable) as the matrix (manure) out of which will grow meat and drink for the marriage feast of Mother Nature's own greatest enemy or opposite, the anima.

The second task is to get a husbandman. I need not stress the obvious sex symbolism of this. The third task is to find one who will set the irons for the plough. Note here a possible parallel to the irons (phallic symbols of psychic power) which pierced Ysbaddaden when he tried to prevent Culhwch and his companions from entering his fort. The next three tasks (four, five, and six), concern the getting of pairs of oxen to plough with: first, two oxen, next, two further oxen, both named; then two horned oxen. The yoking together of each pair is a stressed item, the last two coming from different parts of the country and being said to have been men 'whom God transformed into oxen for their sins'. One can see here a reference to the two parents, and on another level to any two pairs of opposites that have to be joined.

The seventh task returns to the original motif of the land, and we can read between the lines that it is the same place where the thicket formerly was. The giant asks " 'Dost see the hoed tilth yonder? ' " (contrasted to the uncultivated thicket that has been transformed by fire) and immediately reveals his thoughts by saying " 'When first I met the mother of that maiden [Olwen], nine hestors of flax seed were sown therein; neither black nor white has come out of it yet, and I have that measure still. I must have that in the new-broken ground yonder, so that it may be a white head-dress for my daughter's head on the day of thy wedding-feast.' " Olwen is thus, on a deeper level, also the virgin tilth or soil in which the black and white seeds were sown. The black and white seeds sown in it symbolise semen, itself in turn symbolising his own good and bad desires towards her that have not flourished — because it was not his function to sow them. But evil can be undone. And here we perceive a new subtlety: he still has that measure. But it must not be himself who sows the seed — it is to be Culhwch, his 'other side'. In all this delicate handling there is a tacit understanding that the 'hero' is also himself, that side of himself that will live on in the hero when his own present life (that is to say, attitude to life) has gone. If his sowing was a mixture of black and white signifying ambivalence, the hero's will be only white — legitimate and fitting for a bride.

"...Heracles, like Jason, was ordered to tame two bulls, yoke them, clean an overgrown hill, then plough, sow, and reap it in a single day — the usual tasks set a candidate for kingship." (Graves, *The Greek Myths,* vol. 2, p. 117.) This sort of rite was associated with the candidate's fertility, and his marriage to the goddess.

The next five tasks assume that the wedding feast is on. The text is punctuated with bitter-sweet references to it, in which Ysbaddaden as the defeated rival partakes as an observer in his own downfall. These tasks are the getting of food and appurtenances for it. The eighth task is to get " 'honey that will be nine times sweeter than the honey of a virgin swarm, without drones and without bees [a magic food], to make bragget [mead] for the feast' ". The ninth concerns " 'the cup of Llwyr son of Llwyrion, in which is the best of all drink; for there is no vessel in the world which can hold that strong drink [the nectar of love for Culhwch and the bitter cup for himself], save it' ". The tenth is to get " 'the hamper of Gwyddneu Longshank [Garanhir] [10] : if the whole world should come around it, thrice nine men at a time, the meat that every one wished for he would find there-in, to his liking' ". A world of longing is in this phrase. Ysbaddaden will need much comfort at this feast, and therefore adds " 'I must eat therefrom the night my daughter sleeps with thee.' " The eleventh task is to get " 'the horn of Gwlgawd Gododdin to pour out for us that night' ". The twelfth is to get " 'the harp of Teirtu [11] to entertain me that night' ". We may recall the harp that David played to Saul in the extremity of his agony. Ysbaddaden may not be able to bear too much, and so he adds " 'When a man pleases, it will play of itself; when one would have it so, it will be silent.' " So he will nurse his misery, while his successor-self lies in his marriage bed. All the time he comforts himself: " 'He will not give it of his free will, nor canst thou compel him.' "

The thirteenth task (the one which one source omits): " 'The birds of Rhiannon, they that wake the dead and lull the living to sleep, must I have to entertain me that night.' " The waking of the dead refers to Cul-hwch; 'putting the living to sleep' refers to himself. The old order passes.

The fourteenth task is a transitional one. Culhwch is told to get " 'the cauldron of Diwrnach [12] the Irishman [Gwyddel], the overseer of Odgar son

Aedd king of Ireland, [13] to boil meat for thy wedding guests' '". The 'wedding' is to combine the death of the boar and of Ysbaddaden with the delivery of Olwen. The 'cauldron' is the melting pot in which all these diverse contents are to be brewed. It calls to mind, of course, witches and all the alleged good and bad contents of this fateful womb-symbol in which every kind of transformation occurs. It is not fulfilled by Culhwch but by Arthur's men, who seize it, whereon it becomes called Arthur's. They bring it from Ireland to Wales where it is referred to as 'the cauldron full of the treasures of Ireland'. The boiling of the meat may here well indicate the turmoil and transformation in process in Ysbaddaden's heart, he being one of the wedding guests.

Out of the melting pot comes the treasure, heavily disguised. In the fifteenth task Ysbaddaden says " 'I must needs wash my head and shave my beard. The tusk of Ysgithyrwyn Chief Boar [Penbaedd] [14] I must have, wherewith to shave myself. I shall be none the better for that unless it be plucked from his head while alive.' "

At first sight there may be little or no connexion between this and the previous task. This is due to the schizophrenic aspect of Ysbaddaden's character. Just as, at the beginning, Culhwch's 'natural' mother knew but could not face up to the fact that she would be supplanted and died, so Ysbaddaden's character is also split to the extent that, having foreseen the loss of his daughter, the compensation for this has to be veiled in deepest mystery. There is therefore a 'drop through' into what looks like an entirely other world. From wedding feast we turn now to the savagest of all boar hunts.

Who is in fact, however, being hunted? It is Ysbaddaden himself who is being hunted in his soul to yield up that to which he clings. He may not die while yielding it, but has to suffer his deprivation consciously, and only after this may die, having accomplished his task against his intensest conscious desire. So also the boar has to yield up its treasure while still alive — the tusk with which Ysbaddaden is to 'castrate' himself.

I point out here the similarity between the names of Ysbaddaden Pencawr and Ysgithyrwyn Penbaedd, the only two 'chiefs' mentioned in the myth, to realise that there must be some inner affinity between them, and that each has to yield up his treasure while still alive. It may at the same time be pointed out that 'cauldron' and 'head' have a psychological affinity. Each is a 'boiling pot' in which transformations occur. Each is a pregnant cavity, the one predominately 'female', the other predominately 'male', taking also feeling and thinking respectively as psychologically 'female' and 'male'. The 'head' is emphasised in both Ysbaddaden's case (he has to wash his head and shave his beard), and in Ysgithyrwyn's (from whose head — not snout — the tusk has to be plucked). I also point out that, while the cauldron has to be boiled (with fire outside and water in), Ysbaddaden's head has to be washed (with water outside and raging 'fire' inside).

By 'one tusk' there can be no doubt that what is meant is not one tusk of two projecting from either side of the mouth, but the image of a single tusk in the middle of the head. It will be remembered that the tusk must be 'plucked from his head when alive' — there is no mention of mouth or other tusk. The imagery thus calls to mind some fabulous boar-monster not unlike a unicorn, in the Old Testament a symbol of tremendous power and a terribly destructive one.

There are actually in this myth two boars, both made to yield up their respective treasures. The other is Twrch Trwyth (*Terrible Boar*), the hunting of which is described in far greater detail. These are usually considered to be 'doubles', that is to say that one boar is meant, but that two

76

legends have grown up in different places about two boars with very similar attributes, and that both legends are here referred to by the chronicler. This kind of doubling does not particularly worry the psychologist. Local differences always arise in story-telling, and are in the nature of things. Indeed, they go to prove rather than disprove the local genuineness of any myth. A dream with contradictory elements is much more likely to lead to understanding than one neatly constructed so as to conceal the contradictions. In the same way, the fact that the same myth may be associated with a certain spot in one locality and with another spot in another locality does not prove it 'untrue'. Myths cannot be untrue, for the character of mythology deals with psychic factors (not material ones), so wide-spread and common to a large number of people, that they quite naturally vary in their expression according to the particular circumstances, topographical position, or personal quirks of those relating them.

So there are two main boars in this myth (one having progeny, the other not). The stories are very similar, and seem at first sight to be superimposed on one another. What is essential is the psychic feeling, the emotional states or sequences of events or transformation processes which, in the nature of things, can only be expressed in symbolic terms. For instance, were there in the world no boars, it would not mean that the psychic processes symbolised by a boar hunt did not take place. It would mean simply that the psyche would take some other image to hand that could most nearly render what it was trying to express. In dreams it might, and often does, try lots of ways, till ego has the sense to see the common meaning behind them all.

Both boars are of huge dimensions (cf. the giant stature of Ysbaddaden), and each has to render up from his head the wherewithal for Ysbaddaden to shave his beard. The second boar (task twenty-one) is Twrch Trwyth.

77

This comes from the word *twrch,* meaning 'boar', and *trwyth,* which is one of a series of cognate words, and possibly means 'king' — 'King Boar' or 'Boar Son of a King' (as is borne out in later comment in the tale). In English, he is usually known as the Terrible Boar. It is the comb and shears taken from his two ears that Ysbaddaden also needs to shave himself. Towards the end of the myth the 'razor' (cf. tusk) is also said to be taken from him.

It is no chance matter that the boar-motif in this myth has been divided into two aspects. There were, as every folklorist knows, not only two but many boar-myths current in Celtic lands, as there were many such myths in other parts of Europe and in classical antiquity. During the course of our analysis we shall see that there was a very good reason for choosing, of all these, just two. And of the two that aspect of the boar-problem represented by the Twrch Trwyth symbolises a deeper psychic level than that symbolised by Ysgithyrwyn. Deep psychic levels are commonly regarded by the naive ego as 'foreign'. This split in, or these two aspects of, the boar problem is adumbrated here to illustrate the kind of mechanism used by the myth mind and the dream mind, in making use of topographical material to illustrate psychic fact.

The role of the boar might well appear to be that of the father. Culhwch not only had an actual father, Cilydd son of Cyleddon Wledig, and also a 'godfather' or psychic father in Arthur. But there is nothing to prevent him from archetypally having other 'fathers'. Ysbaddaden is his 'father', being the father of Olwen his sister-anima. But Ysbaddaden is also closely connected with the boar, with whose fate he is bound up. The boar, then, on a deeper level, is also something in the nature of a father-figure to Culhwch. He is, however, not directly a father-figure since, being a boar and not a man, his power is derived not from the side of Culhwch's father, but from that of his mother, who is a sow. He thus represents, not father,

78

but again the mother's negative animus, a quality he shares with Ysbadda-den. Arthur can envisage this, and later tackles the boar on Culhwch's be-half.

After I had myself published similar conclusions with regard to the role of the tusked boar in Malekulan religion ("Boar Sacrifice", John Lay-ard, *The Journal of Analytical Psychology,* Vol. I, No. 1, 1955), I came ac-ross Erich Neumann's comment: "The Great Mother... is the sow that far-rows and the boar that kills." As Nature Goddess, she destroys that to which she gives birth, appearing with typical ambivalence as 'female' in her reproductiveness, but in her destructive aspect as 'male'. The fierce male symbol of the boar thus represents the female symbol of the sow in her de-structive aspect. He acts as a 'mask' behind which the devouring mother shelters in order to disguise herself and not be recognised for what she is. But the hero's nature lies in the fact that he does recognise her behind her male guise and so can ruthlessly destroy her — his truly greatest enemy — and, as seen in this myth and in all others of like depth, she is a great ene-my of all mankind lurking in the unconscious of every one of us.

It is this dual aspect of the male and female qualities and bringing it on to a level with Arthur, as the bisexual Self, which gives rise to the two boars found in this myth. Ysgithyrwyn symbolises its more 'male' aspect through the obvious phallic significance of its tusk. With the insistence that Twrch Trwyth's treasure is to be found between its 'two ears' (cf. gen-ital labials), it symbolises the more 'female' aspect of the unconscious Self — a conclusion supported by the fact that it is only after Twrch Trwyth has been disposed of that the 'black witch' or 'hag' appears.

These tasks are still concentrated on the problem of getting the tusk from Ysgithyrwyn. The sixteenth task says: " 'There is no one in the world can pluck it from his head save Odgar son of Aedd king of Ireland.' " This

79

is the same king who owned the cauldron. Tusk and cauldron are thus closely connected, as a pair of opposites of obvious sexual and therefore also symbolically spiritual significance. The seventeenth task goes on to state: " 'I will not entrust the keeping of the tusk to any save Cadw of Prydain.' " [15] The tusk, then, is not only to shave with, but is of value in itself. The name Cadw means 'to keep'; Prydain is Pictland (Scotland). This man has a considerable role to play later in acting as male-midwife in the psychological sense, and is the one who uses the tusk as razor to shave off Ysbaddaden's beard.

The eighteenth task: " 'I must needs dress my beard for me to be shaved.' " But an even more fundamental requirement than the boar's tusk is revealed: " 'It will never settle unless the blood of the Black Witch [sorceress] be obtained, daughter of the White Witch [sorceress], from the head of the Valley of Grief in the uplands of Hell.' " The blood of the Black Witch is here seen as the ultimate need. The Black Witch is, of course, the sow, Mother Nature; she has to be slain in order that the possessive aspect of her may be eliminated and that the life-giving blood of inner freedom for her progeny, which she has hitherto withheld, may be absorbed. They may then live their lives apart from her. The usual dichotomy met with whenever we touch femininity on its deeper levels is met with here also: the contrast between the Black Witch and the White. It is a paradox in this case that the Black Witch is the younger and the one pregnant with the future, once her inner value can be obtained. White witches are usually considered as 'good', black witches 'bad', according to external appearances; inwardly their roles are reversed. The white witch is the evil one because she is the hypocrite, appearing to be good. The black witch has in her the power of nature — of the pregnant unconscious — which has, however, to be wrung from her. Ysbaddaden is certainly now in the throes of grief, knowing that he is to be beheaded in order to make way for his rival. The blood to be shed is partly his. The tusk of the boar is to be used in shaving his own head but by Cadw of Prydain, who is the only man to whom he would entrust its keeping. Thus, intense irony.

The boar is thus seen to be the Black Witch (sow) in male disguise. Note that it is one tusk not two, and it is taken from the boar's 'head'. Boars' tusks, as we have seen from Malekulan evidence, symbolise on one level the *vagina dentata*, the destructive possessiveness of the mother-image ready to devour her young. They are, in this aspect, castrating symbols. This is a single tusk, therefore undifferentiated. The beard may here be taken as representing the head, and is a secondary sex characteristic.

We find that the terms in which the tasks are set carry on the transformation symbolism, as they are psychological symbols referring to real psychic fact. The nineteenth task says: " 'The blood [of the Black Witch] will be no use unless it be obtained while warm.' " This hints at the fact that it is no use 'just killing the witch'. No psychic element can be eliminated, since psychic contents are indestructible. Just as the tusk had to be plucked from White Tusk's head while still alive, so as to preserve the living continuity, so also the blood of the Black Witch has to be transmitted as living substance. Her power must be absorbed into the living structure of the succeeding phase, and thereby will be transformed. If not, it will reconstitute itself in the old pattern and the witch or Devouring Mother principle will continue her havoc in the unconscious. " 'There is no vessel in the world will keep the heat in the liquid that is put therein save the bottles of Gwyddolwyn the Dwarf [Gorr], [16] which keep their heat from the time when the liquid is put into them in the east till one reaches the west.' " The dwarf is a psychological symbol for the acceptance of earth values. Small and 'serving', and inwardly wise, he is in direct contrast to the psychic inflation of the giant. The blood of the Black Witch must keep its heat (living, dynamic power) and not be allowed to get cold, which might well signify indifference to its essentiality. East to west signifies the sun's course through the heavens, and so the hero's life-journey.

The next task refers right back to infancy. " 'Some will wish for milk, but there will be no way to get milk for every one until the bottles of Rhynnon Stiff-Beard [Rhin Farfod] [17] are obtained. In them no liquid ever turns sour.' " The dwarf is also the accepting child, who needs 'milk' as the adult needs 'blood'. The two liquids are complementary in their meaning. This refers to the childlike attitude of acceptance of whatever befalls, which has to be retained throughout life, if life itself is not to become 'sour'.

This ends the tasks dealing with Ysgithyrwyn. They now turn to deal with his psychic twin, the redoubtable Twrch Trwyth.

CHAPTER 7

THE TASKS: TWRCH TRWYTH

One of the difficulties in arranging this material is its inconsequence on the logical plane, though not on the psychological one. Thus, the three tasks just mentioned, dealing with the blood of the Black Witch, follow directly on those concerned with the taking of Ysgithyrwyn's tusk. In the actual fulfilment of the tasks the order is changed, and the slaying of the hag and taking of her blood is not accomplished till after Twrch Trwyth has been killed. The hunting of him is of far greater import, and takes far longer to describe, than the brief mention of the attack on Ysgithyrwyn. This is another indication of the fact that the two boars are regarded as two complementary aspects of one and the same psychic phenomenon.

Of Twrch Trwyth it is later said by Arthur that " 'He was a king, and for his wickedness God transformed him into a swine.' " Thus both boars have eminently human attributes (White Tusk — phallic) but on an archetypal scale. I have also mentioned that the name could mean King Boar or Boar Son of a King. The notion of a man being transformed into an animal 'because of his wickedness' is a wide-spread one in all folk-lore, found also in connexion with belief in the transmigration of souls. It is basically a

psychological concept, indicating regression is the purely animal side of human nature unrelieved by 'reason' and so purely instinctive and *un*transformed in the sense of 'inhumanised'. Extreme animus reactions are among such phenomena, and these, when negative, are something of what the boar symbolises in all mythologies with most surprising regularity. This means, as we have seen, the hostile aspect of femininity (the Great Mother) in male form.

We have seen this to be the case with regard to Ysgithyrwyn being the Black Witch in male guise. The same connexion with the witch is to be found in the case of Twrch Trwyth, but in much more dramatic form when Arthur, after recovering from the strain of hunting him over the whole Celtic world, immediately proceeds alone to the far more desperate encounter with the hag — whose presence or hiding place could not be detected so long as her agent Twrch Trwyth was in the field to conceal her.

The hunting of Twrch Trwyth is so much more important than that of Ysgithyrwyn that not only is he common in ancient Celtic literature, but Lady Charlotte Guest uses his name under the form of *The* Twrch Trwyth as sub-title to the entire myth. In her notes on him (1877 edition, p. 288) she quotes writers as referring to "magic spells. . .like those produced by the circle and wand of Twrch Trwyth", as though he were a magician in human form.

In the twenty-first task, Ysbaddaden declares: " 'There is no comb and shears in the world wherewith my hair may be dressed, so exceeding stiff it is, save the comb and shears that are between the two ears of Twrch Trwyth son of Taredd Wledig.' " A small point may first be mentioned about this, namely that shears consist of a pair of blades in contrast to the single razor-like object that is Ysgithyrwyn's tusk (actually referred to as a 'razor' later on, when both boars have become as one in the chronicler's mind).

More striking, however, is the getting of the comb and shears from "between the two ears of Twrch Trwyth". That this is no chance phrase is shown by its frequent repetition in the remaining parts of the narrative. There is a marked contrast here between the *one tusk* of Ysgithyrwyn and the *two ears* of Twrch Trwyth.

If the 'comb and shears', said to be found between the two ears of Twrch Trwyth, correspond to the one central tusk of Ysgithyrwyn, we thus get the combined image of central tusk between two ears. This, if it be the case, endows all this imagery, which otherwise is well-nigh incomprehensible, with meaning. The tusk thus becomes on the one hand a phallic symbol displaced on to the head, which is an extremely common mythological and psychological motif. On the other hand — and symbols can be taken on many levels — it represents, like any trinitarian formula — a third, transcendant thing uniting two opposites (symbolised by the two ears). However this may be, one is a 'male' number, and two a 'female' one. I suggest here that the basic imagery concerning this aspect of the two boars combined is that of duality united or transformed by a unity transcending the duality. The boar's tusk as symbol of the spirit transcending the duality of life and death (or male and female, or any other pair of opposites) is found in Malekula and elsewhere.

It is of the nature of spirit to destroy in order to re-create, and we have seen this to be a function of the initiating patriarchal mother-image as well. It is the key to this myth that this is so. The head representing the spiritual phallus, symbolic castration (circumcision) of the head, indicated in this tale by trimming the hair or shaving the beard, is equivalent, when undertaken willingly (Culhwch at the hands of Arthur), to a sacrificial initiation into new life. When suffered willingly, it means spiritual death. Culhwch, representing the new order, submits to Arthur. Ysbaddaden, on the contrary, representing the old order about to die unwillingly, tries to avoid this by placing Culhwch's head in his own noose. He uses him as a substitute in what should be Ysbaddaden's own heroic quest, trying to decoy him to what would be his death if he undertook it unwillingly. But Culhwch, on Olwen's instructions, submits to this also, since Olwen is his 'contrasexual side' which understands the paradox.

We have reached the beginning of the initiation process, as adumbrated in the setting of these tasks. The next fourteen tasks are all concerned with preparations for the hunt of the Twrch Trwyth. The first four of these concern the getting of a whelp called Drudwyn [18] belonging to Greid [19] son of Eri. Task twenty-two deals with him direct. Tasks twenty-three to twenty-five are: " 'There is no leash in the world may hold on him, save the leash of Cors [20] Hundred-claws [Cant Ewin]... There is no collar in the world can hold the leash, save the collar of Canhastyr [21] Hundred-hands [Canllaw]... The chain of Cilydd [22] Hundred-holds [Canhastyr] to hold the collar along with the leash.' " These 'hundreds' indicate the giant nature of the whelp that will be needed to hunt the giant boar.

Task twenty-six: " 'There is no huntsman in the world can act as houndsman to that hound, save Mabon son of Modron, who was taken away when three nights old from his mother. Where he is is unknown, or what his state is, whether alive or dead.' " This giant hero has been translated as the Great Son of the Great Mother (Mabon, *Maponus* 'The Great Son'; Modron, *Matrona* 'the Great Mother': Jones, p. xv). His mother has been equated with Rhiannon (*Rigantona*), the Great Queen whose birds Ysbaddaden summoned in task thirteen to ease his pain because "they wake the dead and lull the living to sleep". (Jones, p. xv.) These magic birds are spirit birds reversing the matriarchal order and instituting the patriarchal one, the world of internalised values. Giants are psychic factors of immense power — and none is more powerful than the power of the mother.

Mabon is also one of 'the three supreme prisoners of the Island of Britain', inferior in this respect only to 'one more exalted than the three', Arthur himself, who spent three nights in three prisons, the last three in the 'dark prison under the stone' (Guest, 1877 edition, p. 192). Mabon himself can be connected with the hero Pryderi who as an infant was spirited away from his mother, and she herself was 'punished as though she had slain him' (Jones, p. xv). G. and T. Jones sum up all this as "the story of how the king of the Otherworld changes place with an earthly king, in order that he may beget a wonder-child on an earthly mother." The wonder-child is of course the hero of this and many other myths. The motive of being a prisoner is that of being in fact drawn away from the satisfactions of ordinary everyday instinctive existence, which always, to he who is first experiencing it, appears to be a tragedy; but, if accepted, it can lead to the development of an internal psychic power and understanding far outweighing the straightforward instinctive satisfactions that one has lost.

The King of the Otherworld always at first sight appears, like Pluto, as a destructive ravager, but is in fact the male aspect of the Self, that inner value that transcends and rules external life from the recesses of the soul. All who have been submitted to his terrible visitations and have not succumbed, but have managed to weather the storm and absorb its strength into themselves, partake of this quality of Selfhood, as Arthur did, and Mabon in lesser degree, and Goreu son of Custennin, and now Culhwch. All have been imprisoned in the mother-element from which they draw their strength but from which they now have to be released.

Mabon has the strength that 'no [other] huntsman in the world' has got to prosecute the hunt against the huge power of the matriarchally possessed Twrch Trwyth, because he has both drawn his strength from the mother element of unconscious nature and knows its imprisoning force. In the terms of this task, he is still subject to it since "where he is is unknown, or what his state is, whether alive or dead". One of the main items in the fulfilment of these tasks will be his rescuing from a sea-prison by Arthur and some of the 'oldest animals' — instinctive forces of wisdom and subtlety.

The following two tasks are still concerned with him. Task twenty-seven describes the kind of libido that Mabon will need to prosecute the hunt. As often in dreams, this is here figured as a horse: " 'Gwyn Dun-mane, the steed of Gweddw (as swift as the wave is he!) under Mabon to hunt Twrch Trwyth.' " Horses are often associated with the sea. In Greek mythology Poseidon as a horse stamps his foot and the waters gush forth. We speak of waves in a storm as 'sea horses'. Like wild horses, impetuous and irresistible, a man can drown in them, but if he can ride them in a well-founded ship (as a man rides a horse which carries him), they can support him on his voyages. Horses symbolise libido derived from the mother, the feminine element which in so many mythologies is also symbolised by the sea. Here the likening of Mabon's steed to a swift wave refers to his close contact with the mother world. It is on this steed that Mabon pursues Twrch Trwyth into the waves in one of the final scenes.

Task twenty-eight is still concerned with him: " 'Mabon will never be obtained, where he is is unknown, till his kinsman Eidoel son of Aer [23] be first obtained; for he will be untiring in quest of him. He is his first cousin.' " This task hides (or reveals) a deep secret, the elucidation of which is seen when this double-task is fulfilled. Here I point out only two things: firstly, just as there are two boars, representing two main psychic levels of 'boar-hood' ('male' and 'female'), so also there are in Mabon two levels of which Eiddoel represents the 'male' or more external one, and Mabon himself — the other, deeper, more inward one, directly connected with the source of being, the Great Mother. The first has to be used to find the second. Intellect has to be employed in order to release the deepest emotional faculties. Secondly, the use of the term 'first cousin' indicates this relationship. We have already met with this in the relationship between Culhwch and Arthur, which indicates a similar psychic factor. Culhwch also cannot be 'released' from the bondage of purely natural phenomena without the help of Arthur.

Having earlier called for one huntsman, the duality running all through this myth seems to demand a second. The twenty-ninth task demands the help of " 'Garselit [24] the Irishman [Gwyddelian], chief huntsman of Ireland' ".

Duality also demands two whelps. Only one whelp has been mentioned so far, but the existence of two is assumed. There is also the problem of the leash. This indeed leads us into deep waters. In task thirty, Ysbaddaden demands: " 'A leash from the beard of Dillus [25] the Bearded [Farfawc], for save that there is nothing will hold these two whelps. And no use can be made of it unless it be twitched out of his beard while he is alive, and be plucked with wooden tweezers. He will not allow any one to do that to him while he lives, but it will be useless if dead, for it will be brittle.' " Let us note first the reduplication here of Ysbaddaden's own beard, and that the leash is manufactured out of it; secondly the motif here repeated that the beard must be plucked out of Dillus while he is alive. This may seem at first sight to be just one more gruesome detail, but, as in the case of Ysgithyrwyn's tusk that had to be plucked from his head while he is still alive, and of the Black Witch's blood that had to be obtained while warm, this indicates the need for continuity, and that good grows out of evil if the problem of evil is understood.

Yet a third huntsman is now invoked. The thirty-first task runs:

" 'There is no huntsman in the world will hold those two whelps, save Cyne-dyr the Wild son of Hetwn the Leper [Glafyrawc]. Nine times wilder is he than the wildest beast on the mountain.' " Note that it is Cyledyr the Wild son of Nwython mentioned later, whom Gwyn son of Nudd forced to eat his own father's heart so that he went mad. Cyledyr was finally paired with Mabon son of Modron when they two on their horses plunged into the water after Twrch Trwyth and took from him the shears. Cynedyr's wildness and being the son of a leper illustrate still further the problem of good coming out of evil.

The problem of evil is now deepened. Task thirty-two runs: " 'Thou wilt not hunt Twrch Trwyth until Gwyn son of Nudd [26] be obtained, in whom God has set the spirit of the demons of Annwn, lest this world be de-stroyed.' " Annwn is the Underworld. Gwyn son of Nudd is known as the King of Faerie. In an incident related later he seems to represent the powers of nature as opposed to those of transformed spirit, and as such shows signs of being opposed to Arthur. He certainly is anti-patriarchal, since he forces Cyledyr to eat his father's heart. He also quarrels with Arthur's father-in-law over a girl he stole from him, and as a result it was agreed that he should do battle with him "each May Calends for ever and ever, from that day till doomsday". We enter now into the world of opposites equally matched.

The thirty-third task carries on the same motif: " 'There is no horse in the world that will avail Gwyn to hunt Twrch Trwyth, save Du, the horse of Moro Oerfeddawg.' " *Du* meaning 'black'. It is a black horse that he must ride, symbolising the unconscious and allied to the Black Witch whose inner value (her blood) is the ultimate value.

In task thirty-four the chronicler clearly has in mind Arthur as the greatest of all heroes — the crucial phrase about whom comes in the next task but one. But he demurs, putting into Ysbaddaden's mouth the weak statement: " 'Until Gwilenhin [William?] king of France come, Twrch Trwyth will never be hunted without him. It is improper for him to leave his kingdom, and he will never come hither.' " The king of France gets inserted from time to time into this narrative as a purely lay figure, to heighten superficial effect. The chronicler has his tongue in his cheek in providing him with a perfectly legitimate excuse for not putting in an appearance at so paltry and absurd an affair as the hunting of a mythical boar, knowing full well that Arthur will risk life and limb for it, aware of what it means.

We are, however, now approaching the ultimate issue of Twrch Trwyth and Arthur, and a new motif appears: task thirty-five says: " 'Twrch Trwyth will never be hunted without the son of Alun Dyfed [27] be obtained. A good unleasher is he.' " We have heard previously of leashing, but no unleashing. This means that the quarry is near.

Task thirty-six reveals it and at the same time once more the ambivalence of the whole story: " 'Twrch Trwyth will never be hunted until Aned and Aethlem [28] be obtained. Swift as a gust of wind would they be; never were they unleashed on a beast they did not kill.' " These two appear in the story only once more, when Twrch Trwyth has been finally defeated and his treasures taken from him; he flees out to sea: "From that time forth never a one has known where he went, and Aned and Aethlem with him.' " They seem to be aspects of the Twrch Trwyth, symbolising possibly the two opposites within himself that have produced his own ambivalence, aspects 'unleashed' against himself. Although he has 'made' Arthur and all his host by forcing them to battle and winning it, these aspects then drive or accompany him into obscurity — so often the disguised 'saviour's' role. There is a contrast here also between these two 'swift as a gust of wind' and Mabon's horse 'swift as the wave'. Water is heavy, wind volatile. Mabon as mother's son is borne on the water element which supports and nourishes him. Twrch Trwyth, on the other hand, may be regarded as 'pure spirit', which can be as wholly negative as it can be wholly positive. He was the carrier of it, ultimately the victim — so very much of a saviour in disguise, though an unwilling one and so a defeated sufferer. These two co-beasts Aned and Aethlem, who appear at the moment of Arthur's final victory, evidently act as introducers in the chronicler's mind to the person of Arthur himself. The next task, thirty-seven, puts into Ysbaddaden's mouth the demand for " 'Arthur and his huntsmen to hunt Twrch Trwyth. A man of might is he, and he will not come with thee — the reason is that he is a man of mine.' " Ysbaddaden, fighting against himself in getting Culhwch to amass Arthur and his retinue, is like the boar also a saviour in disguise who 'perishes' when the new order triumphs over the old.

The main point has been reached. The chronicler can now act the buffoon. Task thirty-eight has it that Twrch Trwyth can never be hunted until " 'Bwlch and Cyfwlch and Syfwlch[29] be obtained. . .' " What joke lies behind these squelching words is not divulged, but it is evidently a traditional one. The same three are mentioned towards the end of the long list of warriors invoked by Culhwch earlier on, when he also must have got a bit tired of reciting them. " 'Three gleaming glitterers their three shields; three pointed piercers their three spears; three keen carvers their three swords.' " Three horses are named and three dogs, and with grand inconsequence the name of Arthur's dog Cafall is one of these. Their three wives have joke-names meaning Late-bearer, Ill-bearer and Full-bearer, their three witches (elsewhere, grandchildren) Och, Scream and Shriek, their three daughters Plague, Want and Penury, their three maidservants Bad, Worse and Worst-of-All. " 'The three men shall wind their horns, and all the others will come to make outcry, till none would care though the sky should fall to earth.' "

Task thirty-nine returns to some kind of sense with a demand for the help of what might be thought to be a 'double' of Ysbaddaden Pencawr himself: " 'The sword of Wrnach the Giant; never can he be slain save with that. He will not give it to anyone, neither for price nor for favour, nor canst thou compel him.' "

The fortieth and last task returns to sanity. Culhwch is told: " 'Wakefulness without sleep at night shalt thou have in seeking those things. And thou wilt not get them, nor wilt thou get my daughter.' " Wakefulness without sleep is a requirement of every hero. It means awareness of the Self and of the 'otherness' of things. Each side of the total personality must be constantly aware of the other, ego and Self must be at one. Ego must be constantly aware of Self, and be ready to serve its interests, or let the Self take over and follow it.

It is this latter of the two alternatives (what I have called the 'minor hero's' or 'half-hero's' role of passively letting the Self take over) that Culhwch follows. He replies: " 'Horses shall I have and horsemen, and my lord and kinsman Arthur will get me all those things. And I shall win thy daughter, and thou shalt lose thy life.' " Arthur here represents that part of Culhwch's personality that now takes over and (either personally or through his 'warriors') accomplishes the tasks. Note the duality of the phrases 'horses and horsemen', 'lord and kinsman'. Such duplications have poetic value, but this is in itself a psychic phenomenon reflecting the psyche's need for the expression of basic duality. With respect to 'horses and horsemen', we have just enumerated a number of these and are reminded of Culhwch's entry into Arthur's stronghold riding his steed. The ridden horses symbolise control of, and help from, the inwardly dynamic feminine element in the psyche.

'Lord and kinsman' has also a meaning deeper than mere poetic euphony. The Self is not only 'lord' but also 'kinsman', being no cut-off entity but of the very substance of the personality, its foundation. The actual 'kinship' tie between Culhwch and Arthur is stated throughout the myth as being that of 'first cousins', a psychic cousinship existing also between Mabon and Eiddoel.

The 'cousinship' between Culhwch and Arthur, though between equals (as the term 'cousin' shows) is not a symmetrical one, Arthur being the older and Culhwch's spiritual father. Arthur and Ysbaddaden thus stand in similar but opposite relationship to Culhwch and Olwen. Arthur's and Ysbaddaden's relationship to one another thus centers around two things: on the one hand Olwen, and on the other hand the boar. In the long recitation of these tasks, addressed by Ysbaddaden to Culhwch, Culhwch himself is not mentioned, and nor is Olwen, except by implication regarding her adumbrated wedding feast with him. These two, then, stand aside while others act for them. While Ysbaddaden and Arthur battle for Culhwch's soul (Olwen, his sister-anima), this soul itself cannot rise and fructify without the blood of the Black Witch to feed it with.

Ysbaddaden says " 'Set forward now. Thou shalt not be answerable for food or raiment for my daughter. Seek those things. And when those things are won, my daughter too thou shalt win.' " Such is his dual nature that he knows that, with the aid of Arthur, he will. Moreover, Ysbaddaden will provide the wherewithal for her marriage to him. There is no question any more of giving his daughter 'in return for her portion and her maiden fee'. He will give her freely, though unwillingly, as he will give his life. (The two givings will be the same.)

CHAPTER 8

THE TASKS FULFILLED:

WRNACH THE GIANT

We have now come to the third turning-point in the hero's story. The first was when Culhwch sought out Arthur. The second was the meeting with Ysbaddaden, his first glimpse of Olwen and her telling him to do whatever Ysbaddaden asked of him. The middle part of the story is taken up by the setting of the tasks. Now the tasks are to be fulfilled.

And here we meet with one of the main peculiarities of this whole myth. Though Ysbaddaden has prefaced every task with the phrase 'there is that thou wilt not get', and Culhwch has answered 'It is easy for me to get that, though thou think it is not easy', he does not fulfil one of them himself. He has said 'Arthur will get me all those things', and this is the case, if we include Arthur's men. Culhwch does not appear in the whole tale again, either as taking part on the great boar hunt or in any other way, till, at the very end, he reaps the benefit of Arthur's prowess and marries Olwen. Ysbaddaden himself knows this. When Culhwch in triumph shouted at him " 'And is thy daughter mine now? ' 'Thine,' said he. 'And thou needs not thank me for that, but thank Arthur who has secured her for thee.' "

In fully assessing this, we have to remember that Arthur, though Ysbaddaden's mortal enemy, at the same time is Ysbaddaden's 'man'. The two work
together as negative and positive poles for the release of Olwen to become
Culhwch's bride. They represent deep forces, to both of which Culhwch
submits. One is the cunning old fool, and the other the old wise man; they
work hand in hand. One is passive, the other is active. As functions of Culhwch they represent the fact that by submitting to destruction a man gains
his greatest strength. He thereby places himself under the protection of the
Self which knows all things and comes close to fulfilling the function of the
immanent deity, one of whose aspects is to destroy in order to re-create.
Culhwch has not, however, behaved like this throughout. He is no self-ef-
facing character. He shows all through the utmost self-assurance, if not
bravado, a self-assurance directed even against Arthur himself.

Moreover, he proceeds with complete assurance against Ysbaddaden,
so long as Ysbaddaden appears in the role simply of a possessive father-
figure. That is easy for a youth of Culhwch's calibre, endowed with all the
power of the nature-mother who, in fact, has no husband, so that the father
presents no problem to her son. What does obliterate his ego function, however, and makes it give place to, and rely entirely on, the Self (Ysbaddaden-
Arthur) is the discovery that, underneath the apparently straightforward
father-problem lies a yet deeper one, that of the boar. It is in the boar that
lies the mystery, for it is he that has the treasures of the tusk (razor), the
shears, and the comb that are the object of all this hunt. Culhwch does not
appreciate mysteries, but the Self does, and knows that the ultimate mystery
is no mystery at all. It is the Black Witch or hag, who is not unmasked until
the boar's power has been overcome and its treasures yielded up. She is the
other side of the very nature-mother who had given Culhwch his pristine
strength. It is this ambivalence — this mortally and meanly destructive side

96

of the nature mother-image — that Culhwch could not cope with consciously, and why the Self has to take over at this point.

If Culhwch were a person, which he is not (he is in the myth more of
an ego function), his disappearance from the story at this point would represent a schizoid or epileptoid episode, in which ego is simply incapable of
facing up to the fact that his mother is also his psychic murderess and he
just throws a fit in order to blot out such consciousness. As he is not a
person, but an ego function, this disappearance is an enantiodromia of one
thing into its opposite, and is not psychotic but represents an act of faith
in a power recognised as being superior to itself. In Christian terms this is
what is called 'faith in' or 'laying the burden on' Christ — if by this one
means the immanent god-man who has experienced all human meanness,
pride, cowardice, and frailty but has overcome it 'once for all', that is to
say that, having found out the way, it now knows it. This is the function
of Arthur in the present myth, who ends his struggle in something very like
dismay but holds on till, at the point of worst trial, victory suddenly comes.
And the victory is a final one, gained not for himself but for Culhwch.

While the whole myth, like any true myth, has been a matter of free
association from beginning to end, what follows now is more so than usual.
By free association is meant the logic of the unconscious, which is always
regressive in a positive sense, that is to say going back into the past so as to
pick up the threads of the future — a reversal of the 'two-headed briar' motif wherein the logic of the conscious is obliterated in favour of that of the
unconscious, and a third factor (the transcendent one), stands outside them
both to observe what happens. Although the figure of Culhwch has submitted himself to Arthur, neither is a 'person' in the true sense of the word.
The only 'person' concerned is the narrator or chronicler, who plays with
traditional motifs, all centring round the same theme of the heroic quest

for the missing psychic substance called the anima. He is himself one of a long line of bards, poets, tellers of tales, weavers of fantasies who from time immemorial have let their imaginations be drawn back into the creative vortex in which things turn into their opposites: old values are destroyed and new ones built up, and from which arises the Tree of Wisdom. This is the philosophical tree adumbrated in the 'two-headed briar', the direction of which is now reversed in order to rejoin inwardly the opposites which have been externally parted. The old man Ysbaddaden saw both sides of the question all right, although he could not help himself, being identified only with one. He could not go into the depths to unite them. Nor can Culhwch, who simply stands by. The one who can plunge in is Arthur, the Self figure familiar with the mysteries. The chronicler has at his finger-tips a mass of mythological material originating in dreams and fantasies mixed with historical and semi-historical facts and facts of everyday life. Boar hunting was an outstandingly adventurous pursuit, and was traditionalised as a result of many tellings by many mouths and the collective contributions of many generations of attentive listeners. These will not have failed to add their quotas to the general store. From these the narrator culls such incidents as his memory and the workings of his own inner consciousness suggest, to colour and deepen the main theme he has in mind — at times prompted and deflected, no doubt, in so far as his theme is spoken, by the applause and by suggestions or amendments added by his audience. It is thus that the narrator outlines the Self.

We have already seen how, in the list of tasks, there has been a main theme with many digressions, elaborations and even jokes added to it. This rather enhances the genuineness of the narrative. This is no logical statement in the intellectual sense, with cause and effect worked out in orderly sequence to fit in with a psychological or spiritual theory. It is more in the nature of a spontaneous, organic production arising from a deep mythological level and using, to express itself, what tools it has to hand. So, though it has a general tendency, its fantasy roams as a dog accompanying a man, poking its nose into hedges and ditches, starting a hare here or a bird there, but always coming back in the end to follow the course set by the man. The list of tasks has followed several such hares, but has always returned fairly swiftly to its main theme.

We now enter into a new phase of the narrative in which the apparent digressions are even greater. With the disappearance of ego (Culhwch) in favour of the far more inaccessible Self (Arthur), a process sets in which can at first sight only be described as somewhat bewildering. The surface phenomenon is that the myth, which has been fairly straightforward up to this point, now becomes highly disjointed till, after many apparently inconsequential digressions, it finally gathers itself together in the account of the hunting of Twrch Trwyth and Arthur's ultimate encounter with the hag. Even in piling on the number of the tasks, the chronicler referred to a large number of sub-heroic figures (only some of whose names have been included here) known evidently to his listeners or readers in a world of myth and saga and now unknown to us. Only about a quarter of these tasks, however, receive further mention as being in any way fulfilled, and even these not in the order originally laid down. Such as are mentioned are apt to be expanded in ways that might well appear to be irrelevant to the main issue. Yet other episodes are introduced that have no obvious reference at all to the tasks that have been proposed. On closer study, the perception grows that what the chronicler has in fact done was to drop down to a deeper level of consciousness, and to free associate on that. The method of free association up to the meeting with Ysbaddaden had been all to do with Culhwch as ego figure, and so, despite its mythical quality, had been comparatively easy

99

to understand on straightforward Oedipus-complex grounds. But with Ysbaddaden the motif of deep ambivalence was touched on — that the would-be destroyer might also be the healer in disguise, and that below the father figure still lurked the mother figure in the mysterious entity of the male boar. This is enough to send any simple soul like Culhwch 'into a spin'. He gives up trying to understand, and delegates the problem to 'Arthur'.

This is so typical of a situation arising in deep psychological analysis, when old values have been undermined and new ones have not emerged, that it may not be out of place here to mention that, apart from these new values appearing in dreams as quite inconsequential from the dreamer's ego's point of view, and having to be dealt with always from two opposite angles, one of the greatest helps is the encouragement of what is called 'active imagination' in which the person experiencing this change gives his imagination free play, without interference or ciriticism. This may have unexpected results in bringing to the surface imagery and associations not hitherto recognised as having any connexion with what has gone before in the analysis — or in the experiencer's previous conscious life. Close attention to apparent irrelevancies leads to the best results, as in the consulting room.

The first task selected for fulfilment is, interestingly enough, the last one posed — apart from that of the hero's need for general 'wakefulness'. The thirty-ninth task lies quite outside the general trend of the tasks, which ended with task thirty-seven. In its essence it actually pre-dates the enunciation of the tasks, to deal with the problem of the giant himself. It does not indeed directly mention Ysbaddaden, but is about Wrnach, clearly a substitute for him. In this it gives some indication also of how the chronicler's mind was working in that the last task mentioned and the first to be fulfilled both deal with what was evidently preoccupying him, namely what

Ysbaddaden was really like — what he stood for. The actual description of Wrnach, of his stronghold and of the approach to it, is very similar to that of Ysbaddaden; though in other respects the fact that he has a porter, and the words used by the porter, are identical with the description of what happened at Culhwch's approach to Arthur.

There is no delay after the recitation of the tasks is over. "That day they journeyed till evening, until there was seen a great fort of mortared stone, the greatest of forts in the world." This fort does not recede as Ysbaddaden's did, but otherwise the conversation on entering it is sometimes word for word the same as that with the shepherd Custennin, except for the fact that it is the giant himself who speaks. We have, however, a description of the sort of nature connected with this giant that we did not have of Ysbaddaden: "Lo, they saw coming from the fort a black man, bigger than three men of this world." This giant, then, has blackness associated with him. He is an unconscious figure in Culhwch's own psyche, more unconscious even than Ysbaddaden who, though he was a giant, had distinctly human traits. This brings to mind the Black Witch and the probability that, by comparison with other myths, the great boar itself is black, though this is not actually stated. " 'Whose is the fort? ' 'Fools of men that you are! There is none in the world does not know whose fort this is. It belongs to Wrnach the Giant...No guest has ever come thence with his life.' 'Is there a porter? ' 'There is. And thou, may thy head not be thine, that thou dost ask.' 'Open the gate!' 'I will not.' 'Why wilt thou not open it? ' 'Knife has gone into meat, and drink into horn, and a thronging in Wrnach's hall.' " We are now in the world of ambivalence, where Arthur is 'Ysbaddaden' in reverse. He is not, however, mentioned here by name, any more than Ysbaddaden is.

The prominent figure in the rest of this incident is Cei, with his companion Bedwyr, as also, it will be remembered, at the entrance to Ysbaddaden's stronghold. Cei says that he is a furbisher of swords. The porter says " 'I will go and tell that to Wrnach the Giant and will bring thee an answer.' " The giant says " 'For some time I have been seeking one who should polish my sword, but I found him not. Let that man in...' "

Cei comes in, and talks to the giant with typical double-meaning. He asks the giant whether he wants his sword 'white-haft or dark-haft', and cleans half of one side of the blade. The giant says he would like to have it all like that, adding " 'It is a shame a man as good as thou should be without a fellow.' " Cei answers " 'Oia, good sir, I have a fellow, though he does not practice this craft...I will tell his tokens: the head of his spear will leave its shaft, and it will draw blood from the wind [we have already had this phrase in connexion with Culhwch], and settle upon the shaft again.' " In view of the fact that Cei later slays the giant with his own sword, we can take this as a broad hint which the giant is too stupid to take. His 'fellow' comes in, Bedwyr, who constantly accompanies Cei on his exploits. Cei adds: " 'A wondrous gift has Bedwyr, though [he adds ominously] he does not practice this craft.' " This throws some light on the relation between Cei and Bedwyr, who, from it, evidently here represents Cei's subtlety and double-dealing. After the furbishing of the sword, Cei says to the giant " 'It is thy scabbard has damaged thy sword. Give it to me...' And he took the scabbard, and the sword in the other hand. He came and stood over the giant, as if he would put the sword into the scabbard. He sank it into the giant's head and took off his head at a blow." The scabbard here stands for the giant's muddled head, into which Cei plunges the sword. The sword also symbolises the power of insight (the Logos) that pierces and destroys the blind forces of darkness (the blackness of the giant) or of the unconscious super-conservatism and resistance to change that giants are apt to represent. Wrnach the

Giant is in this respect completely one-sided and utterly inferior to Ysbadda-den, who is a sufferer and an initiator — even if this is so in spite of himself.

There is, incidentally, a hint that in one aspect Wrnach the Giant represents the boar. The account goes on to say: "They laid waste the fort and took away what treasures they would. To the very day at the end of the year they came to Arthur's court, and the sword of Wrnach the Giant with them." Note that treasures and the sword foreshadow the boar's treasures (shears, comb) and the boar's tusk (razor), which are deposited with Arthur. 'The very day at the end of the year' indicates a union of opposites. Ego (the active agents) lay their treasure at the feet of the Self (Arthur), who has through his 'other half' or agent Ysbaddaden, instigated their search.

One other bearing that this incident has on the main tale is the fleeting appearance in it of the fair-haired son of Custennin, already mentioned as leading the way into the giant's fort at the end, thus 'doubling' the character of Culhwch as the young hero. His comrades dub him 'Best of men', *Goreu* meaning 'best'.

This episode, represented as the 'fulfilment of a task', and the following ones until the actual hunting of the boar sets in, are all related as though they were being told to Arthur. It is as if Arthur as the Self is being gradually approached by, so to speak, the whetting of his appetite. Finally he gets caught up personally in the latter stages of the hunt, in which he ends up as being the chief figure. At present he stays in the background and displays only a kind of contemplative curiosity, being roused sometimes, but not always, to take part in whatever may be afoot. Just as Ysbaddaden and Culhwch went through a kind of litany together in the listing of the tasks, so also Arthur has a set phrase with which he always initiates some new quest. Thus, after the getting of Wrnach's sword "they told Arthur how it had gone with them", whereon Arthur, referring to the tasks, says: " 'Which of those marvels will it be best to seek first? ' " There is evidently an order, but it is not the order set out by Ysbaddaden. It is one arrived at by Arthur always in consultation with his men, a kind of 'collective knowing' very different from Ysbaddaden's egocentricity. It gives us a view of the Self as both highly individual and also universal, such as is the nature of all archetypes. By seeking 'those marvels' at all, Arthur shows himself incidentally to be the obedient agent of Ysbaddaden.

CHAPTER 9

THE TASKS FULFILLED:

MABON SON OF MODRON

The 'marvel' to be sought first is chosen collectively: " 'It will be best,' said they, 'to seek Mabon son of Modron...' " This refers to task twenty-six. We have already discussed the significance of this Great Son of the Great Mother, who is also one of the three 'supreme prisoners of the Island of Britain', of which Arthur himself was the fourth and greatest one. It is interesting to note that nowhere in this myth is Culhwch himself described as having been such a 'prisoner'. It is implied by the fact of his being, at the beginning, 'born of a sow', that is to say purely a 'mother's son'. The chronicler, while not stating this directly, nevertheless with his method of free association now brings it to our notice much as a dream would: by presenting as a dream-image some other person known to us having a complex similar to our own, that we can recognise in him but not yet in ourselves. Thus here Mabon son of the Great Mother is an image of Culhwch, introduced in order to make clear the underlying nature of this hero but without intruding it too blatantly. Thus it is rendered acceptable to the listener who would be more superficially interested by the recitation of heroic exploits than by what they really mean in the lives of all of us.

The chronicler, having in the last episode let his mind dwell on the somewhat ludicrous figure of the possessive father (the giant) so easily deceived by Cei's play of opposites, now contemplates the possessed mother's son and analyses deeply into the dual nature of all such mother-boundness. It is by way of introduction to such analysis that Arthur's counsellors, having advised him to seek Mabon son of Modron, add: " 'and there is no getting him until his kinsman Eidoel son of Aer is got first' ". This phrase refers to task twenty-eight, in which it was said that " 'Mabon will never be obtained, where he is is unknown, till his kinsman Eidoel son of Aer be first obtained; for he will be untiring in quest of him. He is his first cousin.' " It was earlier explained that Mabon and Eiddoel symbolised two levels in the character of the same archetypal 'person', of which Mabon stood for the deepest feeling level in closest touch with the Great Mother image and was therefore more 'female'; Eiddoel symbolised his more external, intellectual, or 'male' side. Their 'first cousinship' expressed their close interdependence. Of the two Eiddoel had to be sought first because without the assent of the intellect, however twisted, the deeper emotions cannot be reached or freed.

That was as far as the bald statement contained in the imposition of the task took us. The fulfilment of it takes us very much deeper, being a kind of exposition of what was only adumbrated in the task. To begin with it turns out that not only Mabon was a prisoner, but that Eiddoel was also, though in a different place. "Arthur rose up, and the warriors of the Island of Britain with him, to seek for Eidoel; and they came to Glini's outer wall, to where Eidoel was in prison." There are thus two prisoners, both of whom have to be freed, and Eiddoel first.

We have already hinted at the dual nature of mother-boundness, which is dual in more ways than one. In the first place, through the depths of his mother-bound nature the 'mother's son' may on the one hand be imprisoned by it if he is not able to escape. But on the other hand he is in touch with such deep nature-truths that, once he is delivered from unconscious ties to them and they become conscious (that is to say available for use by an ego steeped in familiarity with them but no longer bound by them), he then has power over them and can make use of them. The fact that Arthur was thrice imprisoned (Guest, 1877 edition, p. 192) but in each case rescued shows the *depth* of his nature (in this story symbolising the ultimate wisdom of the Self — here the male element conscious of its femininity). This gives him the sublimity of being the most 'exalted' of all the 'prisoners'. This expresses the basic truth that only those who have experienced deep trouble in the labyrinthine tangles of the mother-world can, once they have themselves been extricated from them, have understanding deep enough to rescue others (as Arthur rescues Culhwch).

This is the positive aspect of mother-boundness, reached only after long struggle and in this myth appearing only at the very end after Arthur's own personal overcoming of the hag who underlies it all. Its negative aspect is not confined to boundness to the mother only. It spreads to all relationships, under the guise often of being 'free'. One of the paradoxes of this story is that Culhwch throughout appears so free. This is, however, at the beginning, only an appearance of freedom. He was free only with respect to his instinctive animal life. His real freedom from this as a human being began only when he abandoned that freedom by getting Arthur to trim his hair and thus submitting to Arthur's will. That is to say that from one prison he went into another, from that of the mother-world of unadulterated instinct into a psychic father-world, in which instinct is curbed for the sake of internalising it and producing the anima. If Arthur frees him from the mother-world, he must in turn be freed from Arthur representing the father-world, before he can issue forth from it to join his anima in the *hieros gamos* of being united with his own heterosexual self. Arthur freely gives the freedom which he has won for him. This is the psychic process which this myth overtly describes.

There are, however, always false gods obscuring the true ones. Arthur here represents the good internalised father closely allied to the Self. But in external life the process is often the exact reverse, and this is what the interpolated episode of Mabon seems to indicate. As always, the mother-bound who have not been rescued soon enough fall victim to a second boundness, namely unconscious boundness to the father-world, on to which the unconscious mother-boundness is inevitably projected. Instead of feeling imprisoned in the instinctive life, the boy's first feeling is one of being free in it, but when he comes to man's estate this freedom leads into a void or on to a precipice of uncontrolled and unfulfilable desire which may lead even towards crime, madness, outlawry or suicide, or just end in sheer crucified loneliness. These are extremes. But this myth is about extremes. The condition just outlined is that of the father-world 'gone wrong', a primitive father-world fitting a matriarchal society in which the father has no rights and no responsibilities, but utterly unfitting in a patriarchal world such as this myth deals with and which is also the world of large amounts of instinct internalised. It is another form of psychic imprisonment, not deep down as is the mother one, but phallically and quite intolerably exposed, erect and without support in such a society.

This, I suggest, is the reason why Eiddoel, Mabon's second and more superficial personality, is found imprisoned not in any deep place but on a crag, high up and symbol of the negative father-world. He is imprisoned in a fort belonging to one named Glini, who, on the approach of those seeking to rescue Eiddoel, makes a speech. Psychological insight and familiarity

108

with dream-psychology help us to recognise that Glini, as Eiddoel's jailor, represents Eiddoel's own self-imprisoning ambivalence. He appeals to Arthur, saying " 'Arthur, what wouldst thou have of me, since thou wilt not leave me alone on this crag? I have no good herein and no pleasure, neither wheat nor oats have I, without thee too seeking to do me harm.' " Are we not all familiar with the neurotic clinging to his neurosis, the prisoner to his prison, precisely because it is for him a last refuge? And he cannot be blamed for it, because it represents for him his only known way of escape from something even worse, which he knows no way of dealing with. Are we not equally familiar with the paranoid suspicion with which he (or rather the superego in him, which was once his rescuer from the mother-danger but has become an autonomous image of fear split off from the reality of possible help) regards the potential helper? And he has a right to, for never yet has anyone approached him who could allay his fear and arouse hope of being understood and therefore of eventually understanding himself.

Arthur, who has himself suffered, knows this, and does not take his suspicion amiss. (This, in psychological analysis, means accepting willingly and understandingly the negative transference, not taking it as levelled against the psychotherapist, who *must* be tested in this way and misses the point if he takes umbrage or talks of 'resistance' against himself. He knows that his interlocutor has been so often and so deeply deceived that he now cannot for the time being but continue to deceive himself.) So Arthur says " 'Not to hurt thee have I come hither, but to seek out the prisoner that is with thee.' " 'With thee' of course means psychologically 'within thee': the prisoner is his own jailor. Myth telescopes long processes into a moment of time. The jailor gives in: " 'I will give thee the prisoner, though I had not bargained to give him up to any one. And besides this, my aid and backing thou shalt have.' " How different this is from the withholding

109

attitude of Ysbaddaden! The ego yields to Arthur (the Self, the rescuer), as Culhwch had yielded to him in having his hair trimmed.

"The men said to Arthur, 'Lord get thee home. Thou canst not proceed with thy host to seek things so petty as these.' " This is the first of a series of similar admonishments administered to Arthur by his subordinates. It voices a typical 'common-sense' criticism levelled at what may on the surface appear as the obscurity or seeming (from the outside) futility of all psychically healing work. It would appear waste of time for a fine 'head' to busy itself with matters so unworthy of attention as broken down lives or deluded persons such as the man imprisoned on a crag represents. Worse still, is precisely the real 'pettiness' of such persons. Involvement in such 'pettiness' on the part of anyone attempting to deal with it may rightly be considered both morally and socially dangerous or contaminating. But if the helper has already passed through zones of deep meanness and contamination by subtly and morally disintegrating forces within himself, and has emerged from this devastating experience, he will be enriched by it. This is not readily conceivable to the ordinary mortal who has neither descended to such depths nor got the insight resulting therefrom. The helper will be able both to heal and to preserve himself from contamination because he understands the creative forces underlying the meannesses, which have become 'petty' only because they have been repressed and can find no other outlet.

Arthur, 'thrice imprisoned', was such a 'person' (or represents such a function potentially existing within the psyche of everyone). So, while maintaining his dignity, he calls on one of his 'men' (psychic functions) to undertake the task of freeing Eiddoel (the father-bound 'escapist' side of Mabon) from his imprisonment. The 'man' which Arthur employs for this task is Gwrhyr the Interpreter. This psychic function of Arthur's has

appeared several times previously under similar circumstances. It is the one
which, due to the deep transforming experiences which Arthur himself has
undergone, can see below the surface of things to their real meaning. When
the apostles at Pentecost 'began to speak with other tongues' and 'every
man heard them speak in his own language', what was meant is that they
understood the inner language of every man's heart, and that those who
heard them perceived this and so could, in their turn, receive the Word and
have their souls 'rescued'. So also, in the interpretation of dreams their inner meaning (so contrary often to what is 'thought') can, if the interpreter
is familiar enough with the images of the unconscious and can speak and
understand their language, similarly be brought to light and 'rescued' from
unconsciousness.

So Arthur says " 'Gwrhyr Interpreter of Tongues, it is right for thee
to go on this quest. All tongues hast thou, and thou canst speak with some
of the birds and the beasts. **Eidoel, it is right for thee to go along with my**
men to seek him [Mabon] – he is thy first cousin.' " We are now familiar
with the phrase 'first cousin'. The kinship indicated by this phrase is not
of blood but of the spirit. First cousin means spiritually akin. In this case,
Eiddoel and Mabon are one, Mabon being the mother-bound and Eiddoel the
father-bound aspect of one person. A similar double-personality is mentioned in the same breath by Arthur, who goes on immediately to say " 'Cei
and Bedwyr, I have hope that whatever you go to seek will be obtained. Go
then for me on this quest.' " We have already seen how the character of
Bedwyr represents Cei's inner knowledge, Cei being the extravert and Bedwyr representing the introvert aspect of the same person. Without such
inner knowledge Cei would be just a braggadocio or kind of performing
mountebank. With this 'companion' he is a man of subtle wisdom, and
consequent real power.

111

If a man is as double-sided as this Mabon-Eiddoel figure is, this represents in him two foci of awareness: one is deeply hidden and introvert (mo-
ther-identified), and tremendously on the defensive (the 'Mabon' side); the
other is equally inaccessible because too much 'up in the air' and self-opin-
ionated, but at the same time desperately unhappy — represented by Eiddoel imprisoned in the high fort, 'having no good herein'. This is the father-
identified side of him and represents also what in analytical psychology can
be called his inappropriate (to the Self) persona, his mask of intellectual
superiority that he has been driven to adopt through fear of his other, mo-
ther-devoured and potentially mother-devouring side. Unpleasant as such
a mask may be, it is hopeless in psychotherapy to try to oppose it. It is in
fact the bridge between him and the world. If that bridge is broken or felt
to be made inferior by direct attack, the whole personality will range itself
against the attacker, and the psychotherapy will fail. A man has to be taken
at first on his own valuation, before seeking to undermine this in order to
seek the anima so deep-imprisoned in the mother-world. As stated before,
the person's mind, however twisted, must nevertheless be enlisted in the
battle against its own negative side. Its coldness can only be warmed and
so melted by understanding use being made of it. In this way it does not
remain outside the therapeutic process and create havoc because it is unem-
ployed: "Satan finds some evil still for idle hands to do." So Arthur shows
great wisdom in saying " 'Eidoel, it is right for thee to go along with my men
to seek [Mabon].' " This gives the jealous intellect a function and a position
of responsibility in tracking down the anima, which is just what it wants to
do despite appearances. He is addressed by name and is enlisted in the process of self-rediscovery, instead of being either opposed or ignored, which
would have driven him still higher on 'the crag' and at the same time, by the
law of opposites, would have buried or 'imprisoned' the Mabon side of him

still deeper.

Gwrhyr now has recourse to all his arts of divination, and, with Eidd-oel with him (not to speak of Cei and Bedwyr) enquires of the 'birds and the beasts' where Mabon may be. Every word of this tale is full of mean-ing. I will here but call attention to the further duality of 'birds and beasts', creatures respectively of the air and of the earth, of father-world and of mother-world, of intellect and emotion, thinking and feeling. Both have to be enquired from. The creatures thus sought out are, in this order, the Ouzel, Stag, Owl, Eagle, and Salmon. These represent, very roughly, the following elements respectively: maternal spirit-message, or thought; mas-culine spiritual independence, or pride; feminine wisdom (cf. Athene); male intellect; and a leaping, wending principle into the unconscious. Each is older than the preceding one.

The Ouzel of Cilgwri [? in Flintshire, now Cowyd] said " 'When first I came hither, there was a smith's anvil here, and as for me I was a young bird. No work has been done upon it save whilst my beak was thereon every even-ing. Today there is not so much of it as a nut not worn away.' " Thereby it declares its great age, and therefore contact with the past, and is the first to be mentioned of what have been called "the oldest animals". Despite its great age, however, it cannot directly help. Even the smith's capacity for wizardry has been annihilated by her beak. " 'Nevertheless, that which it is right and proper for me to do for Arthur's messengers, I will do. There is a kind of creature God made before me; I will go along as your guide thither.' " And so he conducts them to the next creature. We are reminded of the 'ancientness' of Arthur's gatekeeper, and of Arthur himself. All these figures conduct back into the past, which is equivalent to psychic depth, away from the 'crags' into the heart of the mother-world below, the matrix out of which all life grew up and the ever-renewing source of it.

Each of the creatures mentioned leads one 'depth' lower than the last. This symbolises, psychologically speaking, the progressive uncovering of ever deeper psychic contents, by stages, in a continuous process and without break, so as to preserve the unity of the psyche and leave no 'pockets' of unresolved complex. These 'birds and beasts' are what are called psychologically and in folk-lore the 'helpful animals', and as such often appear in dreams. They are functions of instinct that assist if we are humble enough to ask their help.

The next animal asked is the Stag of Rhedynfre, who also explains his great age, but says " 'I have heard naught of him you are asking after. Nevertheless I will be your guide, since you are Arthur's messengers, to the place where there is an animal God made before me.' "

The next is the Owl of Cwm Cawlwyd (in North Britain) who says " 'When I first came hither, the great valley you see was a wooded glen, and a race of men came thereto and it was laid waste. And the second wood grew up therein, and this wood is the third...From that day to this I have heard naught of the man you are asking after.' " He in turn says he will guide them to the place where is " 'the oldest creature that is in this world, and he that has fared furthest afield, the Eagle...' "

The Eagle of Gwernabwy says " 'I came here a long time ago, and when first I came hither I had a stone, and from its top I pecked at the stars each evening; now it is not a hand-breadth in height. From that day to this I have been here, but have heard naught of him you are asking after. Save that at one faring I went to seek my meat as far as Llyn Llyw, [30] and when I came there I sank my claws into a salmon, thinking he would be meat for me many a long day, and he drew me down into the depths, so that it was with difficulty I got away from him. And my whole kindred and I went after him, to seek to destroy him. But he sent messengers to make

peace with me, and came to me in person to have fifty tridents taken out of his back. Unless he knows something of what you seek, I know none who may. Nevertheless I will be your guide to the place where he is.' "
There could be no better demonstration of the story's symbolism than this image of the eagle, strongest bird of the air, the intellect, superego, or whatever plane his image may be taken on, being dragged down into the depths of the unconscious by the salmon, lord and denizen of the water, one of its most frequent symbols. The superego always seeks to destroy the id. But that is not the way to solve the problem of this ambivalence. Id, the unconscious, sorely wounded by the superego, nevertheless tries to make peace with it — and requests its assistance for its own well-being, and this in fact leads to the solution of the problem and to the rescuing of Mabon.

That the water-element represents the unconscious there could be no doubt even on the evidence of this story alone. Mabon is imprisoned in it (the very opposite of the 'crag' from which his twin 'other self' Eiddoel was rescued). The salmon says " 'As much as I know, I will tell. With every tide I go up along the river till I come to the bend of the wall of Caer Loyw[31]; and there I found such distress that I never found its equal in all my life; and, that you may believe, let one of you come here on my two shoulders.' And Cei and Gwrhyr Interpreter of Tongues went upon the salmon's two shoulders, and they journeyed until they came to the far side of the wall from the prisoner, and they could hear wailing and lamentation on the far side of the wall from them. Gwrhyr said 'What man laments in this house of stone? ' 'Alas, man, there is cause for him who is here to lament. Mabon son of Modron is here in prison; and none was ever so cruelly imprisoned in a prison house as I...' " Tides are 'female'. It is rare to find a woman dreaming about tides, unless she is at the same time menstruating. They are 'moon'-functions symbolising the ebb and flow of two-sided femininity. The prison is a sea or river castle, in which Mabon is. His very name signifies the same fact of being imprisoned in the mother-sea. All through this narrative innumerable characters are referred to, all of them as sons of their father. Mabon, alone in the entire myth, is given the title 'Son of the Mother', and the Great Mother at that. He is the primaeval male force, always potential in the mother. The only two others in the story whom we know primarily as mother's sons (though they are not given this title) are Culhwch and the son of the wife of Custennin (until he comes to be referred to as son of his father as he enters upon his career of 'hero').

The salmon's two shoulders are part of the same basic feminine symbolism. The imagery is the same, once more, as that of the 'two-headed briar'. It represents the duality of the mother-world, and of the mother-boundness symbolised by Mabon's imprisonment, and only by knowing this duality, or this being known by his rescuers, can he be rescued. The two said to be riding to his rescue on the salmon's shoulders are Cei and the Interpreter of Tongues, representing respectively the external and the internal meaning of this imprisonment. A few sentences later these two are said to be Cei and his more usual companion Bedwyr, who represents (with regard to Cei) the same internalised function. The dual meaning with regard to Mabon's imprisonment in the Mother is that, if taken in a negative sense and he were not rescued from it, he would be a mother-bound and so psychically castrated youth; in order to be a 'hero' at all, however, he had to 'go into the Mother' so as to pluck from her the secrets of nature, including his own nature. This is never a pleasant process, but is essential for every hero to do.

Now is the moment for his spiritual birth out of her. The tale goes on with his would-be rescuers asking " 'Hast thou hope of getting thy release for gold or for silver or for worldly wealth, or by battle and fighting? '

'What is got of me, will be got by fighting.' " That is, he has no ulterior
motive save that of making his soul. That is all they have to find out.

"They returned thence and came to where Arthur was. They told
where Mabon son of Modron was in prison. Arthur summoned the warriors
of this Island and went to Caer Loyw where Mabon was in prison. Cei and
Bedwyr went upon the two shoulders of the fish. Whilst Arthur's warriors
assaulted the fort, Cei broke through the wall and took the prisoner on his
back; and still he fought with the men. Arthur came home and Mabon
with him, a free man." It may or may not be chance that Mabon is here
for the first time mentioned without having his mother Modron tacked on
to his name.

CHAPTER 10

THE TASKS FULFILLED:

CANINES, ANTS, BEARD, MAY EVE

The above tale of fulfilling one of the tasks does not yet concern the overcoming of the mother-image, but only the problem of rescuing the hero from it. There is still the problem of destroying her. This is now hinted at, but still in very obscure terms, and with inconclusive results. It concerns overtly the search for the two whelps of Gast Rhymhi [32] who has been mentioned previously only among the names invoked by Culhwch for his boon. There are, in tasks thirty and thirty-one, only references to 'those two whelps' needed to hunt the boar Twrch Trwyth. Gast Rhymhi is evidently introduced here as animal form of the Devouring Mother. " 'Is it known where she is? ' asked Arthur... 'Hast thou heard of her in these parts? In what shape is she? ' 'In the shape of a she-wolf...and she goes about with her two whelps. Often has she slain my stock, and she is down in Aber Cleddyf in a cave.' " The 'two' whelps may once more be taken as expression of the Devouring Mother's duality (another 'two-headed briar' parallel). The Devouring Mother-image lives often in a cave (as she does in Malekula), and here adumbrates the Black Witch or hag whom Arthur finally slays, in a cave also.

The account immediately goes on: "Arthur went to sea in his ship Prydwen, and others by land to hunt the bitch..." This adumbrates the boar hunt, which is soon to take place. Why then Arthur in a ship to hunt a she-wolf on land? Sea and land are once more expressions of duality. "And in this wise they surrounded her and her two whelps, and God changed them back into their own semblance for Arthur." It does not say what this semblance was, but the she-wolf may have been a witch. There is no mention of her death. This short tale now simply ends with "Arthur's host dispersed, one by one, two by two". Perhaps she had been too much for them, and they 'slank away'. This is not surprising, because 'her' animus the boar is still at large, and has not yet been coped with, which must happen first, before the witch, deprived of his protection, can be made to yield.

Whether or not by way of compensation for the humiliation of Arthur's men (whom we now know to represent functions of Arthur — himself Culhwch's internal helper, and therefore of Culhwch's hero-nature itself), we are now given an obscure scrap of a tale about another hero. Gwythyr son of Greidawl, also invoked in Culhwch's list, and described further on, when journeying over a mountain, "heard a wailing and a grievous lamentation, and these were a horrid noise to hear". These came apparently from an anthill. "He sprang forward in that direction, and when he came there he drew his sword and smote off the anthill level with the ground, and so saved them from the fire." Fire has not previously been mentioned, but the imprisoned ants lament very much in the same way as the imprisoned Mabon had been lamenting. They therefore symbolise something similar to Mabon, this time imprisoned not in the water-element, however, but by its opposite element, fire. If water symbolised the passive imprisoning power of the witch, fire might well symbolise in this case the more

119

active and passionate aspect of her destructive side. The ants were grateful for being rescued, and said " 'Take thou God's blessing and ours, and that which no man can ever recover we will come and recover it for thee.' " The chronicler adds, by way of explanation of this not very easy passage, "It was they thereafter who came with the nine hestors of flax seed which Ysbaddaden Chief Giant had named to Culhwch, in full measure, with none of it wanting save for a single flax seed. And the lame ant brought that in before night."

The ants here fall into the category of 'grateful' and therefore also 'helpful' animals; grateful because the hero has first helped them and therefore willing, in their turn, to help him. This is a frequent symbol for psychic contents latent in the unconscious but unable to 'come to life', that is to say to be received into consciousness and so to become operative *in* actual life, unless the conscious itself becomes aware of their 'murmurings' and is humble enough to pay attention to their 'sufferings'. They are in fact ego's own sufferings but of a kind that ego usually does not want to admit, since they belong to those lower or more primitive layers of a person's nature that ego is apt to disregard, as being beneath its dignity to acknowledge. Unconscious contents often find themselves in this position: full of wisdom but 'burnt out', according to the imagery here employed, by the fire of passionate resentment engendered in early childhood against the witch-aspect of the rejecting mother, and therefore also of the internal self-rejecting mother image. It is to the advantage of the rejecting mother image not to be found out and therefore to operate on a level apparently unworthy of ego's attention. Hence, if we carry on this line of thought, the ant as insignificant insect (which, nevertheless, *en masse* can be industrious and highly organised) may symbolise primitive psychic contents. Such contents, having a life of their own desiring to be recognised, repay

attention, as these ants say they will. " 'That which no man can ever recover, we will come and recover it for thee.' " 'Recover' means 'rescue'.
This scrap of a tale refers to task seven. The nine hestors of flax seed there
symbolised, in sexual imagery, the seed which Ysbaddaden had hoped himself to plant in his daughter Olwen. The right to do so was now, however,
passing to Culhwch. This, according to our text, is the process which the
psychic activities called 'ants' have furthered in return for recognition of
them, by gathering together the flax seed or psychic semen which is to be
sown in the 'new-broken ground' of Olwen's maidenhood, ready to receive
it when he has proved himself. The 'lame ant' bringing in the last seed when
this had been overlooked or lost is a typical symbol for the last effort, in
spite of flagging powers, to complete a job. Gwythyr here enables a task to
be accomplished. In the next incident but one, he is significantly checked.

This incident can now, I think, be seen as compensating for the loss
of heart experienced by Arthur's men in their last venture when, despite
their formidable attack by land and sea on the she-wolf, they failed to have
an outright battle with her. We have already seen how Arthur's men symbolise psychic contents of the bigger 'Arthur' or Self side of the hero's personality. They are a numerous body operating with external force. The
ants are similarly a numerous body acting unseen through love. Such com-
parison-by-opposites in terms of psychic imagery is a type of enantiodromia.
It contrasts two aspects of the hero character. From another angle the impetuous demolishment of the anthill might well be likened to an act of an
angry boy, or a frustrated child just working off high spirits, a potential
hero from a more everyday point of view.

The motif of fire is taken up again in the next incident which refers
to task thirty, in which Ysbaddaden required a leash to hold in the two
whelps which were to be used in hunting the great boar. The leash had to

be made from the beard of Dillus the Bearded, twitched out of his beard with wooden tweezers while he was still alive. "As Cei and Bedwyr were sitting on top of Pumlumon on Carn Gwylathyr, in the highest wind in the world, they looked about them and they could see a great smoke towards the south, far off from them, and not blowing across with the wind." Here is a new contrast. From fire in the anthill we are now removed to the top of a mountain in 'the highest wind in the world'. The wind (air contrasting with fire) is directly connected with the fire in that it calls attention to it by blowing its great smoke, but in a peculiar way. 'Not blowing across with the wind' indicates something not belonging to the material world, but to going its own way, a psychic or 'other-worldly' one. Such double-meaning was indicated already by the presence with Cei of Bedwyr, whose appearance with Cei as his double always indicates subtle meaning by way of complementary opposites. We may presume therefore, that in this incident, as elsewhere, there will be some hidden meaning not overtly expressed. "And then Cei said, 'By the hand of my friend [again indicating some problem of opposites, since this is what the reference to 'friend Bedwyr' means], see yonder the fire of a warrior.' They hastened towards the smoke and approached thither, watching from afar as Dillus the Bearded was singeing a wild boar. Now, he was the mightiest warrior that ever fled from Arthur.' " This, so far as I know, is the only enemy of Arthur as such mentioned throughout this tale, with the exception of the boar and the Black Witch or hag.

We are now getting very close to the account of the boar hunt itself, and with regard to Dillus touch here on subtle points of great complexity. There is a certain similarity between Dillus the Bearded and Ysbaddaden in that in both cases the beard is of special importance. In trying to trick Culhwch, Ysbaddaden is at the same time trying to trick Arthur who is on

Culhwch's side. We have discussed the hidden relationship between Ysbaddaden and Arthur, how they are overtly opposed but in the paradoxically
hidden initiating process in fact work hand in hand. The enemy of Arthur
is the boar, whose side Ysbaddaden takes. Unconsciously, that is to say as
agent of an initiation process he does not understand, he brings about its
death, and also his own, and thereby opens the way for the *hieros gamos*
between Olwen and Culhwch which consciously he wished to prevent. In
other words, the forceable shaving of Ysbaddaden's beard was the chief
symbol of his capitulation to Arthur.

Here, however, Dillus is to all intents 'shaving' the boar by singeing
its bristles, and so would seem to be on Arthur's side. But he is said to be
'the mightiest warrior that ever fled from Arthur', a description exactly
tallying with that of the 'king-boar' himself when he comes to be hunted;
he lays waste whole tracts of country and slays large numbers of Arthur's
warriors before he is finally dealt with. In this respect, too, the figure of
Dillus the Bearded would be a parallel one to that of Ysbaddaden, who, in
his double character as paradoxical initiator, both favoured and opposed
the boar.

It is becoming more and more evident, that the present series of interpolated episodes are not only not fortuitous; they serve the purpose of en-
hancing the main story through symbolic analogy (or what Jung might call
'amplification') and revealing depths in it that might not otherwise have received due attention. We have here a very subtle but highly important new
point: "Then Bedwyr said to Cei, 'Dost thou know him? ' 'I know him,'
said Cei; 'that is Dillus the Bearded. There is no leash in the world may
hold Drudwyn the whelp of Greid son of Eri, save a leash from the beard
of him thou seest yonder. And that too will be of no use unless it be plucked
alive with wooden tweezers from his beard; for it will be brittle, dead.' "

Such gruesome, sadistic details are, however, not without meaning. In this case we know by now that a conversation between Cei and Bedwyr is always one having an inner meaning. In the second place, if Dillus is in fact another aspect of the boar, why should his beard have to supply the leash which is essential to hunting the boar (since on it depends the control of the boar-hounds) and why, especially, should it have to be taken from him while alive, for if it were not it would be 'brittle, dead'? We have already noted the connexion of this motif with similar ones: Ysgithyrwyn's tusk having to be plucked from his head while still alive and the Black Witch's blood having to be obtained while warm. This indicates the need for continuity, and emphasises the deep wisdom that evil cannot be destroyed but can only be transmitted into something better, though based on it — and cannot be founded on anything else. A classical example of this truth is the myth enshrined in Wagner's *Parsifal,* that the wound suffered by King Amfortas can only be healed by re-inserting into his wound the very spear that caused that wound. In like vein is the mystical imagery that asserts that Christ is the second Adam, that only sinners can be saved, and that they are saved "through the cords of Adam" himself.

Thus errors can only be rectified by going back to their original source. The dynamic libido leading to the error is *the same* as that which will lead out of it, and the very error itself indicates the line of development the individual is destined to fulfil. The ultimate justification of the rebel against an old order is that he founds a new order, or of a neurotic that the depths of his suffering open up the way to deeper knowledge of the human psyche and of its potential powers than had hitherto been available. In other words, wounds only hurt if we try to cover them up and pretend they do not exist. If gone into, they prove to be doors opening into a deeper world, of a character *similar* to that which had been feared but, taken the other way round, is its antithesis. It is thus a mistake to try to eradicate a fault, or kill a disease. The evil thing which has been rejected can, like an unhappy child, only be turned to good account by being seen as the same principle outlined in task nineteen. The blood of the Black Witch had to be obtained while warm, that is to say while she, though dying, was still alive. Whatever the process of transformation, or of transition, the life-giving matrix must be maintained intact. The vital essence of the old order that has to die is essential to the new one, even though the new order may seem opposed to it.

The symbolism of the 'two-headed briar' operates once again here, as throughout the whole of this mythology. It will be remembered that, when this image was evoked at the beginning of our story, it referred to the two mothers opposed to one another but having a common origin, and ultimately a common purpose also. The two-headed briar grew out of the grave of the natural mother, and so had its origin in her. But the second head was that of the stepmother, the initiating mother whose function it was, under the aegis of the incest taboo, to open up for the hero a new life of the spirit (the search for Olwen the sister-anima), founded on the strength provided by the natural mother but separated from her in order to establish his individuality over against her. This involved for the 'natural mother' a double death, one occurring at the beginning of the story when she actually died. The other comes when, at the end of the story and the apotheosis of it, Arthur on behalf of Culhwch will kill the Black Witch or hag, the internal image of the natural mother in Culhwch's soul, thus clearing away the last obstacle between Culhwch and Olwen and the consummation of his desire.

The suggestion with regard to Dillus the Bearded is that he, also, like these and like Ysbaddaden, has a double nature. He has the nature of the boar, that is to say, the mother's animus, in both aspects, its good one and its bad: one provides strength for the hero but also would overwhelm him

125

if he did not use *that same strength* in order to overcome it as a hostile force within him trying to keep him mother-bound. He must make it his own and thus free himself from the 'bad' mother by turning the bad (possessing) into the good (possessed). This is what is meant by Dillus's beard having to be plucked *while he is still alive.* If dead, the virtue (basic libido) would have gone out of it. There would be nothing to build on for the new life, which *can only grow out of the old.*

This brings us back now to the particular purpose for which Dillus's beard was to be used: as a leash to hold in the two whelps. The hounds that hunt the boar are clearly symbols of the hero's libido in pursuing its aims, and may be thought of thus — and are indeed so in the story when we read of their qualities. They are 'minor heroes' themselves, but have to be held in leash until the time is ripe for their activity. It is remarkable how many times the leash is mentioned in the tasks. Task twenty-three is devoted to it, task twenty-four to the collar to hold the leash, task twenty-five to the chain 'to hold the collar along with the leash', task thirty to the leash itself. Task thirty-five is about a 'good unleasher', and task thirty-six says of the two hounds "never were they unleashed on a beast they did not kill". So six tasks are involved in the subject of the leash, which would seem large proportion did it not have, almost certainly, a deeper meaning, a meaning now linked up with that of Dillus's beard. Here we come down to a level of imagery involving at least two archetypes, that of the cord and of the beard. All cords, strings for holding, leashes and such like may be taken on the body-image level as symbolising that earliest cord in the life of everyone: the umbilical cord through which the blood of the mother flows into the child, and which attaches it to her. At birth, this cord is broken, and the child starts its independent existence. There is however a second cord, that of the spirit, which, like all spiritual phenomena, has two aspects. In an instinctively undeveloped child it remains with him as an incubus, sucking his life back into the personal mother in a negative way because he cannot get psychically free from her, for its power is great. In an instinctively developed one, however, such as Culhwch is, it still flows backwards, but inwardly instead of outwardly, towards the mother-image — but this time the archetypal Great Mother in all her ambivalence. She both provides the energy, and has to be made to yield up the possessiveness with which she seeks to draw it back again into herself, thus depriving the ego of independent life and the power to transform itself.

The degree of 'hero-dom' in anybody's life depends on the extent to which this great umbilical power can be acquired for use against the drag back into unconsciousness. To the extent to which this can be done, the libido thus released is what gives him the power to overcome his internal as well as his external enemies. It thus does not need any great stretch of the imagination to conceive of the leashed hounds, waiting to be unfastened from their restraining cords in order to attack the enemy, as conscious elements of this umbilically based libidinous desire straining towards its source. This is symbolised by the boar representing the mother's positive and negative animus combined. The hero may prove his manhood by attacking the foe that wants to devour him and hold him back, and rescuing from it the treasure of his own umbilical independence which it is trying to withhold. The image has, of course, also its phallic significance, but this is secondary. The unleashing is like a birth scene of the spirit. Hence the importance of the unleasher in task thirty-five.

The other archetype involved in this deep layer of body-imagery is the beard itself. Here we link up with figures such as Mephistopheles, the arch-deceiver and initiator, whose power comes from his hidden femininity, one of the signs of which is his inevitable beard. On one level the mouth, through what is called 'displacement upwards' (and contrasexually), which can be so dangerous from the seducing words it utters, symbolises the female genitalia; the beard symbolises its most prominent external sign. Such archetypal fantasy is part of a system of body-imagery, in which sexes change place and one part of the body comes to symbolise another in accordance with deep psychosomatic mechanisms. These are now beginning to be understood, and have to do with breast-feeding as well as sex, with the former as the basic factor. This explains the close association between the leash and beard as symbolising not only the external sign of female genitalia but also the cord which is first seen to issue from it when a child is born. This imagery deepens the whole concept of the boar as symbol of the devouring mother in her male, destructive aspect. 'The cords of Adam' are another instance of this type of female imagery in male form.

That we have now got down to a birth level would seem to be supported by what follows, when Cei has finished his speech: " 'What is our counsel concerning that?' asked Bedwyr. 'Let us suffer him,' said Cei, 'to eat his fill of meat and after that he will fall asleep.' Whilst he was about this, they busied themselves making tweezers. When Cei knew for certain that he was asleep, he dug a pit under his feet, the biggest in the world, and he struck him a blow mighty past telling, and pressed him down in the pit until they had entirely twitched out his beard with the tweezers; and after that they slew him outright."

This method of killing by trickery is an extremely feminine one, very unlike Cei's usual heroic deeds, and it will be noted that it is done so on the recommendation of Bedwyr, who, as we have seen throughout, represents Cei's inner or 'female' side. It is also not unusual in mythology that of the two main enemies (the 'male' and 'female' ones based ultimately on the two parents), while the 'male' element can be tackled direct, the 'female' is so powerful that she can only be defeated by means of trickery. A well-known example of this is Marduk killing the great sea-monster mother-image Tiamat, first having tricked her by catching her in a net after every direct onslaught had failed. Dillus is such a female power in male guise. In the imagery here used Dillus can only be 'undermined', and pushed into the pit dug for him. The subsequent description of how Cei 'pressed him down into the pit' accords with the fact that his beard symbolises the umbilical cord, which does indeed come out of a hole.

The beard-leash-umbilical-cord is here the 'treasure' recovered from the womb of the destructive male-mother-figure, just as later the ultimate 'treasures' are similarly extracted from the boar. It will be remembered that in the episode dealing with Mabon son of Modron, the 'treasure' extracted from the sea-prison was Mabon himself. It is in the order of natural birth that the object to come next is the umbilical cord. The seizing of this on behalf of the hero symbolises that the hero is now free to act on his own accord. There now ensues, appended to this episode of Dillus the Bearded, a scene which bears this out.

This is the fact that Cei, chief henchman of Arthur, and also an extravert aspect of himself, who has accomplished this feat with the aid of his companion Bedwyr, the introverted one, now leaves Arthur for good. This is quite clearly part of the archetypal pattern that, however much help a man may need in his journey to find his soul, the ultimate issue has to be fought out alone. No man chooses this path. He has it forced on him by circumstance or by the nature of things, for, universal as the problem may be, and therefore however much help a man may get from others versed in it, in the very last instance a man's soul is his unique own, not quite like any other, and personality triumphs over all collective concepts or set methods. So Arthur, from now on, gradually loses friends, helpers and warriors. His counsellors prove to be bad ones. Even his body-servants fail him. Even though he has overcome the boar, he has to face the ultimate hag alone.

This anticipating is necessary for the understanding of what happens now. The incident is particularly human in that, as so often in myth and equally often — if not invariably — in real life, this momentous separation seems to come about as the result of a quite unnecessary tiff. The account goes on: "And then the two of them [Cei and Bedwyr] went to Celli Wig [33] in Cornwall, and a leash from Dillus the Bearded's beard with them." Celli Wig is, as we know, Arthur's (as Pan-Celtic Self) own stronghold and symbolises the centre of his soul, or his soul-cavity. In Culhwch's boon-list, the seer *par excellence* saw from Celli Wig to Caithness; the marksman *par excellence* shot a wren between the legs in the middle of Leinster, aimed from Celli Wig. It is, as all such recepticals, female, and in this respect resembles the pit into which Dillus the Bearded was pushed. But the direction of events is here reversed. The leash from his beard was taken from Dillus when in his hole, but now it is brought to Arthur and put into his. For in a sense Arthur is at the moment (as throughout the fulfilment of all these earlier tasks) using Celli Wig not so much as a seat of government as a funk-hole, from which he sends out others to do his dirty work while himself skulking, or at least sitting in safety, at home, until the actual problem of the boar hunt comes up. That rouses him to bestir himself. This is so typical of human behaviour, and as a rule so unnoticed. Arthur was not sitting in Celli Wig in state, above all petty squabbles and inconveniences. Though as the Self he is above it all, knowing beforehand the outcome, as Man he is in mortal danger, as subsequent events will prove.

It needs a shock to rouse a man in this condition of apparent security, and the first shock now comes, apparently brought on by Arthur's own 'superior' foolishness. Cei and Bedwyr have now come with the leash to

130

Celli Wig: "And Cei gave it into Arthur's hand, and thereupon Arthur sang this englyn:

> Cei made a leash
> From Dillus' beard, son of Eurei.
> Were he alive, thy death he'd be.

And because of this Cei grew angry, so that it was with difficulty the warriors of this Island made peace between Cei and Arthur. But nevertheless, neither for Arthur's lack of help, nor for the slaying of his men, did Cei have aught to do with him in his hour of need from that time forward."

What lies behind this taunt is not quite clear. Whether Arthur was hinting that, had he himself been Dillus, Cei would not have survived, or whether the taunt was that Cei had obtained by trickery what he should, if he were a real hero, have obtained by battle, the fact is that Cei took umbrage, and appears no more in this story. Bedwyr does, however, from time to time, possibly because he is the introvert having knowledge of inner mechanisms, whereas Cei is the purely extravert. However this may be, Arthur, though starting out on the boar hunt the master of countless hosts of warriors, becomes gradually more and more deprived of helpers, until he finally meets the Black Witch all alone. He has to face the ultimate test of killing her not in the glory of battle but horribly in a cave, all by himself. Such is the fate of the real hero.

"And then Arthur said, 'Which of the marvels will it now be best to seek? ' " to which reply is made " 'It will be best to seek Drudwyn the whelp of Greid son of Eri.' " In the next episode we see that Greid son of Eri, its owner, has been another of several 'prisoners' whom Arthur sets free. It is assumed that the whelp is obtained.

The next episode is the last before the boar hunt actually begins. In spite of its apparent irrelevance, it is a statement about the everlasting conflict between the opposing forces of nature and of transformed nature, of mother-right and father-right, and of the flesh and the spirit, in which Arthur intervenes on the side of the spirit. Nevertheless the mutual opposition has ritual sanction endlessly. The opposition is here in the form of two men quarrelling over a maiden who has been equated with Cordelia the daughter of King Lear. If ever there was a 'father's daughter' in the positive sense, it certainly was she. There is in this probably a hidden reference to Olwen, though it is nowhere stated in the text. The account begins, "A short while before this" as though it were an afterthought, and goes on "Creiddlad [34] [Cordelia] daughter of Lludd [Lear] Silver-hand went with Gwythyr son of Greidawl [35]; and before he had slept with her there came Gwyn son of Nudd and carried her off by force." This looks at first sight very much like Culhwch's father carrying his stepmother off by force, whereby the element of father-right triumphed over the matriarchal world of untransformed nature. But the present seduction is the other way round, as may be seen from the personalities of the two men concerned. For, as seen in the comment on task thirty-two, Gwyn son of Nudd was the King of Faerie, connected with the Underworld of the Mother. On the other hand Gwythyr was father to one of Arthur's three wives (who all bore the name of Gwenhwyfar) and so was his father-in-law (Guest, 1877 edition, pp. 262-3), thus representing the patriarchal social system and personal responsibility. So this represents also a conflict between the two sides of Arthur: the world of external reality symbolised by his father-in-law, and fantasies of unreal omnipotence connected with the faerie king, who stole the maiden properly belonging to the representative of the patriarchal principle.

The two fought. "Gwythyr son of Greidawl gathered a host, and he came to fight with Gwyn son of Nudd. And Gwyn prevailed..." This symbolises the original dominance of primaeval nature, which is in the course of this episode to be reversed in the interests of a ritual equilibrium between the two. "And he took prisoner Greid son of Eri..." Whoever 'takes prisoners' in this myth is on the matriarchal side, that of nature refusing to be transformed. As owner of the whelp Drudwyn to be used in hunting the boar, Greid is again on the side of the spirit. Gwyn also took prisoner a number of others, including "Gwrgwst the Half-naked" and others, but that which shows him in truest colours in his opposition to father-right is his taking of yet another prisoner, "Nwython [36], and Cyledyr the Wild his son, and he slew Nwython and took out his heart, and compelled Cyledyr to eat his father's heart; and because of this Cyledyr went mad." This is the only case in this myth of anybody going mad, with the exception of Culhwch's 'natural' mother, who went mad through being forced into her husband's patriarchal pattern. She only recovered her sanity by following her own true sow-nature (*uncompromising* nature) by giving birth to Culhwch among the swine. We have, in the course of this myth, advanced a long way towards patriarchy and the combatting of this matriarchally possessive 'natural' and self-destructive attitude. Now, as a last fling before its doom overtakes it with the boar hunt, the force of nature inimical to human control once more asserts itself in this incentive to parricide.

The 'parricide' in Arthur's soul had shown itself in his staying put in Celli Wig while others fought his preliminary battles for him. He hoped thereby, from the safety of his mother-citadel, to be able to remain aloof from the conflict and maintain an appearance of calm dignity without being involved. But now Cei has left him. He no longer has that shield between him and the world of his own inner conflict. He has to rouse himself, to vindicate his own position of all-father. In fact his very existence is threatened as the sequel shows, though he is not yet aware of this.

133

So at first Arthur acts mildly, still keeping his dignity. "Arthur heard tell of this, and he came into the North [37] and summoned to him Gwyn son of Nudd and set free his noblemen from his prison..." The North is the point of the compass in which Ysgithyrwyn was ultimately slain, and also the direction from which the boar Twrch Trwyth will make its onslaught against Celli Wig. It is in the North also that the hag or Black Witch has her home, living in a cave there, where Arthur ultimately slew her as his final task. Topographical position is also, in this myth, symbolic of psychic configuration.

Arthur frees these 'noblemen' (powers of his own) whom Gwyn had imprisoned, but no punishment is meted out to him. It seems that, though Arthur will ultimately be victorious over the forces of unredeemed nature, the fact of the conflict must never be lost to mind, and to remind the world of it a special kind of peace was made. "And peace was made between Gwyn son of Nudd and Gwythyr son of Greidawl. This is the peace that was made: the maiden should remain in her father's house, unmolested by either side, and there should be battle between Gwyn and Gwythyr each May-calends [38] for ever and ever, and from that day till doomsday; and the one of them that should be victor on doomsday, let him have the maiden." The 'maiden' in any case symbolises something very deep in Arthur's character, an anima-like figure symbolising libido that may be influenced one way or another unless under the protection of a father-figure. The intellect must function, holding the balance between the two opposing forces of blind nature and transformed nature in Arthur's own soul. In terms of Arthur as the Self the problem is an endless one to be resolved only at doomsday. In terms of Arthur as Man, the battle has to be fought out here and now. This is the time when a man faces the father-problem within himself, which has to do with the release of the anima, before the ultimate mother-problem can be solved and the whole man be set free. (Rivals fighting for the right to mate with the moon goddess is an old theme concerning fertility.)

"And when those lords had been thus reconciled, Arthur obtained Dun-mane the steed of Gweddw, and the leash of Cors Hundred-claws." It is through a union of opposites that anything new is born. What Arthur now obtains as a result of this union of the two 'lords' is Mabon's steed. Arthur never rides this — or any other steed — himself, but Mabon does. This steed of the Great Mother's son is brought into the story here apparently to show why the matriarchal Gwyn son of Nudd was not punished but only deprived of his prisoners. The mother-principle must not be destroyed. It must only be deprived of its possessiveness. The leash of Cors Hundred-claws was mentioned in task twenty-three as being the one needed to hold the whelp Drudwyn. The title Hundred-claws is a terrifying image. It indicates that the leash (umbilical cord) is now, in Arthur's hands and no longer in those of the destructive male-mother image, to drag him back into the unconscious. The stage is now set for the great boar hunt to begin.

CHAPTER 11

THE TASKS FULFILLED:

YSGITHYRWYN, MENW, CAULDRON

At last we come now to the first stage of the boar hunt. The mother-bound heroes have been rescued from prison, the leash representing the umbilical cord leading to the Great Mother in her positive aspect and to be used against her in her negative one has been obtained. So also have the hounds, and now the steed. There has been one preliminary skirmish with the hag in the form of the she-wolf. Arthur has been deserted by his best right-hand man, so has to rouse himself and use all the resources left at his command.

"After that Arthur made his way to Llydaw [39], and with him Mabon son of Mellt and Gware Golden-hair [Gwallt Euryn] [40] to seek the two dogs of Glythfyr Ledewig [41]." It is of interest at the same time to note the picking up of two former motifs: Mabon is the liberated Great Son of the Great Mother; 'Golden-hair' recalls Goreu, the 'lad with curly yellow hair' who also had been a prisoner of the matriarchal system. This pair and the pair of dogs they seek out carry on the motif of united opposites. "And when he had obtained them, Arthur went to the west of Ireland to seek out [two men again, one of whom was] Odgar son of Aedd king of Ireland..." This latter was the original owner of the cauldron mentioned in task fourteen, to be obtained shortly under dramatic circumstances, a cauldron full of the wisdom and wickedness of femininity. "And after that Arthur went into the North and caught Cyledyr the Wild; and he went after Ysgithyrwyn Chief Boar."

Arthur is now not only aroused. He goes to far confines of the Celtic world, to Ireland, to start the hunt. The whole Celtic world stands for a psychic image of Arthur as Self, who now starts at its periphery symbolising his outer consciousness, as far away from its center at Celli Wig as possible. It was in the North that Gwyn son of Nudd had imprisoned Cyledyr the Wild, whom he had sent mad by forcing him to eat his father's heart (desecration of the father principle). No wonder that Arthur should seek him out: he would have more reason than anyone to avenge the crime that he had been compelled to commit. Madness lends strength and passion for a one-pointed task. So Arthur does well to return to him his sanity by providing the proper outlet for his rage, helping to slay the boar that carried the phallic emblem of the mother's domination over the male principle. That Cyledyr the Wild is but a function of Arthur himself is clear from the fact that he is not mentioned again in this context. He is an image of Arthur's own internal rage, brought in here by the chronicler to indicate to those not bluffed by Arthur's external composure what power of frustrated manhood lay in him.

The account of the hunt and slaying of Ysgithyrwyn is short and sharp. All the hounds so far mentioned take part in it: two pairs, with the addition of Drudwyn the whelp. So far, though Arthur has been in the background more or less in control of things, he has not himself entered the fray. Now "Arthur himself took his place in the hunt, and Cafall, Arthur's dog, in his hand. And Cadw of Prydain mounted Llamrei[42], Arthur's

137

mare, and he was the first to bring the boar to bay. And then Cadw of Prydain armed him with a hatchet, and boldly and gallantly set upon the boar and split his head in two. [See Appendix III.] And Cadw took the tusk." The chronicler adds "It was not the dogs which Ysbaddaden had named to Culhwch which killed the boar, but Cafall, Arthur's own dog."

Even now, Arthur does not actually kill the boar, but his dog does. He enters the combat only when the very centre of the problem is reached (for which the boar is only a mask) when he personally engages the hag. Llamrei and Cafall are themselves symbolical, being respectively female and male. The bisexual nature of the Self which Arthur symbolises is now becoming evident; also the double-naturedness required of anyone who would dare to attack such a monster, and without which any such project would fail. Wisdom comes from the female side and action (attack) from the male. Though Arthur does not himself ride the mare, it is nevertheless the mare's rider who deals the final blow, presumably after Cafall has reduced the boar to impotence.

The nature of the blow by which Ysgithyrwyn is slain is, however, of prime importance. The hatchet "split his head in two". To emphasise the meaning of this, we must anticipate and quote what happened when Arthur himself finally and single-handedly slew the hag; striking her with his knife "across the middle until she was as two tubs". Each was therefore split into two. Two aspects of these two killings must be stressed here. Firstly, they are accomplished with no such knightly weapon as a sword (the only mention of which in this myth was in connexion with Wrnach the Giant). In the case of Ysgithyrwyn it is a common hatchet, and in the case of the hag a knife, and we may imagine the blood spurting out. If read of in a newspaper today, both these murders would read like the most sordid of crimes. This is no chance thing or unfair analogy: highest and lowest join. The

138

hero has to go into the most horrid depths of shame, crime, and sordidness. All the really great heroes have done this, for example Hercules in clearing out the Augean stables of mountains of dung. This is why Culhwch is no first-class hero, since he lets all this be done for him. But Arthur is. He plumbs the ultimate depths, and from them draws his nobility.

The second and more basic aspect of both these killings is the division into two. Here we have yet another aspect of the 'two-headed briar' with which the story opened, which runs all through it like an undercurrent, and comes openly to the surface again in these two ultimate scenes. 'Division into two' means what has been termed 'differentiation' but might here be more aptly described as 'discernment'. It is found in some form or other at the beginning of almost every creation story. Its manifold symbolism includes the break-up of an original chaotic situation into its two main component parts, bringing with it as third thing an element of differentiated consciousness into what had before been a confused mass of primary undifferentiated psychic matter. This element of consciousness is also the element of individuality now able to discern the different characteristics of the two opposites out of which it arose. The two elements can symbolise the parents and the third thing arising out of them, the child. Or the third thing may come from without and be the intelligence that divides, and thus prepare the way for the emergence of the fourth, the new life or understanding that arises as a result of it. This is a case in point. The hatchet 'divides', and 'out' of the division comes the tusk. To take another analogy, the husk or outer covering of a seed, which has reared in itself that seed, splits into two. The need of new life emerges, and the husk dies, having fulfilled its task.

In the case of Ysgithyrwyn, the boar is killed, but its tusk is preserved. The corruptible body is got rid of, but the incorruptible thing which has

139

grown out of it is kept. There is even mentioned in task seventeen a special 'keeper of the tusk', who is no less than Cadw of Prydain (Cadw means 'to keep'), the minor hero who rode Arthur's mare and actually split open the boar's head. I have written elsewhere of the 'divine' nature of the white tusk as symbolising the hero's own latent spirituality delivered from the black body of corruptibility. ("Boar Sacrifice", John Layard, *The Journal of Analytical Psychology,* Vol. I, No. 1, 1955.) I have also pointed out that the image conceived of this tusk not as one of two tusks issuing from either side of the jaw, but rather of a single unicorn-like tusk issuing from the boar's head. Attention has also been called to its phallic nature. Now 'phallus' is also a synonym, in the case of a woman, for the male child issuing from her womb. The male child is often, in fact, 'her' phallus, which she would like to hold on to and not let free. These are psychological findings of prime importance for the understanding of human life. This scene of splitting the boar's head in two and rescuing the tusk from it thus symbolises parturition, in which the boar's head stands for the womb of the Black Witch from which the 'male child', in the form of the phallic tusk, is 'delivered' by Cadw, acting as male midwife and keeping it in trust for Arthur. Arthur in turn keeps it in trust for Culhwch, who finally gets it in the form of Olwen his spirit-bride. She, like the tusk, is 'moon-like', incorruptible, and is his 'only wife' — just as the tusk has been an 'only tusk'.

This body-image symbolism of the head as the male womb of the initiating protagonist being split open (sometimes in anger and despair), thus being made to yield up out of itself something of great value, is not only mythological; it occurs in modern dreams and active fantasies. I shall here analyse at length a parallel instance of this. A dreamer who had been rescued from a severe breakdown had, during a phase of negative transference against his analyst, the visual experience of taking an axe and splitting the analyst's head in two. Out of the cleft there then poured forth black vomit which the dreamer recognised as being his own; in the midst appeared a letter from an anima figure dating from long ago, which gave an important clue for the further prosecution of the analysis. In his breakdown, he had been subject to terrible nightmares in which almost everything he valued seemed to be being destroyed. He made the typical mistake of identifying his ego with these valued objects, all of which were of an inflationary kind. The analyst, however, took the line that what was being destroyed *had* to be destroyed, in other words that the apparent destruction was the work of the Great Mother in her initiating aspect, avenging herself on the false values he had built up through lack of discrimination between the 'two mothers'. The external mother had given physical birth to him but had denied him his individuality; the internal mother was his own true nature that had been thus repressed. It was the latter Great Mother who was outraged and was out to destroy her enemies — the false constructs he had built up in order to hide from himself his own denial of himself. It was therefore not ego that she was attacking, but ego that she was trying to save from them. The 'two mothers' were in conflict. Which would he believe?

At the same time there were in his life two men, to whom different sides of himself looked for help. One appeared to him to be an authority on psychic matters, but was not an analyst. The other was, but frankly admitted that he was in the dark along with the dreamer. He had, however, faith in the initiating process. His formerly 'friendly' internal structure, connected with superimposed values derived from the actual mother, offered the appearance of safety in the form of the inflated order to which he clung like grim death — but which in fact was death to him. The analyst sided with the destroying elements.

This led the analysand, with one side of his psyche, deeply to suspect

141

the analyst for siding with the destructive forces. At the same time he experienced what was to him a new sensation of belief and warmth. These
latter gradually triumphed over his fear, till he was able to accept the destructive forces with gratitude, and finally himself to side with them, seeing
more and more clearly the contrasting attributes of the two mother-images.

In the situation he had found himself in at the time of his breakdown,
both these mother-images had been projected on to men. The 'earth mother' was projected on to the authoritarian man who seemed reliable; he
wished to 'build up' the dreamer's ego and did not appreciate the virtue of
his destructive side. The other image was projected on to the doubtful char-
aracter (as it appeared to him) of the analyst. The latter, however, did not
accept this one-sided division into opposites, but strove to focus both images upon himself, so that they could be worked out in a single relationship.
The only difference was in the accent upon 'authority'. He disclaimed all
personal authority by constantly reiterating that he 'did not know', but
that something else did know. This something else was the autonomous
psyche within the dreamer himself, which was both active in the destruction of the false values, and would in turn do the building up once the false
structure had collapsed. The analyst had basically to observe and point out
both processes, agreeing with both — the ruthless destruction and the warm
glow of tender feeling that lay behind and in fact prompted its destructively
creative act. Out of the two combined arose the dreamer's new personality,
a resurrected self now able to cope with both internal and external problems.

This brief description of basic psychotherapeutic attitude has been
gone into here because of the light it throws on the mutual relationships between Culhwch, Ysbaddaden, Arthur, Olwen, and — ultimately — the boar.
A pivotal phrase is Olwen's 'counsel' to Culhwch at their first meeting, when
she refuses to go with him till he has 'made' himself, "Lest sin be charged to

142

me and thee". She knows it will be difficult, so prefaces her words by saying " 'There is, however, counsel I will give thee, if thou wilt take it.' [Then
comes one of the keys to the whole myth:] 'Go ask me of my father. And
however much he demand of thee, do thou promise to get it, and me too
shalt thou get.' [She adds warningly:] 'But if he has cause to doubt at all,
get me thou shalt not, and 'tis well for thee if thou escape with thy life.' "
Ysbaddaden, we know, symbolises the mother's negative animus. Culhwch
here corresponds to the analysand, baulked of his desire, cut off from his
own inner consciousness, the 'hero' not knowing what to do. In his admitted
ignorance he has submitted himself to Arthur, though without subservience:
he threatens to ruin his honour if not assisted. This is like a typical beginning to a good psychological analysis, the seeker rightly laying the burden
upon the analyst while still not trusting him. The trust, when it comes, will
be shot through with critical attitudes quite necessary to any vital relationship. Bitter hates will have to be expressed if the analysis is not to peter out
through blockage of essential libido; and thoughts of revenge will follow if
the analysis fails. The analyst must know how to take all this with satisfaction, as Arthur does, honouring the seeker not in spite of, but because of it.
He knows that this expresses the basic ambivalence that rules all life, and
that its projection upon himself is an honour indicating the all-importance
of the relationship.

Arthur himself says that he has never heard of her: " 'Ah, chieftain,
I have never heard tell of the maiden thou tellest of, nor of her parents.' "
He thus addresses him with respect, as a good analyst regards any — even the
most apparently unsuitable or undesirable — who come to seek his help. He
does not pose as an authority, but confesses his ignorance, thus putting himself as low as the seeker and on a par with him. But he adds 'I will gladly
send messengers to seek her.' He will gladly bring into play what faculties

('messengers') he has, to seek out the seeker's anima and tempt her from her hiding-place, that is to say the seeker's own ambivalent emotional powers, which are so largely unknown to him. In seeking the anima, Culhwch runs up against her most ferocious enemy, the mother's negative animus, Ysbaddaden Pencawr. This is the hostile father-figure who seeks to destroy. But to destroy what? Overtly he seeks to destroy Culhwch, but only if Culhwch identifies himself with his own fear, that is to say with that aspect of Culhwch represented by Ysbaddaden. The natural thing would be to oppose him immediately. But none can oppose the Great Mother or her agents head-on. She is not only too powerful, but she is dual, in such a way that in opposing one side of her the other is strengthened. The only thing then is to submit.

For Ysbaddaden is not only Culhwch's mother's negative animus. He is Olwen's father, who with the same ambivalence as the Great Mother, has one side of him which ultimately wishes her good. The good he does is to make Culhwch into a man by violently opposing him. By this means he rouses in Culhwch the spirit of opposition to the possessive aspect of the mother-image, which Culhwch could not become aware of if his protagonist was a woman. This, in terms of psychological analysis, involves the negative transference dug up and exposed within the framework of the positive one. Without the two no real individuation process is possible. The seeker learns that he may hate as well as love the same object, and so his inborn hate or aggression need no longer be turned against himself, that is to say against his anima. She is the greatest enemy of, and releaser from, the negatively possessive mother-image.

In psychological analysis of patients more or less unaware of this ambivalence and leading what are called 'normal' lives, this negative side has to be fished out. It takes a long time and much deep probing to turn such

144

people into 'heroes'. In such cases the analyst himself has to provide the element of attack, or wait long before the inner enemy appears. But a seeker already in a state of breakdown is in a different category. He is already on a deep level in the grip of forces that can no longer appear to him to be purely external, as those of more ordinary folk are apt to find. He is conscious of being attacked not only from without by known people but also from within. He feels the surge of uncontrolled impulses. If, as our dreamer did, he has the good fortune to be aware of his nightmares, these are much more valuable than his conscious terrors, since in them may be seen the operation of the Terrible Mother divested of human form: of natural impetuous or insidious forces such as fire, water, storms, things falling or crushing, exploding, wild animals attacking, or things creeping, poisoning, infecting with sickness, suffocating, and so on.

These are, particularly the more violent ones, what in our myth are symbolised by the boar. The man already broken down is willy-nilly a 'hero' in the sense that he must find his way through these terrors or perish in the attempt. What then does Culhwch do? Does he manfully do battle with Ysbaddaden and slay him, as any straightforward, clean-limbed, soldierly young braggart (as his bold talking would suggest) would do? Had this been the case, he might have won a wife in the material sense but only at the price of missing his chance of individuating himself. His anima appears in all her beauty and tells him to submit and carry out her father's orders.

This is the cue for the good analyst dealing with breakdowns. The dreamer is struggling against his fate, which is to say the operation of an interior will far stronger than his own conscious will. This will in fact break him if he does not submit. He cannot realise this so long as he identifies ego with the false values he has built up. His ego is in fact swamped in the

145

struggle against his better self, and, being so, is projected upon the analyst whom he hopes may help him out. What he cannot do of himself, the analyst must do, that is to say to take sides with the autonomous psyche, which the dreamer is in the condition of thinking is his worst enemy.

What now again does Culhwch do when he has accepted the anima's counsel? He says proudly that he will — and then does nothing. He leaves it all to his 'lord and kinsman Arthur' to do them for him. This can be taken on two levels. Arthur may be taken to be either the Self, or, as in the case of this dreamer seeking help, at first the analyst. I say 'at first' because, if the analysis goes as it should, the two merge into one. The seeker's Self projected on to the analyst causes belief in the autonomous psyche gradually to percolate through to the seeker. As one piece of apparent destruction after another is seen to have a healing intent, he gradually shifts his ground. He thinks of himself less and less as the victim of unkind forces, realising that he is himself the 'attacker' in rejecting them.

Innumerable facets of the seeker's personality come under review from the two angles of external and internal reality, the gap between the two growing smaller as the internal dichotomy is more and more clearly defined. It is acknowledged as being in the nature of things and the most creative factor in life. Personality comes out of the split. This is what is symbolised in our myth by splitting Ysgithyrwyn's head and getting hold of the tusk. While the head has been said to be the male womb of consciousness, there is a general progression of this head-womb from being partly male to being entirely female. The same general progression from 'maleness' to 'femaleness' was also strikingly illustrated in the case of our dreamer by two dreams, both preceding the vision already spoken of. The first was that the analyst split the dreamer's penis lengthwise with something like a knife. The second was that the analyst split the dreamer's whole body in two from the chest down

146

towards the genitals, not quite reaching them. The process of transformation by which the phallus gets gradually turned into a womb is here illustrated. In the first dream of the split penis the wound was a dorsal one, similar to subincision such as was formerly practiced by Australian aborigines with the avowed purpose of simulating the female vagina, with the resulting blood representing the menstrual flow. This is a ritual act symbolising the psychic fact that the novice so operated on as part of the initiation process is now married (as a female) to the male tribe. And this in turn symbolises submission to the spiritual world which thus appears as an attacker but is really a healer, taking a boy out of the mother-world and initiating him into the world of men. The analyst is here cast in the role of the operator, performing the *opus* of initiation on the novice, hurting to heal. Any who have witnessed initiation rites know how the operator and his confederates comfort and cosset the boy after the operation is done. He is in the dream an internalised figure, symbol of a psychic function of the dreamer himself, his own 'internal analyst' released through contact with the external analyst.

The next dream shows the whole body taking the place of the phallus, and so broadening the affect to include the heart. But the splitting did not quite reach the genital region, still somewhat separated in the dreamer's psyche from the seat of deeper emotion. The subsequent visionary experience in which the roles were reversed, the splitting motif transferred to the head, and the subject now taking the active role rather than the passive one, was due to such deeper emotion having been touched on. The subject was not yet quite ready for this and so reacted with anger. Such was the solid basis of the analytical relationship, however, that this negative reaction produced a positive one through the subject taking the initiative into his own hands more or less consciously. It also brought into the open the female element in all this bisexual symbolism. As in the case of Ysgithyrwyn, the head of the protagonist functioned as a male womb spilling forth the bile. The subject recognised this as symbolising his own anger (more accurately still his anguish, or male labour-pains).

In both the visual experience and the dreams the role of the analyst corresponds with that of the boar. Before being attacked and hunted by Arthur and all his men, the boar had previously laid waste all their country-side. Thus in the dreams, the dreamer had been attacked or violated by the analyst. The analyst can be for the patient an image of the Self, including the image of both parents, or, deeper still, of both 'mothers'. He is thus, for the patient's psyche, bisexual. If a man, he carries, under his external manliness, the feeling attributes of the mother, without which dynamism he cannot work and the more conscious he is of it the better will be his work. If a woman, she can function as successful analyst only in so far as her natural femininity is clothed with, and transmitted through, the penetrating power of masculine thought.

A last and very important aspect of the analogy is that, though Arthur first seeks out the boar, the boar then turns the tables on him and 'seeks out' him, driving him headlong in retreat. In just the same way does the analysand gradually get stripped of his neurotic defences till the truth of his inner personality or something near it is laid bare. The idea of this terrifies him till it is found, when it in fact proves to be his salvation.

The analysand's defences are thus laid bare. Paradoxically enough, the defences diminish the stronger he finds himself. Strength now comes from the Self (the centre) rather than from the periphery. With this he has the power to ward off the last assault of the 'external analyst' who, however understandingly and lovingly he may have handled his analysand in his dual capacity of huntsman and lover, now comes to symbolise an external

authority. He has to rid himself of this in order to establish his own individuality, an individuality always ultimately untouchable. Ysgithyrwyn,
symbolising the more intellectual aspect of the boar as Self-symbol, can be
divided up and slain; Twrch Trwyth symbolising its more female and therefore ultimately its more basic aspect cannot. The successful, depth analyst
cannot be 'slain', in so far as he has been internalised. The psychic ferment
goes on working within the pupil wherever the master has gone or whatever
he may become.

Culhwch is a braggart, but does not realise it. In Ysbaddaden he meets
this quality in himself face to face. Culhwch is also a bully. He has bullied
Arthur, and Arthur's gatekeeper, and has, through his companions, mis-
handled several of Ysbaddaden's men. Ysbaddaden is a bully also. Yet Culhwch finds his anima in possession of this angry shadow, his mother's anger
that has been automatically taken over by him without knowing it any more
than she knew of hers. It had sent her mad when faced with it, that is to say
when faced with making a relationship to her husband. The problem which
she rejected Culhwch now has to face. Just as his mother had rejected his
father, so he had rejected or not even known about his anima. Meeting with
his own overwhelming anger and possessiveness in Ysbaddaden had two results. Firstly it justified this anger, since out of it Olwen was born. This is
important. It 'justifies' the negative transference in psychological analysis.
On a deeper level, because he now sees it in Ysbaddaden, it makes him conscious of an anger potentially within himself that he had never known. It is
the potential anger of all matriarchal men at the possessiveness of their
women-folk, a possessiveness showing itself in the rejection of themselves
as husbands by the women whom they have fertilised. Such a rejection
gives to the men freedom of promiscuity (since there are no marital 'ties'),
that is to say 'nature'-freedom, but it denies to them the deeper freedom

of relationship. This involves both wife and anima, who represents for a
man that inner relationship with himself which makes tolerable anything
like marital fidelity. The anima thus also gives rise to spiritual value. And
spiritual life, whatever the theologians may say, begins with anger, that is
to say with the child's self-assertion over against the possessive mother-
image, which is equivalent to saying against self-regard in its negative com-
placent sense.

Ysbaddaden is the image of such self-regard, absorbing everything into itself and giving nothing away. It is enraged if anything from outside
threatens it as Culhwch does. But Ysbaddaden in turn threatened him.
Self-regard is the blockage to all development. Faced with Ysbaddaden's,
he now realised his own. Out of that realisation appeared Olwen, the anima
who is the object of his desire, but at the same time withholds herself
lest he should think she was a woman whom he, as promiscuous all-having
man, could just take as in his state of matriarchal freedom he would take
any other. Were he not in the service of Arthur, his spiritual and transforming lord, he would doubtless either have killed her father and raped
her, gone off in dudgeon if he could not, or else himself got killed. But
she speaks out of his depths, giving him the double view of things that only
the anima, standing between two worlds, can give. She tells him that Ysbaddaden, as his anger, is neither to be despised nor disobeyed. It has to
be served, at whatever risk to life and limb it may entail. So only will he
get her. It is, therefore, ultimately his own anger that he kills.

Of all the ambivalent figures in this story, Ysbaddaden is the most
self-tortured and divided one. He is a figure of the Self in its most negative
and divided aspect; the devil who divides and is in torment, and therefore
wants to divide everyone else so as not to experience his own dividedness
but only see it in them. In this Olwen is his opposite on the female side.

On the male side it is Arthur, who from ages past has united the opposites within himself and so is the 'lord'. In this age-long aspect he is the Old Wise Man. He is, however, not the Self in its entirety. Deeper than Arthur, Ysbaddaden, or even Olwen, is the entity of the Terrible Boar. Even the boar is not an absolute Self, for, though symbolically bisexual, he yet does not completely unite the opposites. The boar as a composite figure is, however, much nearer to the Self than any other image in this myth, since, like the 'cauldron' which contains the 'treasures of Ireland', the two boars between them produce, when overcome, the 'treasures' which, other than the hag, are the main object of the hunt.

Three incidents are now related before the final hunt begins. The first is highly suggestive with regard to the theme we have just been handling. "And after Ysgithyrwyn Chief Boar was slain, Arthur and his host went to Celli Wig in Cornwall..." We have already seen how this stronghold of Arthur's represents one of the deep recesses in his soul and is ultimately connected with the boar. Ysgithyrwyn symbolising the more external, male aspect of the evil is therefore not met with too close to Celli Wig; Twrch Trwyth, who symbolises its more 'female' aspect, comes nearer to penetrating and thus disrupting Arthur in his inmost citadel.

The second is revealed: "and thence he sent Menw son of Teirgwaedd[43] [one of Culhwch's original six companions] to see whether the treasures were between the two ears of Twrch Trwyth — so mean a thing would it be to go to fight with him, had he not those treasures." If the boar's head symbolises the uterus and genitalia generally of the mother in disguised male form (the mother's animus), what should the two ears, between which the treasures are to be found, symbolise but the two guardians of its entrance, the vaginal labia. The treasures are ostensibly the comb and shears, in other words the dread teeth of the *vagina dentata* so long as they are not removed, but

151

individuation symbols once they are. Were all this not the case, were the boar not a disguised symbol of femininity, why should it be "so mean a thing" to go to fight with him? Hunting the boar in real life was in those times a highly masculine, necessary and noble occupation, often even reserved for kings. On what possible grounds should this be considered 'mean' were it not known that the boar symbolised a female being who normally should be respected, honoured and protected if not even loved, and therefore, certainly not attacked. But if the treasures were of the kind stated, if they were the most dangerous weapons for castrating men, then even the crime of attacking a woman is justified, for she is the Devouring Mother in male guise who must be destroyed, before she destroys.

We have already seen Arthur put in this dilemma when he was seeking to rescue Mabon from her clutches in the form of the sea prison, and his men said "thou canst not proceed with thy hosts to seek things so pretty as these". He then consented to send others to carry out this task; now that the ultimate issue is at stake, all the forces at his command are going to be employed.

The doubt about Twrch Trwyth's destructiveness is also soon resolved. "However, it was certain that he was there; he had already laid waste the third part of Ireland." The task is so great, and the myth is therefore so like life, that it is full of setbacks. "Menw went to seek them out. [Twrch Trwyth is here referred to in the plural, with his seven young pigs, to help him in the battle against Arthur and his hosts] He saw them in Esgeir Oerfel in Ireland. And Menw transformed himself into the likeness of a bird and alighted over his lair and sought to snatch one of the treasures away from him. But for all that he got nothing save one of his bristles. The other [the boar] arose in his might and shook himself so that some of his poison caught him. And after that Menw was never without scathe."

The boar's witch-power is now beginning to show itself. Menw's boldness was rewarded by a poisonous wound.

The third incident before the full boar hunt begins is the getting of the "cauldron of Diwrnach the Irisman". The placing of this incident just here not only confirms the view that the chronicler, in selecting some tasks for fulfillment and omitting others (and adding some not even mentioned) is indulging in 'free association' of a psychologically most pointed kind. It confirms also the view that the two boars are identical in the sense that they symbolise both male and female parental images, and so, in this respect, are interchangeable. For this incident refers to task fourteen, which in the list of tasks precedes the hunt not of Twrch Trwyth but of Ysgithyrwyn, and there the use to which it was to be put was to "boil meat" for Culhwch's wedding guests. Cooking — for good or for evil — is a well-known symbol of gestation.

The symbolism of the witch's cauldron brewing mischief is too well known to be enlarged on here. There is, however, in the Mabinogion tale called *Branwen Daughter of Llyr,* mention of a "cauldron of rebirth" into which dead bodies were cast and next day arose "as good fighting men as before, save that they were not able to speak" (Jones, p.37). The human symbolism of this cauldron is made evident when one named Efnisien, who had committed a shameful act, was cast into it, whereon "he stretched himself out in the cauldron, so that the cauldron burst into four pieces, and his heart burst also". There was a "Lake of the Cauldron" from which the cauldron had been fetched on the back of a "monstrous man" followed by a woman of whom he said "this woman...at the end of a month and a fortnight will conceive, and the son who will then be born of that wombful at the end of the month and the fortnight will be a fighting man full armed" (Jones, p.30). There is mention in another poem of the Cauldron of the

153

Head of Annwn (the underworld), which "boils not the food of a coward". The motif of the cauldron in our myth is likely to be about, therefore, the birth of a hero, and death to such as are not heroes. It is in any case a womb-symbol of great power for good or evil.

Arthur sends a messenger to Odgar son of the king of Ireland "to ask for the cauldron of Diwrnach the Irishman [Gwyddel], his overseer. Odgar besought him to give it. [As the context later shows, he seems to have known resistance was useless.] Said Diwrnach, 'God knows, though he should be the better for getting one glimpse of it, he should not have it.' And Arthur's messenger came back from Ireland with a nay. Arthur set out and a light force with him, and went in Prydwen his ship, and came to Ireland, and they made for the house of Diwrnach the Irishman. The hosts of Odgar took note of their strength; and after they had eaten and drunk their fill Arthur demanded the cauldron. He made answer that were he to give it to anyone, he would have given it at the word of Odgar king of Ireland. When he had spoken them nay, Bedwyr arose and laid hold of the cauldron and put it on the back of Hygwydd, Arthur's servant. . . His [brother's] office was always to carry Arthur's cauldron and to kindle fire under it. Llenlleawg the Irish-man [Gwyddel] seized Caledfwlch [44] [Arthur's sword] and swung it in a round and he slew Diwrnach the Irishman and all his host. The hosts of Ireland came and fought with them. And when the hosts were utterly routed Arthur and his men went on board ship before their very eyes, and with them the cauldron full of the treasures of Ireland. . ."

This shows the importance of the cauldron, and the last phrase "full of the treasures of Ireland" provides at least some clue again as to why this account of it should be brought in here. It is true that "the treasures of Ire-land" has a wide connotation, but in this context it is at least noteworthy that the same reference to 'treasure' was in the last incident connected with the boar. The next passage, in which the boar hunt begins in earnest, tells of Arthur also going to Ireland in order to track it down. Cauldron and the boar are symbols for the same thing, namely the immense power of the female element both to destroy and to give birth. The hero is he that can acquire the cauldron and overcome the boar. The treasures are inside the cauldron (since it is nothing if not female) whereas they are outside the boar (upon its head), the boar symbolising the masculine aspect of the powerful feminine principle. The power of the female invested in the cauldron is needed by the hero in all his battles with the boar which now ensue.

CHAPTER 12

THE TASKS FULFILLED:

THE HUNT OF THE TWRCH TRWYTH

The stage is now set for the mortal battle that ranges over the whole Celtic world. "And then Arthur gathered together what warriors there were in the Three Realms of Britain and its three adjacent islands, and what there were in France and Brittany and Normandy and the Summer Country[45], and what there were of picked dogs and horses of renown. And with all those hosts he went to Ireland, and at his coming there was great fear and trembling in Ireland. And when Arthur had come to land, there came to him the saints of Ireland to ask his protection." This is one of the few Christian references in the text. It shows incidentally how the boar was their enemy also. "And he granted them protection, and they gave him their blessing. The men of Ireland came to Arthur and gave him a tribute of victuals. Arthur came to Esgeir Oerfel in Ireland, to the place where Twrch Trwyth was, and his seven young pigs with him. Dogs were let loose at him from all sides. That day until evening the Irish fought with him; nevertheless he laid waste one of the five provinces of Ireland. And on the morrow Arthur's war-band fought with him: save for what evil they got from him, they got

nothing good. The third day Arthur himself fought with him, nine nights
and nine days: he slew of his pigs but one pigling." Arthur is now for the
first time personally engaged.

Now comes the question of who Twrch Trwyth is. The boar is
'human' — previously referred to as 'son of Taredd Wledig'. "His men asked
Arthur what was the history of that swine, and he told them: 'He was a
king, and for his wickedness God transformed him into a swine.' "

Then Arthur seeks for a parley. "Arthur sent Gwrhyr Interpreter of
Tongues to seek to have a word with him. Gwrhyr went in the form of a
bird and alighted above the lair of him and his seven [sic] young pigs." It
may be pointed out here that boars do not usually lie with their young.
This is the function of a sow. The chronicler has let the archetypal meaning
of the boar as a mother-figure slip out, in spite of his male disguise. (The
Interpreter of Tongues is now functioning.) "And Gwrhyr...asked him,
'For His sake who made thee in this shape, if you can speak, I beseech one
of you to come and talk with Arthur.' Grugyn Silver-bristle made answer.
Like wings of silver were all his bristles; what way he went through wood
and meadow one could discern from how his bristles glittered." This is an
image of moonlight. As well as the fact that Olwen is herself a moon-
maiden, and that Ysbaddaden suffered under the new moon, this is another
reference to the moon. It faintly hints at the world-wide pig-moon symbolism already mentioned but does nothing more, except to connect it with
the only pig reported in this myth as being capable of using human language.
This may presuppose an element of consciousness which the moon-aspect
of pig mythology represents.

"This was the answer Grugyn gave: 'By Him who made us in this
shape, we will neither do nor say aught for Arthur. Harm enough hath God
wrought us, to have made us in this shape, without you too coming to fight

157

with us.' " This implies the interesting admission that these pigs, including the great boar-sow himself, are not happy in their lot. This is important. No angry or destructive person is. To know such a fact is half the battle in psychotherapy. Perhaps Arthur hoped to cash in on this when asking for a parley. But the Devouring Mother is implacable. Rage blinds her even to her own good. In any case, these pigs are archetypes, and it is of the nature of archetypes that they are 'types'. Human beings can change, but archetypes, like angels, are unchangeable precisely because they are not human, but represent isolated 'typical attitudes' and as such, by definition, remain constant. It is the essence of this story that pigs are not human, but symbolise only an attitude of mind, which here is that of the mother's blindly proud and destructive animus, an attitude that can 'possess' a person to his or her own destruction, even against that person's conscious will.

Another factor in this is that 'every jot and title of the law must be fulfilled'. The Terrible Mother in the form of the boar has to be killed. Any compromise would only weaken the 'hero' by putting off the inevitable battle. Whatever may be meant by 'God', blind fate, divine purpose, or what you will, His purpose in turning these humans into pigs was to create a 'hero' by forcing him into conflict with this near-ultimate archetype of self-destructiveness. Gwrhyr Interpreter of Tongues, accepting the despairing challenge of Grugyn Silver-bristle, replied, "I tell you, Arthur will fight for the comb, the razor and the shears which are between the two ears of Twrch Trwyth." Note that the 'razor' (tusk) is here included with the comb and shears. Both boars are in the chronicler's mind here rolled into one, and remain so until the end, when all three implements are eventually taken from Twrch Trwyth. "Said Grugyn, 'Until first his life be taken, those treasures will not be taken. And to-morrow in the morning we will set out hence and go into Arthur's country, and there we will do

158

all the mischief we can.' " Like Judas, he seals his fate, and at the same time in this deep myth of double-meanings, provides the means for Arthur's (and Culhwch's) hero-dom.

"They set out by sea towards Wales; and Arthur and his hosts, his horses and his dogs, went aboard Prydwen, and in the twinkling of an eye they saw them. Twrch Trwyth came to land at Porth Cleis in Dyfed [a harbour in Pembrokeshire, at the estuary of the Alun]. That night Arthur came as far as Mynyw [St. David's]. On the morrow Arthur was told they had gone by, and he overtook him, killing the cattle of Cynwas Cwryfagyl, after slaying what men and beasts were in Deu Gleddyf [Milford Haven] before the coming of Arthur." Cattle were domesticated and used symbolically later than pigs, so that this attack on cattle might be thought of as part of the matriarchal mother's resentment at any change.

"From the time of Arthur's coming, Twrch Trwyth made off thence to Preseleu [Preselly]. Arthur and the hosts of the world [sic] came thither. Arthur sent his men to the hunt. Eli and Trachmyr, and Drudwyn the whelp of Greid son of Eri in his own hand" and a man and two other dogs not previously mentioned; "and Bedwyr with Arthur's dog Cafall in his hand." This is the second mention of Bedwyr since Cei defected. Then Arthur "ranged all the warriors on either side of the Nyfer", the river Nevern. Then came three brothers who, though not previously mentioned "had won great fame at the slaying of Ysgithyrwyn Chief Boar." The boar "stood at bay. And he then slew four of Arthur's champions... And after he had slain those men, again he stood at bay against them there, and slew Gwydre son of Arthur...[and three others]. And then he himself was wounded." This is Twrch Trwyth's first recorded wound.

"And the morrow's morn at point of day some of the men caught up with him. And then he slew...the three servants of Glewlwyd Mighty-grasp

159

[Gafaelfawr, Arthur's gatekeeper], so that God knows he had never a servant left to him in the world, save only Llaesgymyn [Slack-hewer], a man for whom none was the better. And over and above those he slew many a man of the country, and Gwlyddyn the Craftsman [Saer], Arthur's chief builder. And then Arthur caught up with him at Peluniawg [and he then slew three men]. And thence he went to Aber Tywi [Teify]. And there he stood at bay against them, and he then slew Cynlas son of Cynan and Gwilenhin king of France [whose help had been recommended in task thirty-four]. Thereafter he went to Glyn Ystun, and then the man and dogs lost him."

"Arthur summoned to him Gwyn son of Nudd [King of Faerie] and asked him whether he knew aught of Twrch Trwyth. He said he did not. Thereupon all the huntsmen went to hunt the pigs as far as Dyffryn Llychwr [Loughor]." This seems to mean the seven young ones, since the great boar himself has managed to elude the chase. These turned at bay, for "Grugyn Silver-bristle and Llwydawg [46] the Hewer [Gofynnyad] dashed into them and slew the huntsmen so that not a soul of them escaped alive, save one man only. So Arthur and his hosts came to the place where Grugyn and Llwydawg were. And then he let loose upon them all the dogs that had been named to this end. And at the clamour that was then raised, and the barking, Twrch Trwyth came up and defended them. And ever since they had crossed the Irish sea, he had not set eyes on them till now. Then was he beset by men and dogs. With might and with main he went to Mynydd Amanw [the heights between the counties of Brecon and Carmarthen], and then a pigling was slain of his pigs. And then they joined him with life for life, and it was then Twrch Llawin [47] was slain. And then another of his pigs was slain... " Then two other named pigs are slain; this makes five pigs in all. The one originally slain by Arthur has been forgotten by the chronicler, for the account goes on about Twrch Trwyth:

"Not one of his pigs went with him alive from that place, save Grugyn Silver-bristle and Llwydawg the Hewer."

The account goes on to tell how at another place Arthur caught up with him, and then he stood at bay and slew three men "and many a man and dog besides". Then Grugyn Silver-bristle parted from them, was pursued, and finally slain, but not till he had himself killed many men. Then Llwydawg was chased, and slew three men, including the King of Brittany, and two of "Arthur's uncles, his mother's brothers", and then he too was slain. There has here been a successful assault on, and subsequent weakening of, Arthur's maternal line of strength.

That finished Twrch Trwyth's young brood. I have given these extracts from the boar hunt in order to give an impression of what this hunt was like, with the boar in its cunning and constant flight alternating with moments when it was brought to bay, when it appeared as a fearsome warrior slaying minor heroes as well as dogs — the same applying to its two chief young pigs. There is on Arthur's side a similar ambiguity. At one moment great hosts (on one occasion from the whole world) were ranged against this foe, at others it was a matter of single combat in personal fight.

Now all the great boar's brood are slain, and a new and even more deeply archetypal phase begins. The river Severn plays an important part, and then the sea: "Twrch Trwyth went then between Tawy and Ewyas, Arthur summoned Cornwall and Devon to meet him at the mouth of the Severn. And Arthur said to the warriors of this Island: 'Twrch Trwyth has slain many of my men. By the valour of men, not while I am alive shall he go into Cornwall. I will pursue him no further, but I will join with him for life. You, do what you will.' " Arthur's objection was apparently because his chief seat was there, at Celli Wig, said according to the Triads

161

to be "one of the three national thrones of Britain, and one of King Arthur's chief seats of empire, in which he was used to celebrate the high festivals of Christmas, Easter and Whitsuntide" (Guest, 1877 edition, p. 275). The other two seats were "Caerlleon upon Usk, and Penrhyn Rhionydd, in the North". Celli Wig was also, according to the Triads, one of the three archbishoprics of Britain.

In terms of this myth it symbolises the last deep stronghold of Arthur's soul, where absolute defeat or absolute victory are the only alternatives. There is a story that "when Medrawd, Arthur's wicked nephew, usurped the government of the island during his uncle's absence, he went to Gelliwig, and dragged Gwenhwyvar from her throne with contumely, and left neither meat nor drink in the court, 'not even so much as would feed a fly', but consumed and wasted all. The fatal battle of Camlan was fought to avenge this insult" (Guest, 1877 edition, p. 275). This is the kind of fate to his own female soul that Arthur dreaded if the boar Twrch Trwyth were to penetrate into his stronghold or even enter the area in which it was located. It would represent ultimate defeat. For in this matriarchal conflict between uncle and sister's son, we see also the essence of the problem of the mother's animus writ large in terms of relatives, as it is writ large as inner conflict in terms of Arthur and Twrch Trwyth.

This stronghold is that of Arthur's soul, wherein the ultimate battle with the force symbolised by the boar has to take place. And this is emphasised by the fact that, of the five times that Celli Wig is mentioned during the course of the myth, three are intimately connected with the boar, and two, only indirectly so. The indirect mention occurs in connection with the list of people whom Culhwch invokes when claiming Arthur's help to win Olwen; it includes " 'Drem son of Dremidydd [Sight son of Seer], who saw from Celli Wig in Cornwall as far as Pen Blathaon in

162

Prydain' ''. Prydain means Pictland (Scotland), and Pen Blathaon, Caithness — a long cry up the coast of Britain from Cornwall. This indicates direct vision, a soul quality. It also includes "Medyr son of Medredydd (who from Celli Wig would hit a wren on Esgeir Oerfel in Ireland, exactly through its two legs)". This is Aim son of Aimer, shooting to a ridge in Leinster in Ireland, and indicates sureness of intention. The third is when Cei and Bedwyr presented Dillus's beard to Arthur in Celli Wig, and Arthur forthwith picked the quarrel with Cei that resulted in Cei leaving him to fight his battles with the boar alone. The fourth mention was when, after the efforts involved in killing Ysgithyrwyn, Arthur retired to Celli Wig, whence he sent his messenger to spy out whether indeed the 'treasures' were to be found between Twrch Trwyth's ears. The fifth mention is when Twrch Trwyth, in spite of all Arthur's efforts, does penetrate into Cornwall and the most desperate battle takes place. After this Arthur once more retires into the fastness of Celli Wig "to bathe himself and rid him of his weariness". In other words, he retires within himself to cleanse and to revivify himself in the deep waters of his inmost being.

This concept of Celli Wig, a seat of government and therefore symbolising the central recess of Arthur's soul, raises the whole question of the significance of the topographical descriptions insisted on throughout this myth. That a boar hunt should range from the west of Ireland, across the Irish Channel to West Wales, thence to South Wales as far as the river Severn, and now be threatening Cornwall, clearly indicates some psychic concept. It shows that the whole thing is 'magical' — whatever that may mean. But to the mind used to dealing with the internal logic of dreams and of mythology, it is not absurd, and turns out to be an accurate account of psychic processes that would be difficult to describe succinctly in other terms. Here, as often in mythology, the structure of the psyche, or the successive levels found in it, are pictured topographically, as though the earth itself were a map or chart on which progressive psychic happenings can be traced out. The same phenomenon is met with in dreams, in which the layout of the land, and the varying features of it, symbolise different parts of the psychic structure of the dreamer, the whole founded on a universal archetypal pattern but each feature of it, and the relationship between these features, coloured by the dreamer's own characteristic peculiarities.

This myth of *Culhwch and Olwen* is not an individual dream, but is a collective phenomenon portraying the psychic condition of the best (that is to say most integrated) elements in the Celtic race throughout the period in which it was conceived and handed down. (It was doubtless altered during the process.) Though it includes many Irish elements, it is more specifically a British myth originating east of the Irish Channel which at that time divided the Celtic race in two, with a subsidiary division between Wales and Cornwall represented by the river Severn. This latter represents Arthur's last protection before the seat of his soul in Celli Wig is reached.

If this is so, we may now understand why the whole hunt should begin so far away. This is the farthest point away from Celli Wig that it was possible for any Celt to reach within the confines of his racial or linguistic territory, that is to say within his 'world', barring Scotland itself, which is brought in incidentally (Cadw of Prydain, Pen Blathaon), and references to Brittany and Somerset. In psychic terms this symbolises the outermost extension of Arthur's personality, the periphery of the Self-circle of which Celli Wig symbolised the significant centre point of a therefore integrated ego (possibly Wales and Cornwall) in a wider Self; the Self being at once the greatest and the smallest, the whole surrounded by its circumference as well as the central point around which the circumference revolves. In his possession (figuratively conceived) of all that this circumference contained, Arthur stands as the great emperor, lord of the whole Celtic world. But in the centre he was himself a man of inner problems, on the solution of which depended his lordship of, and the well-being of, the whole territory.

This is an image not only of a man's external relations, but of his internal relations too. The circumference is the persona which a man maintains with reference to the world of everyday activity, including the mask he wears for the protection of his personality. This mask may truly reflect his inner personality, or it may not, but be a false one erected only to keep off the buffets of the world. In every individual it has elements of both, but for the purpose of self-knowledge or transformation of the personality it must be pierced and the real truth of inner personality exposed. This is the last thing that any 'normal' person wants. It is the 'hero's' prerogative to undergo the pain and terror that it involves. No hero even, however, would ever submit himself to this if he knew beforehand what it would involve him in. Arthur set out to help Culhwch, but in the end found himself fighting for his own life.

The progress of the battle shows that, starting so bravely against 'so mean a foe', Arthur himself not only loses large numbers of his warriors, but himself gets wounded. The tables are turned on him. When Arthur, already in distress, had sought to parley with Grugyn Silver-bristle, he replied: "Until his [Arthur's] life be taken, these treasures will not be taken. And tomorrow in the morning we will set out hence and go into Arthur's country, and there we will do all the mischief we can." It is now Arthur who fears that he will be destroyed if this force which the boar represents succeeds in penetrating his soul-stronghold. The devil lies still and hidden till he is aroused. Then woe betide the 'hero' who has dared to uncover the passions within himself which will destroy him unless, through weakness accepted and turned to strength, he manages to overcome his own state of unconsciousness and turn external disaster into internal victory.

What we have seen is, in the progress of the fight against the boar, the equally progressive piercing of Arthur's own psychic defence. From "the west of Ireland" the boar is hunted into the north, where one half of the boar-problem (the father one) gets dealt with and Ysgithyrwyn is slain. From there the hunt leads to Twrch Trwyth (the mother half), though not until the 'cauldron' of inner knowledge (a female attribute, also from Ireland) is fetched. Thence over the sea through Wales and so down to the Severn the hunt proceeds, getting ever nearer to Arthur's home, his inmost psychic refuge.

One thing to be noted is highly paradoxical. Ysgithyrwyn is sought out and slain in Ireland, and Twrch Trwyth, though roused from his lair in Ireland, is chased out of it across to Wales and finally disposed of in Cornwall. The paradoxical nature of man's psyche is externally male but internally female. Natural man is as a rule unconscious of his feminine side; he thinks of himself usually as being wholly male. So it would be quite natural to use as symbol for a man a male object, in this case Ysgithyrwyn. His female side, unknown to him, would, equally naturally, be projected across the water to Ireland (as the English and Americans commonly project theirs on to Paris). The seeking of the boar in Ireland would be equivalent to the modern Anglo-Saxon going to France for the satisfaction of certain impulses that he thinks he cannot satisfy at home, and there finding what in these terms would be called his 'manhood', whereas the real problem lies of course within himself. So, in this case, the more superficial problem of the slaying of Ysgithyrwyn is accomplished in Ireland, whereas the more internal problem, aroused there, pursues the 'hero' home and has to be faced in his own land and finally alone in his own soul.

This, in terms of our myth, is the recesses of Celli Wig. But, just as there is a persona by means of which a man protects himself against the external world, so also there is a corresponding inner function by means of which he protects himself from knowledge of his inner self. It is therefore of interest to note that, in this myth, the name Celli Wig is never used alone, but is in every case referred to as Celli Wig in Cornwall. This mode of referring to places is of course not unusual in this story, but in this case it is not used by Arthur who, in his fear that Twrch Trwyth might penetrate to Celli Wig, does not mention this stronghold, but only says 'Cornwall'. This is understandable on the assumption that a man does not speak of his own soul, of which as a rule he does not know very much (and which in any case belongs to those intimate things one does not speak of) but rather concentrates on that which protects it. Here Cornwall is indeed Arthur's last line of defence. Thus, while Celli Wig symbolises the hero's inmost self, the surrounding country of Cornwall acts as a kind of sheath to it, that which protects a man from too close contact with anything that might threaten its complacency or the false safety of its secret hiding-place where evil things might flourish, unknown either to himself or to the world at large.

This is a female attribute, a quite necessary protection for ordinary folk, but one which stands in the way of that ultimate self-realisation which is the 'hero's' task. It can be penetrated only by something with equal feminine power but in male guise, which calls forth the hero's inward masculinity to withstand it, as the ultimate sequel in this myth will show. This explains Arthur's violent reaction against the possibility of Twrch Trwyth's penetrating into Cornwall. Even the 'hero' quails before the ultimate issue, since, having had his defences torn off him one by one till there is nothing left but the prospect either of psychic disintegration or conquest over himself, he is in a position of extreme danger. Only faith in his own integrity can ultimately avert it. This is not faith in ego, but faith in the Self which brings apparent calamity but also brings 'healing in its wings' (here the two ears of the Twrch Trwyth). The calamity must be recognised as being directed not against the personality but for it. Through the destruction of the false values, other values that have been lost by the personality externally through the operation of the incest taboo may be regained internally; the fury of outraged Mother Nature can be overcome, and the destructive weapons seized from her and turned into weapons for the creation of a new inner life.

These weapons are symbolised by the razor, the shears and the comb. The battle for them is a desperate one. The 'victim' or 'hero' of it (for they are ultimately the same — no 'hero' chooses to be one, he has it forced on him) always fights to the last ditch to avoid the pain, not knowing, or only gradually glimpsing, the inner development that will result.

So also Arthur. He and the boar in this respect are 'twins'. He is the image of the Self in its positive aspect, as Twrch Trwyth is part of its negative one. But Self is inoperative unless (unlike Twrch Trwyth, who is inhuman, has not been subject to the incest taboo, and has no fear) it becomes human and suffers from human weaknesses. As man, Arthur is mortally afraid. In the topographical soul-imagery used in this myth, he could not brook the danger of Twrch Trwyth pursuing him into Cornwall so near to home. In other words, he still hoped to put off the reckoning which would result if his inner defence were pierced and so his soul laid bare. He did not in the end succeed in preventing this, but did his utmost to.

The method employed reveals for the first time the fact that the boar is not actually to die, as the Self cannot die. What is of paramount importance is the getting of the razor, shears, and comb from between

Twrch Trwyth's ears, which cannot apparently be done on land, but can only be done in the watery element. "And by his [Arthur's] counsel a body of horsemen was sent, and the dogs of the Island with them, as far as Ewyas, and they beat back thence to the Severn, and they waylaid him there with what tried warriors there were in this Island, and drove him by sheer force into Severn." The hunt is now reaching its climax. Three of the main sub-heroes in this myth are named, and all pursue him into the water. These are, firstly, Mabon son of Modron, now riding "Gwyn Dun-mane the steed of Gweddw" of which horse it was said in task twenty-seven, "as swift as the wave is he, under Mabon to hunt Twrch Trwyth". This 'mother's son' is well acquainted with the sea (the Mother), and so is well suited for this task. The second is Goreu son of Custennin, another 'mother's son' turned into a 'father's son', who reappears again at the very end to cut off Ysbaddaden's head. The third is Menw son of Teirgwaedd whose recent attempt at Twrch Trwyth had been a failure and had only resulted in getting himself injured. These three went with Twrch Trwyth into the Severn "between Llyn Lliwan and Aber Gwy".

Before going on to the remarkable scene that follows, it is useful to explain that Llyn Lliwan (Llinlivan) is thought to be the site of the Severn Bore. Lady Charlotte Guest (1877 edition, p. 294) gives the following quotation from the account of this which Nennius wrote in his eighth century *De Mirabilibus Britanniae*, "Marvels of Britain": "There is another wonder, which is Oper Linn Liuan, the mouth of which river opens into the Severn; and when the tide flows into the Severn, the sea in the like manner flows into the mouth of the above-named river, and is received into a pool at its mouth, as into a gulf, and does not proceed higher up. And there is a beach near the river, and when the tide is in the Severn, that beach is not covered; and when the sea and the Severn recede, then the pool Liuan disgorges all that it had swallowed from the sea, and that beach is covered therewith, and it discharges and pours it out in one wave, in size like to a mountain. And if there should be the whole army of that country there, and they should turn their faces towards the wave, it would draw the army to it by force, their clothes being full of moisture, and their horses would be drawn in like manner. But should the army turn their backs towards the wave, it will not injure them... "

This account not only describes the bore in physical terms, but also gives some indication of the emotional impact on the observer of it; what it symbolised to men of that age in terms of its overpowering attraction to those who let themselves be so attracted, and its ability to annihilate them. The image of a whole army being thus drawn in is as physically absurd as that of all the hosts of Arthur pursuing one wild boar over the length and breadth of three countries. But it is psychologically no wonder: if we concede that the sea, as its world-wide symbolism proclaims, represents the Devouring Mother, it is a fact that she is as dangerous. The armies having to turn their faces from her in order not to be drawn in, are parallelled by Perseus being unable to slay the Gorgon if he faced her directly, or Mithras having to turn his head when slaying the bull. There is a symbolic affinity between the bore, and the cauldron which had to be acquired before all was ready to hunt the boar. Both are mother symbols of the greatest possible power, with this apparent difference: whereas the cauldron was also a Cauldron of Rebirth and of 'treasures', the Severn Bore would appear to be only destructive. However, with the double meaning which all this symbolism has, it is in this same Severn Bore that Twrch Trwyth is in fact made to yield up the razor and shears.

Other observations have here to be made. It was "between Llyn Lliwan and Aber Gwy" that the boar was driven into the Severn. The symbolism of 'between two things' is now becoming familiar to us, primarily in the treasure having to be found 'between the two ears'. It will be appreciated that boar and Severn can now be symbolically one in their outraged primitive female destructiveness, and it will be seen below that both yield up, at one and the same time, the ultimate treasure. Nor does the symbolism of duality end here: two men are drowned in the process, just as two go riding off with the boar, and this too will be seen to have an inner meaning.

The chase now reaches its first climax. After the three auxiliary heroes had pursued the boar into the Severn it is said: "And Arthur fell upon him, and the champions of Britain along with him. Osla Big-knife [48] [in Culhwch's boon-list, he bore a short, broad dagger with a marvellous bridging property] drew near, and Manawydan son of Llyr [hero of the third Branch of the Mabinogi in which a wild white boar appears], and Cacamwri [49] Arthur's servant, and Gwyngelli [50], and closed in on him. And first they laid hold of his feet, and soused him in Severn till it was flooding over him." The boar is now upside down. This is a sign for the reversal of fortune, when inner and outer truths change places, and values change hands. So it is now that the boar yields up his treasures and that, in changing hands, what had been symbols of destruction now can become symbols of power and victory. (All does not happen at once, however, nor, when it does, without payment. The sea and the boar demand their due.) "On the one side Mabon son of Modron spurred his horse and took the razor from him, and on the other Cyledyr the Wild, on another horse, plunged into Severn with him and took from him the shears." The earlier anti-patriarchal outrage of Cyledyr is now avenged on the Otherworld (Mother-world) beast.

"But or ever the comb could be taken he found land with his feet;

171

and from the moment he found land neither dog nor man nor horse could
keep up with him until he went into Cornwall. Whatever mischief was come
by in seeking those treasures from him, worse was come by in seeking to
save the two men from drowning. Cacamwri, as he was dragged forth, two
quernstones [millstones] dragged him into the depths. As Osla Big-knife
was running after the boar, his knife fell out of its sheath and he lost it; and
his sheath thereafter being full of water, as he was dragged forth, it dragged
him back into the depths." Here these two men symbolise respectively the
feminine and masculine principles; both needed in the fray but both, having
performed their functions, no longer needed, and so may 'die'. The manner
of their dying is symbolic of what they were. Cacamwri is dragged down
by two quernstones. One quernstone would have been enough to drown
any man; two signifies female. They grind cereal — 'female' produce.
Osla Big-knife, on the other hand, clearly because of his weapon, represents
the masculine principle, which also succumbs — but not, however, of itself.
Knife and sheath are well-known sex symbols, of which the sheath is female.
It is this — his feminine side — which, despite his valiant masculinity,
betrays him; it gets caught by the Mother (filled with water), and drags him
"back into the depths". The meaning of their perishing is that, in the
ultimate issue, Arthur must be alone.

Twrch Trwyth is now in the area of Celli Wig. The stronghold, symbol of the soul, is feminine. It represents a man's most precious inwardness,
his refuge, and the centre of his being; the matrix (mother-symbol) from
which he issues forth for his work in the world, and to which he can retire
if pressed. On the material plane, it is also the centre of all organised life.
It must be kept inviolate. It is the point of greatest danger if it is threatened (for if the capital city goes, the whole country has gone). But it is the
point of greatest strength if it can be kept intact, as focal point from which

all defence as well as civil expansion proceeds.

This it is that is now threatened by the boar representing, by contrast, all that is most destructive in the feminine psyche disguised as male. This supreme anxiety is expressed powerfully: "Then Arthur went with his hosts until he caught up with him in Cornwall. Whatever mischief was come by before that was play to what was come by then in seeking the comb. But from mischief to mischief the comb was won from him." The denouement is sudden. This may be partly because Arthur has to do battle with a yet stronger force, behind the boar, the Terrible Mother, Black Witch or hag. Her hostile intent is only hidden by the boar as her indomitable agent, and, for ordinary folk, her almost impenetrable disguise.

Robbed of all his power, now transferred to Arthur, the boar goes back into the mother element from which he came: "And then he was forced out of Cornwall and driven straight forward into the sea. From that time forth never a one has known where he went, and Aned and Aethlem with him." They represent another duality, and so together are a symbol of primitive and unresolved femininity and doubt (*Zwiespalt*). This is a poignant scene. Disappearing into the sea is symbolic of very many things: suicide (I know of dreams in which a child, despairing of mother-love, drowns itself in her element, the sea), baptism, and consequent rebirth. The parable of the Gadarene swine, dealing with a man with an unclean spirit whom no man could bind ("no, not with chains"): when he saw the Lord, he cried out "What have I to do with thee...thou Son of the most high God? I adjure thee by God, that thou torment me not....Now there was nigh unto the mountains a great herd of swine feeding. And all the devils besought him, saying, Send us into the swine, that we may enter into them. And forthwith Jesus gave them leave. And the unclean spirits went out, and entered into the swine: and the herd ran violently down a steep place into the sea...and were choked in the sea." (Mark V: 1-16) For the man this was salvation. For the pigs — suicide or baptism, or both? The boar is not killed. Being an aspect of the Self, he cannot be because he represents a perennial problem, arising anew in every man, and indestructible.

"And Arthur went thence to Celli Wig in Cornwall, to bathe himself and rid him of his weariness." He has now thus 'come home', and enters his soul unscathed. He also 'bathes', which the boar has just done. The two thus have a close affinity, which we should respect, being opposite aspects of the same symbol, the Self.

One word more remains to be said about the symbolism of the 'razor and shears' on the one hand, which were taken from the boar in Severn, and on the other hand the 'comb', which was taken from the boar at the last moment when Arthur's ultimate stronghold was threatened, that is to say in his utmost extremity. Razor and shears are both cutting instruments, and therefore phallic. Both, particularly the shears, symbolise the *vagina dentata*. But this also is phallic, serving the destructive feminine principle in male guise. The comb, on the contrary, symbolises that feminine wile that can coax a man's hair into being cut. It represents a feminine function of a very subtle kind — seeming so harmless but being in fact as dangerous as the razor and shears, though so disguised as to appear negligible or even non-existent as a hostile force.

Such disguised forces are even more formidable than those which can be recognised more easily. They are like the spider's web that seems so beautiful, that the last thing that could be thought of it was that it was the lair of a Devouring Mother. I therefore suggest that, as there are two main stages in every conflict with the parental images, in this bi-parental problem it was once more the father-aspect symbolised by the razor and shears that was first depotentiated and that it was the mother-aspect, symbolised by the comb, which threatened to elude defeat ('detection') entirely, and which needed the utmost ardour to deal with it.

CHAPTER 13

THE TASKS FULFILLED:

THE SLAYING OF THE HAG

Once her disguise, consisting of the boar and its maleness, has gone, the Witch can no longer conceal herself. Arthur has been 'returned' by the boar's ravages to his inner sanctuary, and the boar himself has disappeared into the sea. Through the channels of free association which are the logic of the psyche, the chronicler proceeds: "Said Arthur, 'Is there any of the marvels still unobtained? ' Said one of the men, 'There is: the blood of the Black Witch, daughter of the White Witch, from the head of the Valley of Grief in the uplands of Hell.' "

This refers back to task eighteen, where Ysbaddaden said: " 'I must needs dress my beard for me to be shaved. It will never settle unless the blood of the Black Witch be obtained...' " — and then proceeded to describe her in the same words as are now repeated.

The first task we have to undertake is to examine just what is meant by "the Black Witch, daughter of the White Witch". We are inevitably reminded of the problem of the 'two mothers' with which the myth opened and which the whole story is about. We have now come full circle back to it, but here the order of the two women is reversed. Black as a colour associated with women means basic pregnancy. Black can be 'gone into', where white cannot. White represents in this context the incest taboo, and therefore the initiating stepmother, while black symbolises the Earth Mother (Demeter, as represented by the black sow). She is the great life-giver and the great destroyer, unless this destructive aspect of her can itself be destroyed in order to be made to yield up its inner treasure, its 'blood'.

We have said that we have now come full circle, with the order of things reversed. In the beginning the sow, mother of Culhwch, who can be thought of as the Black Witch, came first. She was the 'mother' out of whom came, or who superseded her, her contrary-minded opposite, the stepmother, who can be thought of as the White Witch. The latter can therefore be thought of as her 'psychic daughter', just as Persephone was called the daughter of Demeter — although the two are known to have represented two aspects of the same Great Mother principle. Demeter is queen of living, pulsating, passionate matter unconscious of itself. Persephone is Queen of the Dead, that is to say of the spiritual world of inner values, introvert as opposed to her extravert mother, and therefore acts as the initiator. It will be remembered that she was raped by Pluto, just as in our myth the stepmother was raped by Culhwch's father, when he incontinently slew the stepmother's former husband and "carried her away by force". She is the 'patrilineal mother' and the initiator who sends Culhwch forth on his hero's journey to find the anima. She is here symbolised as the White Witch, the White Goddess or moon-mother, in the same way as Persephone is also a moon-mother, the Moon representing the transforming aspect of the feminine principle. The Moon Goddess shines in the darkness and represents the principle of inner consciousness.

She begins in our story as the stepmother, and is finally constellated most fully in Olwen, towards whom, from the beginning, the stepmother points the way. Her opposite principle is the Black Sun, an expression used in alchemy and meaning the life-warming principle (here female, black) hidden behind its own darkness and so unconscious of itself. Neither of these principles can realise itself without the action of the masculine principle which the feminine principle itself conceives, as Culhwch's mother conceives him and brings him forth without nevertheless knowing what she has brought him forth to do. This is the Black Sun's function, to give birth unconsciously. The function of the Moon Goddess, or the White Goddess, is to *know* what the son she has brought forth must do, which is, with her help, to find out and to reveal to the Earth Mother or Black-Sun quality in himself what her own inner nature is and to absorb it into himself. This inner nature of the Earth Mother is "the blood of the Black Witch", the counterpart to the moon-maiden Olwen. Without this necessary earth-counterpart to the purity of the moon-maiden she cannot safely be won, since without it she would represent madness — moon-struckness, lunacy. With it the hero combines both female elements in a final synthesis becoming himself thereby all-wise, and, since now he has the wholeness of femininity within him, symbolically hermaphroditic. He has attained the status of the Self.

The blood of the Black Witch is 'dragon's blood', she being the ultimate 'dragon' which must be slain in order to obtain and drink the blood which she has been withholding because of her primitive possessiveness. What then is slain is the refusal of nature to yield up its treasure, that is to say its own mother-boundness clinging to the past. While undelivered, the blood is like a child unborn, awaiting its deliverer. It represents the basic reservoir of all instinctive life as yet unconscious of itself. When the citadel which contains it (the mother's body) is stormed and the 'blood' is released, instinct then becomes conscious and is turned into spiritual life. In this respect the blood of the Black Witch and Olwen are one, for Olwen the anima is the 'blood of the black witch' transformed and made assimilable to consciousness. 'Blood' means the inner truth that is behind both day-time sun and the Black Sun combined. It represents, as in the highest religious symbolism, the ultimate meaning of life.

This can, however, only be attained to by reversing, in the psyche, the forward movement of normal extravert life. As the growing boy normally moves forward out of the maternal aura into the man's world to make his way in it, eschewing for a time all women, this is at first a healthy freeing of himself from the matrix of unconscious action and dependency. But, just as in extravert life he then turns back to find a female mate, or, if he does not, proves himself to be 'unnatural', so also a healthy psychic life demands an inward 'turning back' to re-contact one's origins and source of dynamic life, the female element within. The forward process extern-ally must, if any ultimate truth is to be found (and this, like all hero myths, is about ultimates), have as its counterbalance an inward movement in the opposite direction. This is what is called in psychology a 'positive regres-sion', a movement backwards to the mother-image inwardly, to wrest from it the treasure which it withholds. It is this backward movement in the psyche that causes the relative positions of 'mother' and 'daughter' in our myth to be reversed, and the Black Witch who in the beginning was psychically 'mother' to the White Witch (the stepmother) now becomes her 'daughter'. "The Black Witch daughter to the White Witch" symbolises this backward movement of regeneration and reclamation, in new form, of that which had been lost. It is a symbol of Redemption of deep earth-roots that had to be discarded externally, in which sphere they would rep-resent psychic boundnesses and paralysing bad-mother influences of every kind, but which must be recaptured inwardly if full life and the creation of soul-substance are to be had.

One further word about the otherwise obscure phrases used in enunciating task eighteen: " 'I must needs dress my beard for me to be shaved. It will never settle unless the blood of the Black Witch be obtained...from the head of the Valley of Grief in the uplands of Hell [51].' " Without knowing much about Welsh mythology and not knowing how much is known about its Underworld in terms of written records, the implications psychologically are of great interest. We have by now some inkling of why Ysbaddaden's beard had to be shaved. This is a castration symbol, with both positive and negative meaning. Negatively it means an unwilling sacrifice — it is in the end actually a symbol for Culhwch's triumph and Ysbaddaden's death. But positively, if undertaken willingly, it means the voluntary sacrifice of unrestrained natural libido for the sake of acquiring inner control and ultimate spiritual union (the *hieros gamos*) with the anima, through the internalised process of reversal that we have described. This probably explains the otherwise obscure allusion to the need of the Black Witch's blood to "settle it". The implication is that the beard would otherwise be too unruly even to cut. The Black Witch's blood is here used as if immersion of the beard in it would represent a kind of blood-baptism, giving to it an order and pliability contrasting strongly to the phrase used of it in task twenty-one, "so exceedingly stiff". 'Stiff' means 'uncompromising', resistant to any change.

We seem here to sense the subtlety of Ysbaddaden's mentality, knowing what should be done but being unable to submit, precisely because of the 'grief' that this would entail. "Grief in the uplands of Hell" is a truly wonderful phrase, not a meaningless figure of speech. Hell, Hades, the Underworld in all mythologies represents the mother-world of the

Unconscious. Even in Christian apocryphal writings (see M.R. James), Hell is represented as a woman sending out her husband, Satan, to bring in men's souls for her to devour in her insatiable jaws, often depicted in mediaeval paintings as the jaws of some chimerical monster. Hell is the Devouring Mother, and her emissary Satan (or what corresponds to him, for this is universal symbolism, not only Christian) is in our myth symbolised by the boar. The boar is everywhere either an unclean animal or a terrible menace, for this reason. It will devour anything, dead or alive, in actual fact. Its maleness is like the 'maleness' of Satan, which should not deceive us. He is well known to be the arch-deceiver, and among his deceptive guises is his apparent masculinity. But he is, like the boar throughout all mythology, from Ireland to Greece, to Egypt, to South-east Asia and out into the Pacific, basically the emissary of the Devouring Mother with her devouring teeth. In line with the same symbolism that turned Twrch Trwyth upside down when 'soused in Severn', the boar is a woman turned head to tail, with the head and mouth symbolising (as in the mediaeval paintings) the woman's *vagina dentata*, her (with action reversed, as in all this symbolism) devouring genitalia, always seeking to destroy that which she has brought forth.

This devouring crevice is, in psychic imagery, what is meant by the "Valley of Grief" (the 'vale of tears' in modern linguistic figurativeness, so robbed of power by forgetfulness of its original meaning). But the Valley of Grief is not a valley in the ordinary sense as being somewhere low or deep down. It lies elevated "in the uplands of Hell", that is to say, in terms of this mythology, on the boar's head, a point emphasised in the text itself when it speaks not simply of the valley but of the 'head' of the valley. "Between the two ears of Twrch Trywth" is an equivalent image to that of the valley on the hill.

The whole imagery is that of a colossal 'delivery' or 'deliverance' of psychic elements, both male and female (see Appendices), which, in possession of the devouring 'male mother' representing the totality of the unconscious, are a deadly menace, but when 'delivered' — as a child may be delivered in an almost impossibly difficult and dangerous birth scene — by the male hero and his male confederates, become their own spiritual powers.

This represents the 'birth out of the father', which *is* the 'second birth'. It is the process of psychological rebirth, which always basically comes out of a 'man', since it is the complementary opposite of physical birth out of a woman. It also takes place, as we have seen, in terms of body-image, at the opposite end of the body, the head instead of the genitalia, this symbolising consciousness as opposed to the unconsciousness of being born physically. Such symbolism goes through all mythology. A supreme example is the birth of Athene from Zeus's head. In more commonplace folklore the Germanic hare that lays the Easter eggs is male, and is commonly pictured as wearing trousers and carrying the eggs in a basket, symbolic of his anima — that part of the male which gives birth to the spirit child. Psychologically also this is the case. The anima of a man gives birth (or withholds it). In the case of a woman, she needs a positive animus to fertilise and make conscious her latent spiritual womanhood, so often held in check by the withholding animus.

All these things go by opposites. In our myth, while the masculinity of the boar masks and serves the purposes of the Great Mother, it will be noticed that Arthur has as his steed not a male horse, but his mare Llamrei, symbolising his female dynamic side. For his voyages to Ireland, he used his ship Prydwen, also a female symbol. The name Prydwen is also used by other chroniclers as that of his shield, also a female (protective womb) symbol. So male and female elements combine, but it is the male element in the fighting that is uppermost, with the female latent behind.

The headlong chase is now over, that is to say the urgent masculine aspect of the affair which, despite the protestations of some of Arthur's attendants that it was not worthy of so great a man, nevertheless could wear a semblance of nobility. Most hero stories end with this, the appearance of what may popularly be thought of as a fair fight against manly odds well won. The popular version of George and the dragon is of this type. He also had to first fight to win a maiden. Usually depicted poised elegantly on a horse, he is immaculately clad, while under him cowers the submissive form of the dragon which he has overcome. This is of course a travesty. The true psychic hero at his last gasp, sweats with blood and toil, with humiliation and disgust, both at himself and at the enemy he has to slay. In the last instance this is his own feminine meanness, possessiveness, half-conscious trickery, conceit, false courage and a whole host of horrors lurking hidden in the recesses of his wretchedly unformed soul. These are the bases of witchcraft that spread themselves like a net under his feet, bedevil his relationships, and keep him cut off from himself. These all are symbolised by the dragon or the Black Witch.

The basic symbolism of the dragon fight as a counter-*vagina dentata* contest is conventionally depicted by the hero's spear aimed into the dragon's mouth and is clear enough. One hidden meaning is that it shall pierce down the throat and through into the heart, so that the victim's heart's blood may flow. It may be required that it be drunk by the hero in a last orgy of mess and filth, by means of which he contacts the depths of his own nature and, knowing and absorbing what he is, then rises out of it with clear eyes and with his full strength, now master of his fate. This is the true nobility of the hero: he knows himself, and does not shrink from this dread battle of mutual meanness and cruelty. Worst thing of all, the battle is with a woman — and old and hag-like at that. On this deep level the hero that fights a hag is nearer the truth than he to whom the truth is glossed over by calling it a dragon, thus giving the fight a certain air of external nobility. The first-class hero's fight is *not* noble, from any conventional point of view. But it is so, unseen to any external eye, internally. The hero is the one who will risk all, including what is thought of him, and yet triumphs, precisely because he has been true to himself.

Such a hero is Arthur. "Arthur set out for the North and came to where the hag's cave was." As will be recalled, the North is the unconscious, haphazard area. The cave, as mother symbol and last refuge of the pursued, or innermost reserve of psychic contents, is the very centre of the personality. In this respect it corresponds to Celli Wig. It may also, if we are to follow the free association of the chronicler, correspond on another level with the sea-mother, into which Twrch Trwyth has just plunged. Arthur can be thought of, therefore, as plunging after him and reaching, symbolically and by way of opposites, the cave where the hag lives who has caused all this dire mischief. We can also recall the imagery of Mabon's sea-prison. Sea, stronghold, and cave are symbols for one thing, the Great Mother: the first her earliest primaeval form, the second her cultural one, the third her individual one in the recesses of man's soul. If the cave itself is her in her protective aspect, the hag within it is the last remnant of her destructive side, so dreadfully appealing to pity that it would seem terrible to murder her. But in these matters of the soul murder has to be done. She is an archetypal figure, who cannot change. Either the hero murders her, or she murders the hero. Pity cannot be allowed. Other myths demonstrate this, as that of Cupid and Psyche in Apuleius's *The Golden Ass.* Psyche, on her journey into the underworld to obtain from Persephone the box of beauty ointment which finally releases and immortalises her, is forbidden to succour any unfortunates who come her way. She herself had just been contemplating suicide, and needed every ounce of strength for her own purposes. She must not yield to the temptation of pity, for pity in the last instance is self-pity — no attribute of a hero. The hero is one who also knows how to look after himself, and that it is only in so far as he can do so that he can be of real use to anyone else.

The next piece of our text, preparatory to the last fearful struggle, is full of subtleties by way of the union of complementary opposites. These are seen in the pairs of helpers that Arthur now has. It needs close observation of the text, and memory of what has gone before, to realise how closely woven the apparently haphazard introduction of the various characters really is. "It was the counsel of Gwyn son of Nudd and Gwythyr son of Greidawl that Cacamwri and Hygwydd [52] his brother be sent to fight with the hag." It will be remembered that the first two are respectively King of Faerie and Arthur's father-in-law, representing the opposites of fancy and fact, or of unconscious and conscious processes. The interesting thing here is the reconciliation of opposites, as in their May Calends fights. Neither is ultimately wrong, but both are necessary. Of several previous mentions of "Arthur's two servants", Cacamwri has been one while the second has varied. In the final bout with Twrch Trwyth, he represented a female aspect, and lost his life. So as a narrative-teller the chronicler has slipped up and resurrected him.

Cacamwri and Hygwydd now enter the cave: "And as they came inside the cave the hag grabbed at them, and caught Hygwydd by the hair of his head and flung him to the floor beneath her. And Cacamwri seized her by the hair of her head, and dragged her to the ground off Hygwydd, but she then turned on Cacamwri and dressed them both down and disarmed them, and drove them out squealing and squalling." This is hardly a

184

dignified kind of fight-to-the-death for a mighty hero or his representatives
to be engaged in. Nevertheless it is so; this is what psychic heroes are made
of. Analysis of the unconscious is rarely dignified in the conventional sense,
yet it is a vital process of great consequence. Note once more the importance of the hair, so far mentioned only in connection with men. This is
a fight in which no quarter is given: what she does, they do. That is part of
the retribution — her sins now find her out. She has 'castrated' men symbolically by demanding that they have their hair cut off if they are to enter
into her mysteries. Now she suffers the like, but wins this first bout of the
battle. But what of Arthur's two servants, whom she drove out "squealing
and squalling"? Are they thus pigs too? It is sure that Arthur himself
may be one in the shadow aspect of his nature...

"And Arthur was angered to see his two servants well nigh slain, and
he sought to seize the cave. And then Gwyn and Gwythyr told him, 'It is
neither seemly nor pleasant for us to see thee scuffling with a hag. Send
Long Amren and Long Eiddil [53] into the cave.' " It is the counsellors of
course who say this, not the servants who do his bidding and take the
knocks. They hold aloof and do not wish their master to be mixed up in
such dirty work, still less themselves. One could understand Arthur's
father-in-law taking up this attitude, but that Gwyn son of Nudd, the Faerie
King of the Underworld should also, is surprising. It evidently means that
no one but the hero himself can free himself, that he will get no praise, and
will be lucky if he is not blamed. We moderns may well think of all the
obloquy cast in its early days on psychology for dirtying its hands with such
things as sex, sex fantasies, and inner knowledge generally. They are still
considered by many as rather nasty, or at least unhealthy preoccupations.
We are actually dealing with matters of real spiritual consequence, for out
of the depths arise the heights; the deeper and more slimy the pit, the

185

greater the value that can be obtained from it. Out of the cords of Adam salvation comes. Arthur's 'cords' also are being stirred up. For the first time he is angry — in truth angry at himself for his own shrinking from the task.

Note that the servants do not refuse to do Arthur's bidding. They then rank higher than the counsellors in hero-dom. Arthur then consents to send them into the cave, as even Arthur does not yet know that he alone must do the deed: "And they went. But if ill was the plight of the first two, the plight of those two was worse, so that God knows no one of the whole four could have stirred from the place, but for the way they were all four loaded on Llamrei, Arthur's mare." This is another quaternity. Long Amren and Long Eiddil appear from their common appellation of 'long' both to be phallic. While Long Amren and Long Eiddil together represent the male element in the attack, Cacamwri and Hygwydd may represent the female element. What is really remarkable is their being all four rescued by being loaded on the back of Llamrei. This confirms our evaluation of her as representing a positive feminine side of Arthur's character.

In this penultimate scene before Arthur's final onslaught alone, we have thus not only a quaternity composed of his four servants, who now are 'absorbed' into himself by way of his mare Llamrei, but a quintessence, Arthur himself being the fifth element. Arthur himself is also dual, being composed of ego, his male person, and Llamrei, the female element on which he relies — the dynamic feminine function on which all else depends. Note that he does not ever ride her. She acts as a soul-mate rather than a steed. She rescues and supports his four 'functions' (the four servants), while he, thus freed, now goes in single-handed to fight the hag to the death. There are thus here six elements in all in this personality of Arthur's: the four servants, probably coupled together as complementary opposite

186

masculine and feminine functions; as 'superior' aspect of the quintessence is Arthur's ego; and as 'inferior' (supporting) aspect is the mare Llamrei — a kind of anima in animal form. The two are 'married', since she is his mare and he is her master.

"And then Arthur seized the entrance to the cave, and from the entrance he took aim at the hag with Carnwennan [54] his knife, and struck her across the middle until she was as two tubs. And Cadw of Prydain took the witch's blood and kept it with him."

The terror in Arthur's heart at making this attack may be gathered from the fact that even now he does not apparently touch her directly — he is perhaps too afraid; he takes aim at her from the entrance. The knife attack has obvious phallic significance, but the emphasis is on the 'entrance to the cave'. Our text gives 'seize the cave', but Lady Charlotte Guest has: "Arthur rushed to the door of the cave, and at the door he struck at the witch." With the extreme exactness of the archetypal symbolism used by the chronicler, this may be significant. Lady Charlotte's version would simply reduplicate the image of the phallic entry. In the text here being used, however, the translation is so much more carefully accurate that, although at first sight it might be less dramatic, closer examination brings to light far greater subtlety and depth of archetypal meaning. The two levels of interpretation are now so clearly defined as to demand desperate treatment. They also demonstrate the difference between Freudian and Jungian types of thinking, though I should like to emphasize that both are valid, and that the two complement one another, and that in a thorough psychological analysis both should be used.

To take first the Freudian level, the cave would represent the womb or uterus, and the entrance the vagina. Seizing the cave would be equivalent to depotentiating the *vagina dentata* so as to make entry without annihilation possible. This interpretation amplifies the following one on a more personal and body-image level.

The other, Jungian interpretation concerns what is called the *mandala*, a Sanskrit word indicating a circle, or square within a circle, or circle within a square (or sometimes triangle or diamond); this is an object of contemplation and represents by basic imagery the innermost structure of the soul. The image can be a circular mound or mountain with a square inner chamber, a moated castle, the flat world with four quarters surrounded by a river, a Garden of Eden with four internal rivers, or any one of innumerable possible forms on this kind of model. But always basically it is the same. The circle is a magic one to keep out what is not desired and keep in what is, and for this purpose there are gateways or doors intended to exclude or to draw in. The ultimate purpose is to concentrate attention on central things. In body-image this is the womb — the creative producing centre. This fits in with the Freudian concept of libido being ultimately sexual. In the spiritual life of a man it is his soul, his female element. Both of these are often represented by a cave, with an entrance for going in or out.

In this myth, we have now reached the central point, and for this reason the myth is soon to end. Arthur is now faced with his innermost problem, which is the ultimate mother-problem; or, as Jung would put it, confrontation with the unconscious in its most basic form. In the smaller crystal focalising the Self at the supporting end of the diamond body (see diagram page 202), we see this 'cave' or soul-cavity, inhabited by the hag (Black Witch): nature violently hostile to change or any kind of conditioning or settled order.

An important inverse conception is as follows: at the moment when 'Arthur' is finally forging his diamond body, as a spiritual character in our myth, he is shown physically as penetrating the cave of the hag by aiming his knife at her. Visually, this can be viewed as the diamond entering or establishing itself or its power in the circle or sphere. In mandala terms and representation, this is precisely bringing order into chaos (circling the square or diamond or triangle). The knife is the cutting edge of the diamond body.

Doing an old woman to death is hardly an edifying tale. The chronicler, however, has been at such pains all through this tale, particularly at its beginning and at its end, to deal in dualities. He has here given us the quaternity of the four servants, neatly divided into two pairs, with Arthur and his mare as supraordinate figures. He was certainly aware of archetypal structure in a way that modern man has forgotten, and which he is only now rediscovering. (The circle is not specifically mentioned.)

"Arthur struck her across the middle until she was as two tubs"? One has to be very simple, as well as a bit erudite, if possible, if one is to understand the archetypes. By simple is meant childlike (not childish). This is a supreme example of hidden symbolic meaning on two opposed levels, which demonstrates psychological thinking. It shows the basic duality: psychic structure combined with down-to-earth body imagery.

On the level of body image, the hag's body viewed as an actual body, 'two tubs' can only mean either of two things. This is, I believe, an archetypal image which the translators have misunderstood by saying 'across'. Lady Charlotte Guest has the more non-committal 'clove her in twain'. The archetypal imagery is in terms of complementary opposites (same but opposite) which the word 'across' does not fit in with. The split is longitudinal, from top to bottom, dividing right from left. On the level of body image, the 'two tubs' are either the buttocks or the breasts. These two body images are more closely connected psychically than might be suspected by those not familiar with the psychological phenomenon of displacement. Of the two, the image of the cleft might make the buttocks seem

189

more apt, and at the same time call up the image of the closely placed gen-italia. We may be sure the chronicler would not shy at this. We are here, however, down to the rock-bottom of basic facts in the consciousness of an individual, and for the very small child consciousness is centred on the mother's breasts.

That we are apt to forget such simple things, so that they have to be veiled in symbols, is part of the natural process of growing up, when we discard childish things. We have, as years advance, to 'grow down again' in order to recapture psychically what we have lost physically, to regain sym-bolically what was once bodily fact. The two-ness of the breasts is both fact and symbol. A woman has two breasts; she also has two attitudes. Nor is this necessarily a neurotic symptom. It may become neurotic only if the basic, necessary, and creative split in all human nature is not known to her, either as head knowledge or in 'natural' feeling. This is not natural from 'nature's' point of view, but it is natural and basic from the human point of view because of the operation of the incest taboo. The terms 'good breast' and 'bad breast' are now commonplaces of Kleinian psychology (derived from Freudian and also incorporated in Britain into Jungian psychology). They represent a way of expressing the basic duality of human nature. They do not refer to right or left breast specifically as being good or bad. 'Breast' in this sense means 'feeding motherhood'.

This is the concept of the 'two mothers' with which this myth began. It was then an external one, symbolised by the natural mother and the initiating stepmother. These had first to be separated, in order to be later joined (for Culhwch) by the single uniting figure of the sister-anima Olwen. That was the young man's ego-problem. Now with Arthur, the ancient symbol of the Self, the splitting process repeats itself, but is internalised. If Culhwch's mother was a sow, so also is the hag. At any rate she is the

Black Witch who lies behind the boar, the female counterpart that sent him forth. The first of Arthur's two pairs of servants were routed 'squealing and squalling' as though they were pigs. Now Arthur himself attacks her with his knife — a counterpart of Ysgithyrwyn's tusk. The 'boar' in the form of Arthur (the latter having vanquished him), instead of being her agent, is now taking his revenge on her.

The Kleinian concept of the 'two breasts' — equivalent to the 'two mothers' — is that the 'good mother' satisfies her child, both physically and with other forms of motherly love. The 'bad mother' does not satisfy in either of these ways. But the meaning of the Arthurian figure is not so simple as this. For in this myth the original mother image actually becomes fourfold. In the beginning she is the bountiful, 'good' earth-mother (the fertile sow). But her jealousy of the father turns her into the 'bad mother' refusing to be transformed or civilised, and dying. All stepmothers begin by being 'bad' simply because they are not the natural mother. But this stepmother knows her initiating role (this is a very advanced state of fairy-tale) and therefore becomes the culturally and spiritually 'good mother'. In this way good and bad change places. Now at the very end of the tale, the process is completed by being internalised: the 'mothers' are no longer externalised. Just as the psyche of any child has the images of the external world introjected into it, and finally as grown adult has to face them internally and divide the 'good' mother from the 'bad' inside himself, so, this being a universal problem, Arthur is shown tackling it inside his cave. It is an easy task for nobody. It involves the birth pangs of psychic separation so that the individual anima can emerge, belonging to no parents, but the 'hero's' own.

Another form of the separation is of the 'blood' from the 'body'. This means the attainment of inner truth. The body is killed so that the

191

blood may be drunk. There can be few more basically animal images than this. Yet it is of the highest spiritual significance, as more than one world-wide religion, and particularly the highest of them, shows. This rite goes back to most primitive times. The killing of the dragon (the mother) to drink its heart's blood is one instance of it in many mythologies. The best example, however, combining the splitting of the body and the effect of the blood, is one of the very earliest. It is the Babylonian myth of Tiamat, who was at once the primaeval chaotic sea and the leviathan (or behemoth) that inhabited it. She gave birth without a husband to all the gods before ever there were any men or land. Then, like all primitive earth-mothers, she started devouring her children till the survivors took counsel among them-selves. The elder ones having failed to deal with her, they sent Marduk, who finally cleft her in twain. He took one half of her body and made of it the sea, confined within its borders; and he turned the other half into the clouds, locked with a lock so that they would not flood the earth, but so that the rain from them could be used only for man's benefit, and at his will. Between these two the land arose. From the blood which spurted out when he pierced her with his sword through the mouth (a good sex symbol) and right down to the heart, there grew the beasts and cattle and, finally, men.

In our myth, the boar Twrch Trwyth finally disappears into, or joins itself with, its own element, the sea. That is to say, in terms of this imagery, he rejoined the sow (for sow, hag, sea all symbolise the mother when she becomes chaos again). The Babylonian myth stresses the waters above and below the land, and reminds us of all the other divisions into two: the light from darkness, land from sea, male from female, and so on. Finally, it sig-nifies the two basic divisions of the human psyche caused by the incest taboo.

There is also a third level of meaning. It is like an act of parturition, out of which, as the following scene shows, the hero is born. The splitting of Ysgithyrwyn's head was a birth scene producing the tusk; the treasure was taken from between Twrch Trwyth's two ears; now Arthur, in his ultimate onslaught on the hag, acts as midwife for the production of the hag's blood. This then inebriates Culhwch and his companions, as it were (cf. the blood of Christ at Communion — a positive victim), with its heady wine and leads to the climax.

Note: Further psychological discussion of the overcoming of forces of evil is given in Appendix I.

CHAPTER 14

THE FINAL SCENE:

CULHWCH WINS OLWEN

"And then Culhwch set forth, and Goreu son of Custennin with him, and every one that wished ill to Ysbaddaden Chief Giant, and those marvels with them to his court. And Cadw of Prydain came to shave his beard, flesh and skin to the bone, and his two ears outright. And Culhwch said, 'Hast had thy shave, man? ' 'I have,' said he. 'And is thy daughter mine now? ' 'Thine,' said he. 'And thou needst not thank me for that, but thank Arthur who has secured her for thee. Of my own free will thou shouldst never have had her. And it is high time to take away my life.' And then Goreu son of Custennin caught him by the hair of his head and dragged him behind him to the mound, and cut off his head, and set it in the bailey-stake. And he took possession of his fort and his dominions.

"And that night Culhwch slept with Olwen, and she was his only wife so long as he lived. And the hosts of Arthur dispersed, every one to his country.

"And in this wise did Culhwch win Olwen daughter of Ysbaddaden Chief Giant." So ends the tale.

Thus Culhwch does nothing of himself, but he reaps the benefit of Arthur's suffering and psychic heroism. The hag's blood is not mentioned again because this, being a female thing, signifies an inward attribute. On the crass physical level, it has direct reference to menstrual blood or to the bloodiness accompanying birth. The drinking of it (it has of course been 'drunk', though in a peculiar way that will be referred to shortly) is symbolic and represents the counterpart of what Arthur has done in facing up to the 'hag within himself', that is to say 'swallowing' the truth which we all fight to repress and to forget about: that we were in fact all born, in the words of one of the Church Fathers, "between the anus and the urethra", or, in more vulgar language, "between shit and piss". The 'son of a sow', Culhwch, should not find too great a difficulty in admitting this, not so much difficulty as the rest of us. It means that, in terms of 'culture', we come from the lowest of the low. The mystical, and practical, result of this is that, through this admission, we become the highest of the high. "He was made man for us, and for our salvation." This myth is about no less depths and heights than this. *He* was also born out of a virgin. It is the virgin goddesses of classical antiquity, like Artemis, who sent out the boar against their enemies. Culhwch's natural mother was 'virginal' towards marriage and towards culture and the spiritual life. Culhwch himself became 'virginal' in the opposite direction by submitting himself to culture through the symbolic castration he sought and obtained at the hands of Arthur. Culture is here equivalent to spirituality in the sense that it implies the curbing of primary externally expressed natural desire in order to produce an inner experience.

The curbing of desire brings us back to that odd phrase of Ysbaddaden Pencawr's which we have already noticed: "I must needs dress my beard for me to be shaved. It will never settle unless the blood of the Black Witch be obtained, daughter of the White Witch, from the head of the Valley of Grief in the uplands of Hell." We have already discussed its female genital significance: Twrch Trwyth's head representing the 'male uterus', and Dillus the Bearded's beard symbolising the female pubic hair. In this complex hermaphroditic symbolism where male represents female, the head symbolises the genitals, and so on (a symbolism which is absolutely real in dream life and in mythology). The male beard throughout this myth symbolises that very hidden and destructive power in a man that comes from his negative feminine side. It is a phallic symbol under female guise, and signifies extremes of jealousy, bitterness, and implacable hostility. Such are the attributes of a woman's negative animus, all operating within the manly breast in the form of an ice-cold, withdrawn, negatively virginal and possessively destructive anima-image, which destroys him from the inside if he cannot express it by destroying others. These may seem rather strong words; why else, however, should Cadw of Prydain come with such fury as "to shave his beard, flesh and skin to the bone"? We have not heard of 'flesh and skin' before. These matters have been hidden from us until this crucial moment. Moreover, the symbolic bodily location of this 'flesh and skin' is clearly stated when the text goes on to say 'and his two ears outright'. This phrase is familiar to us as applying to Twrch Trwyth, lurking behind the 'manly' mask of Ysbaddaden Pencawr; the hag in turn lurks behind the mask of Twrch Trwyth. There is here a double layer of unmasking. The ultimate danger is the hag, and it is *her* pubic hair, vaginal flesh, and external genitalia that are here being robbed of their destructive power, in manner parallel to that of Arthur slaying the hag.

All this fits in with the character of Ysbaddaden: jealous, destructive, and zealously possessive of his daughter Olwen, whom he has so far kept imprisoned in his stronghold against deliverance by any suitor, as a mother refusing to give birth to the child within her womb. Now comes the birth scene. The ramparts of the stronghold have been destroyed, the gates torn off, the withholding portals robbed of their power to close in again. Culhwch the hero and deliverer shouts in triumph, disregarding the giant's sufferings: "Hast had thy shave, man? " The giant says, "I have." "And is thy daughter mine now? " She is. The giant is delivered of Olwen, as Zeus was delivered of Athene. The sister-anima is born. Conceived by the father but then withheld by him, this father's daughter, delivered on behalf of the mother's son, her opposite, now comes to him as bride. The son takes over from the father, and he and the daughter are now one.

But Ysbaddaden is not yet dead. This complex old man, who has known all along he had to die, is not unconscious (as the witch was) in his yielding. The witch can't know. She never does. She is unconsciousness, the force of nature, and unrelieved by thought, dies unknowing. Thought is a masculine attribute which women can have as well as men (witness the stepmother), once they admit the man as mate and not only as son. Being a witch, she is an absolute archetype, more so than her forerunner the nature woman, Culhwch's mother. She, though she had to die, accepted death, knowing nevertheless that there was some other kind of womanhood — the stepmother — who would succeed her, though still resenting it. The nature woman died somehow of her own accord, half-knowingly. But the Black Witch (in contrast to the White Witch) knows nothing of this. She fights to the last ugly, treacherous, extreme gesture, and dies fighting. Ysbaddaden, however, is quite conscious of the fate that awaits him, and is resigned. He has done his best to set Culhwch's feet in the trap set for himself, but, such is the nature of transforming fate (spiteful to the last degree if looked at with blind eyes, but wonderfully wise when understood), this brings about the very death he feared, and now accepts. He says: "Of

197

my own free will thou shouldst never have had her. And it is high time to take away my life."

Even so, however, he is given a degrading death, but a phallic one. In contrast to the witch killed secretly inside her cave (as a child murdered in the womb), he is strung up. His head is cut off and set up on a bailey-stake, exposed for all to see. What, then, is the significance of the hair of his head? This is quite different from that of his beard; in fact contrasted with it. The beard is cut off, but the head hair is kept, as part of the phallic structure of the head. It is used as a string to drag him by. Culhwch willingly sacrificed the hair of his head, thus yielding up his masculine animal possessiveness. (There is no mention anywhere of Culhwch's beard. He may indeed have been too young to have one. Symbolically this may mean that he has not yet had time in his short life to develop a negatively possessive anima such as the beard here symbolises.) Ysbaddaden makes no willing sacrifice of his grown one, in spite of all his assertions that he must dress it. It looks as though the loss of his beard but keeping of his head hair is but another indication that it was his female possessiveness that was his undoing, and not his straightforward masculinity.

Whereas the witch was slaughtered in a cave, his head was exposed upon a mound — the reverse of a cave. On the level of body image there is an obvious symbolism in this connected with the exposed nature of male sex values compared with that which is concealed within the body of a woman. Another aspect of body imagery is that it may be that the mound symbolises the breast, with Ysbaddaden's head on its stake representing the 'bad nipple'. The hero seizes the good one. "And he took possession of his fort and his dominions"; the fort of the breast, and the immense power it wields.

In the final scene, Culhwch has with him Goreu son of Custennin, another but younger hero of the Culhwch type — the next of a continuous line of heroes who will fight the same fight from generation to generation till the end of time. On the other hand, Goreu takes over the role of Arthur, finishing off the gruesome work that Arthur had begun. In this respect he represents past as well as future — a sort of *puer aeternus* tackling the father problem eternally while it is left to the Old Wise Man aspect of the Self to have prepared the way by achieving the far more difficult and inward task of tackling the witch. In this respect Goreu and Arthur represent respectively the young and old aspects of the hero (Culhwch) problem. The part of the hero function that is the actual attack on the giant is Cadw of Prydain, once again male midwife. As rider of Arthur's mare Llamrei and therefore in touch primarily with Arthur's feminine side, he is in a position to cope with the female aspect of the hermaphrodite giant Ysbaddaden, both in its negative and its positive roles, and deliver the anima from him.

There are thus, in this final scene, four heroes alluded to in all, that is to say four hero-functions: Culhwch as ego; Arthur representing the Self, by nature hermaphroditic and having a female aspect as well as a male one; of these, the female side, being the more fundamental, acts first, and is symbolised by Cadw of Prydain; and Goreu, symbolising the Self's male aspect, depotentiates the giant's masculine aspect.

In addition to these there are four further characters who (now that the boar has been absorbed into the general psyche) go to make up the final psychic picture. These are Ysbaddaden Pencawr, and Olwen, deriving her life-blood as it were from that of the hag, and the eternal sorceress, herself in her black and white presences. These may be represented by using the diagrammatical presentation of the well-known Chinese Taigitu, as shown on page 200.

Here the circle symbolises the total psyche of the hero. Above is

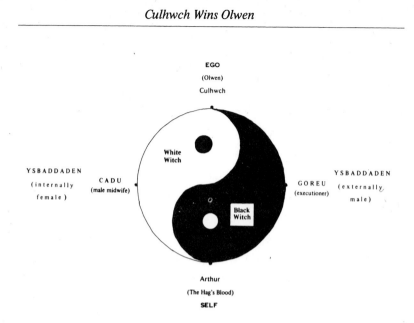

Culhwch, the focal point of the ego. Below is Arthur representing the essence of the Self. Across the median line lies Ysbaddaden Pencawr, the ambivalent father figure, externally male (to the right), internally female (to the left). The life-line of psychic power flows upward from the Self to the ego by means of the two subsidiary hero-figures: first, to the left, Cadw of Prydain as male midwife; secondly, to the right, Goreu as male executioner. The life-line is also the curving umbilical cord carrying the virtue of the hag's blood, obtained by Arthur, to Culhwch and Olwen at the top.

It is through this most primitive of biological channels from mother to child, now spiritualised and under the control of men (the male aspect of the Self now predominating over the female which, however, is still basic to the whole structure), that the problem of the 'two mothers', posed at the outset of the myth and underlying it throughout, is now solved. The Black Witch symbolising the totally matrilineal mother-image dies. On the diagram, this portion is now becoming white from its centre. That is to say

200

that her destructive power, her creative inner power, the blood, is transferred to the White Witch (the patrilineal moon-maiden as opposed to the sow mother) Olwen, and so, through her, to Culhwch the ego, through the action of Arthur, the Self. On the diagram, the White Witch portion is shown turning black through the infusion of blood at its centre. Obtaining the blood was the result of Arthur's personal struggle with, and victory over, the female possessiveness within himself. He does not keep it for himself, but passes it straight on to be the life-blood of Culhwch and Olwen, cementing their union in their youthful *hieros gamos.*

In one sense, Arthur is the real hero of the myth, the everlasting prototype from which the lesser hero Culhwch, his godson, draws his strength. In the next 'chapter', it would be Goreu the learner, Culhwch's still younger mate, who would do the same. And so on, throughout the ages, the boar hunt will go on, revealing behind it the yet greater terror of the hag, whose jealous greed is the worst thing on earth, but whose blood is the most precious.

APPENDIX I: THE DIAMOND BODY

The diagram below is an image of psychic structure in its perfection, a structural image of the Self. Looked at geometrically, as it can be and often is looked at, it is in the form of a crystal founded on a square with upper and lower supporting or containing points. This is the 'diamond body' of the philosophical systems. The Eastern concept of producing from out of the mortal body, while living, a diamond body, through meditation and right living, comes from such areas as Tibet, Indian, China. It includes 'marriages' or unions of opposites in all directions, between top (ego) and bottom (Self), between the four other points represented by the four parents, etc.

In Jungian psychology, the ego is most often conceived of (when considered diagrammatically) as being *contained* in the Self, which is 'larger' than it. For our purposes here, however, we have further differentiated out the Self as being focalised at the supporting end of the crystal. Two further crystal concepts,

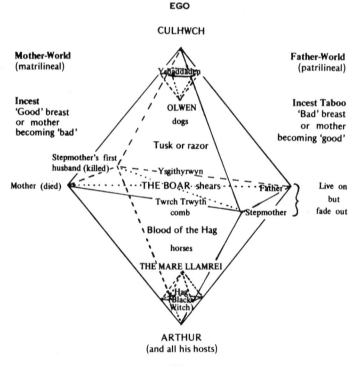

202

re-inforcing, if you like, the points of the conglomerate crystal, show a subsidiary 'opposing' point of the Self as the mare Llamrei and a subsidiary 'opposing' point of the ego as the sister-anima, Olwen.

The Self as a whole has as super-ordinate quaternity the four parents, who have controlled the young ego. They can be considered as external. The Self extremity, however, is not only supported by warriors, counsellors, etc., at Arthur's behest, but, at the final, crucial moment, by four servants. These, especially the latter, can be considered as internal agents.

In terms of the myth itself, each diamond body has a centre, which represents the central problem with which it is immediately concerned. Seen from the inside, the diamond body is a cave, or a container; the outside represents the personality as seen from without, that is to say the effect it produces on its environment, and it partakes of the nature of a persona. In the case of the Arthur sub-crystal, this is an archetype, representing the essence of a particular character-attitude – here that of the hero. Seen from the inside, this archetype is a crucible in which the inner conflict of the hero has been fought out. Like an alchemical vase, the outside is sealed, but this is precisely on account of the very intensity of the battle or transformation process that is going on inside; none of it must escape in the form of projections on to outer things, and all takes place inwardly.

Arthur first had to fight the boar and wrest from it its prize – razor, comb, and shears. (These were external acts, and can be likened to projection into the world; this precedes internalisation.) This victory, accomplished with so much hardship, forged for him his diamond body, a firm thing resistant to all attack, itself pointed in all six directions and so ready to defend itself against all comers but itself unwoundable. Then only can he with profit and assurance turn inwardly, to face the real enemy inside himself, in the recesses of the soul where conflicts within the personality are fought out to their bitter end. These are conflicts unseen by the outer world, but they are nevertheless intense and either integrating or disintegrating. The myth describes the recesses of the soul as a cave, where, hidden, lurks the hag, as it were, secretly sending out her boar and all his brood to lay waste his countryside, destroy his cattle, and kill off his warriors. This means Arthur's own internally destructive female side. The issue is whether she is to be allowed to operate from inside unseen and therefore unknown, or whether she is to be tracked down to her own lair and there fought and made to yield up her inner power.

Arthur triumphs over the hag. He draws her blood – the ultimate prize of all this battling – which Cadw of Prydain keeps to be handed on for any who follow the hero's path. This life-blood is the fluid element which Arthur wins through his own fearless sharp-pointed single-mindedness, which is not to be deterred by false advice which suggests that he not get too involved with basic filth. He thus turns out to be the diamond body in its *positive* aspect, and that is why, coupled with his extreme ancientness, and with his indestructibility in face of all these trials, he has been regarded throughout this analysis as symbolising the Self.

Another aspect of this is that Arthur, as Self, is paradoxically self-less, in that from all the battles he undertakes, no credit or gain is taken for himself. All are kept primarily for Culhwch. There is no real paradox in this since, though the Self contains within itself all things (as we know it to contain its own ego, persona, anima, shadow, four functions, etc.), it is, from another aspect, itself an impersonal unity, or an anti-ego with a relation to the ego of the human personality which it informs. The success of that human's life depends on how far this personal ego can bow to this impersonal but nevertheless highly dynamic Self, which forms the basis of his own individuality. This is what Culhwch did in submitting himself to Arthur. The Self can give help precisely because, in its age-long life, it has, over and over again, taken the hero's role and fought his battles, with ego following behind and accepting the gifts. In this respect Culhwch, as has been said before, is only a half-hero, the ultimate hero being the Self itself, here represented by Arthur.

We have now seen that the name 'Arthur' can be taken in two senses: as representing the totality of the Self, comprising the whole gamut of 'Arthur's hosts' — individual warriors, servants, dogs and horse; and as an 'individual' within the Self, the Arthur that strives and fights as a man does. It will not be possible in our discussion to keep these two aspects of Arthur entirely apart, but it may make things clearer if we regard the individual Arthur as one of the representatives of the larger Arthur, which we have called the Self. (The concepts of the structure of the psyche and of the Self are due to Jung, and are among those used in analytical psychology. The earlier findings of Freud form the basis of psychoanalysis. The two approaches do not necessarily contradict one another.) One looks, so to speak, from the bottom upward, starting with archetypal concepts connected with Self and reaching upward to find out how ego seems to be handling them. The other approach starts from the ego and reaches downward towards the world of archetypal imagery. Both are valid and complement one another, and both should be used in any thorough psychological analysis. Each extremity operates from its own level, reaching upwards towards ego or downwards towards the Self as the case may be.

The two factors constantly intermingle. The concept of an individual ego within the Self reflects the view that the Self itself is complex, and holds in it all possibilities of human behaviour, though in not personal but archetypal form. That is to say everything emanating from the Self represents not just individual reaction but typical reaction of some kind or other. Among such reactions is that of the hero, which is an archetypal figure of perfection that does not exist in any person in pure form. It represents an awareness of psychic potentiality that never emerges into overt life in unadulterated form, since in any average person it is controlled and modified by many other factors. But it can and does emerge quite pure in mythology, which is one way we have of finding out about it. Moreover, everything that emerges from the Self has two aspects, so when we say that Arthur may symbolise both Self and ego this may sound paradoxical but is the way with the dual nature of archetypal images. As with the sibyls of classical antiquity, they utter truths which can be taken either way round. This does not impair their validity. We simply have to hold both concepts (really a single concept with two aspects) in mind, because they intermingle in such a way that as a rule they can only be separated theoretically but not practically.

So the Arthur at the supporting end of our diamond body is that part of the Self that is nearest to consciousness and which not only experiences the actual suffering, but is also the link with Culhwch. This aspect of Arthur is primarily an archetype, though, as we shall see, he shows certain weaknesses which give him a partly human character.

If Arthur is mainly archetype and only in small measure human, his mare Llamrei is pure archetype. Arthur's own human wife Gwenhwyfar (Guinevere) is only once mentioned, near the beginning, when he names her only as one of his possessions that Culhwch could not request, though he can demand almost anything else. She is not mentioned again. Her place as anima figure is taken by the mare Llamrei who, as an animal and therefore existing on a psychic layer so much deeper than the human Gwenhwyfar, clearly belongs to the world of archetypes. She is the only actual female thing mentioned when the Self, at the extremity of Arthur's career, is finally faced with having to confront the witch alone; and this is an accurate description of the female attribute of the Self, at such a time.

One remarkable thing, however, is that, though she appears at two crucial moments, in neither instance is she ridden by Arthur himself. She acts as soul mate or companion of mother-type rather than as wife. This is particularly evident when she appears rescuing the four servants and carrying them away loaded on her back. She is mentioned also when she is ridden by Cadw of Prydain: mounted on her, he splits Ysgithyrwyn's head in two in a way similar to the splitting of the hag's body which follows Llamrei's intervention in the fight with her.

Cadw of Prydain took the boar's tusk and also keeps the slain hag's blood. Arthur himself does not touch these things but has them kept (though this is not overtly stated) for Culhwch. He, as Self figure, personally has no need of them. That he also does not ride Llamrei is understandable only on the supposition that, just as Arthur himself represents the male side of the Self (which is by definition bisexual) in its parental aspect, that is to say the godfather, so Llamrei symbolises its female side, the godmother. Their counterbalance is heightened by their lack of contact. In this case she would be equated (on a deeper level) with the stepmother at the beginning of the myth, while the hag herself would be equated with the untamed natural mother. Beginning and end concur, and those forces which at the beginning were symbolised by the two mothers appear at the end as far more basic figures, respectively as the untamed and untamable destructive witch and the tamed serviceable mare. As universal mother-figure, Llamrei the mare would belong no more to Arthur personally than to Culhwch or to any other hero figure. And this he shows by not riding her himself and thus claiming exclusive possession of her, but by delegating this function. The mother is also trustee for her son. So Cadw of Prydain rides the mare, thus symbolising the passing of power from godfather (the Self) to 'son' (ego), from past to future, from old to young, from unconsciousness to consciousness. The 'father' risks all and offers himself to the 'son', through the intermediary of the mother (the horse being psychic energy from the maternal side) and of her male representative, Cadw of Prydain, who in this context is a double for the 'son', keeping the tusk and the blood for him. (In some Northern mythology, the horse is said to have given birth to the world.)

Apart from the stag mentioned in the interpolated incident of the 'oldest animals', there are in the main part of the myth only three kinds of mammal: the boar (with its young), the dogs, and the horses (and mare) used in hunting it. Dogs and horses are servants and helpers of Man. Having been at least partly domesticated and thus separated off from the purely natural, non-human aspect of mother-nature and so brought into the service of man, they have become part of man's world, and so, in myth, symbolise parts of the hero's character, that is to say the character of a rational being knowing what he is about. They are opposed to the irrational factors still untamed and rampant in human nature, here all lumped into one and symbolised by the boar, agent of the archetype of the Great Mother and in herself the sum of all untransformed natural forces — wild. Of the two kinds of domesticated animal here mentioned, the function of the horses is to 'carry', while that of the dogs is to 'attack'. Here we find the two sex characteristics once more symbolised as complementary opposites working in harmony: the horses, including the mare, symbolising the female function of carrying, bearing, supporting, but not actually fighting; and the dogs the male penetrating function of attack. While the boar, representing purely natural functioning, is undifferentiated, being physically male and symbolically female (both attributes being so fused and intermingled that it has taken quite a bit of analysis to sort them out), the dog and the horse are clearly differentiated, and therefore more closely allied to human consciousness. Here also we have a duality, even within the animal kingdom, in so far as it has been partly domesticated by man.

The diamond body has a central point, invisible in the midst of it, which may be called 'the fine point of the soul'. Recalling the six outer points, this is the seventh and ultimately the most important one. All, for the soul's sake, depend on this central point: not only what it is, but what ego *thinks* of it. For it is always ambivalent. Being in the middle, it always faces two ways. It partakes equally of consciousness and of the unconscious. In sexual terms it is bisexual or hermaphroditic.

When it now comes to an examination of the central points in the structure of the sub-crystals, we find a difference between the two diamond bodies. It is clear that if we want to get *inside* this diamond body, we can only do so by thinking of it as a hollow space or cave, as indeed every solid body is when values are reversed. This concept is provided by the myth itself, which at this point in Arthur's career has been concentrated on the hag sitting within her cave, with

Arthur outside and fearful of entering it. While Llamrei the mare is Arthur's complementary opposite in the sense of co-operating with him in the attack on the hag, the hag herself is even more of an opposite. She represents the absolute antithesis of everything that is noble in Arthur. Not only is her sex different (an attribute shared by the helping Llamrei). She is actually utterly opposed to him to the point of wanting to destroy him, and of him consequently wanting to destroy her. She is the ultimate hostile, unscrupulous, devouring-mother image now stripped of every disguise and seen for what she is, old as the hills, the prime instigator of evil against mankind, she who wishes to annihilate men's souls. She and Arthur symbolise the ultimate antitheses in human life. Yet she is a part of the greater (Self) Arthur, that which could turn him into a tyrant instead of a beneficent ruler if she were not robbed of her power.

With the ego sub-crystal, however, the picture is very different. Culhwch never comes near the hag. He never sees her. He might never even have heard of her. As half-hero only, he has no inkling of the mother problem that lies hidden behind the father one. He is prepared and willing to defy the father image, Ysbaddaden, without suspecting that Ysbaddaden's outraged possessiveness of his daughter is in fact the sign of being internally hag-ridden, as all 'giants' are. They are but male representatives of the matriarchy which will not at any price allow its daughters to have real mates who might challenge its authority. So Culhwch, as male ego-figure, makes no progress, as it were, beyond the father problem. Therefore, for him the central figure in his diamond body is not the hag, the ultimate but as yet unknown enemy, but the image of the matriarchal father, Ysbaddaden. This is in fact the problem of the youth as yet not fully established in the world of men, in contrast to Arthur, who is so familiar with it that he commands hosts of warriors (a worldful of them) but who knows, in his deep wisdom, that this is not the ultimate victory: it is that of overcoming Death itself in the form of the super-archetypal devouring-mother image within the soul.

This is also, incidentally, an instance of the contrasting problems connected with the first and second halves of the life of what we might call the normal individual with a good instinctive background, Culhwch representing the battle of youth, and Arthur that of the mature man. The hag fight takes no note of twists and turns such as counter-Oedipus problems, which we have to deal with in great quantity, with youths of today. The hag herself is such an adept at twists and turns that even neurotics may draw comfort from this greater fight in which she reveals herself only at the end, after the boar, her advance agent, has run the gamut of escape mechanisms and finally been tracked down.

In the total Self crystal, the two mothers and their two husbands are seen at the four quarters of the central part of this diagram, each pair married diagonally across it. In the middle, where all these cross, is the Boar, the central transforming image of the myth, combining both mother image and father image in one symbol, Culhwch's Ysbaddaden and Arthur's hag. He, like all these central figures, does one thing and means another, sets out consciously to destroy, but unconsciously initiates, this being accomplished by his or her own death, whereby the treasure which he has guarded is yielded up. He is symbolically hermaphroditic. His male aspect is depicted above, his female aspect below. The phallus belongs to Youth which wields the tusk — phallic symbol. The womb symbolism (birth of the anima out of the father's head) is the ultimate problem of the second half of life and of old age. It can only be tackled by a figure of hoary antiquity (though ever young) like Arthur. The hag's Blood is a female symbol of deepest wisdom and a knowledge of opposites. The whole upper pyramid can be seen to be aggressively phallic, the whole bottom (inverted) pyramid may be seen as a container for the blood.

Thus the whole of this larger diamond body is seen as a union of opposites between ego and Self, of which ego to begin with is purely masculine in a matriarchal way (that is to say uncontrolled), but Self is as nearly as possible bisexual, being masculine of the patriarchal kind that has absorbed into itself the female function, and is itself a container as well as being male. They are in the relation of Son to spiritual Father. This is not only a static relationship. It is a dynamic one, and the whole time-sequence of the combined hero's task in its main lines can be followed by reading this diamond body from top to bottom. The fact that Culhwch uses these gains only to attain Olwen the sister-anima and thus to complete only his own ego-diamond, personally avoiding the whole problem of the hag, is of lesser importance. We are here contemplating the whole 'ideal' process as it is accomplished by the matured man.

The respective meanings of razor, shears, and comb are also shown in this diagram, in the actual order in which they were seized. Having two contrary opposite blades, the shears have the double-meaning of facing both ways. We must also note the left-hand and right-hand symbolism. On the left hand of the quaternity are Culhwch's 'natural' mother, who died, and the stepmother's first husband, also representing the old order and therefore having to be killed. They represent the Mother-World, which gives birth to the body but is psychologically incestuous, since the mother-child relationship is not broken by any intimate or spiritual relationship with the father. On the right is the Father-World: the father, cause and upholder of the incest taboo between mother and son, and the stepmother who is his second wife, the patriarchal, cultural and spiritual one with whom he has a real relationship.

It may be well here to repeat once more the contrasts as regards ego and Self. These represent two aspects of the individual, as it were often in opposition, acting in a sense as mirror opposites. While participating in the same action of the individual in question, they in fact look on it from diametrically opposite points of view. Ego does not want to suffer. It wants to live and enjoy life from day to day without being bothered and with as few obstacles as possible to the straightforward satisfaction of every natural desire. Self, on the contrary, having been present when the world began, knows the secrets of creation and the purpose of it, and has itself suffered throughout the ages in learning its lessons. It is

208

itself a pair of opposites (as shown) and, understanding the opposites, has grown wise in the knowledge that all things have to be transformed. It knows that only a willing acceptance of this fact can open the eyes of anyone to his true nature and to what he was born for, and that he must face up to the contradictions within himself if he is to get any real satisfaction out of life and to fulfil his destiny. Self, therefore, seems a cruel taskmaster to those who do not submit, but proves to be the initiator into new life for those who do. Culhwch submitted, but, being only a half-fledged hero, got so far as to face up to the angry father image of Ysbaddaden and made all his out-of-hand promises. Nevertheless from that time he fades out. Arthur himself (like a good godfather) had to arrange the fulfilling of the tasks. The Self once again 'became man', and goes through all the blood and sweat of the hero in the thick of the fight; he also suffers his humiliations. True, these latter are glossed over somewhat, but nevertheless Arthur has been closely threatened at Celli Wig, and has to undertake the degrading task of killing the hag himself.

The servants had failed to conquer the hag. He had allowed himself to send them because of the apparently wise but in fact unwise advice of his two counsellors. See here the conflict within himself. These counsellors represent two sides of him which both try to persuade him to adopt the 'common-sense' attitude that this fight is not really so important and is not worthy of employing all his energies on; it is also very far from being dignified. But now he can no longer avoid the direct personal issue: his whole personality has to be staked on it. He must now brace himself alone, using every faculty at once, to face this ultimate horror. It is the issue of his own completely opposite side, so different from the noble Arthur the world knows (and that he also might like to think he is).

If he stands divided in any way, he will fail once more. The situation he now finds himself in is one calling either for the resolution of a hero or for action born out of despair. The one thing that does not come within the range of possibilities is that he will be admired for undertaking the deed. That has been plainly ruled out. He would be admired, rather, for abandoning it as being a mean and unworthy act. As for the other two possibilities, despair or heroic resolution, it is on second thought doubtful how valid such a distinction is. Those who know the depths of the psyche know how very near to one another these two motivations lie. The chronicler inclines, however, to the view of its heroic nature, since it is not, on the surface, the hag who attacks an unwitting victim, but the hero who seeks her out. This does not mean that the hero does not know the mortal danger he is in. It means, on the contrary, that he is even more aware of it than any unwitting victim who gets caught unawares. A victim does not know the danger until it is on him. The hero is he who knows clearly what the danger is, could turn his back on it (though he could never pretend that it did not exist), but does in fact not only face it but seeks it out to encounter it, knowing also the probable results if he does not do so.

So now, in our myth, all forces are gathered together within the hero himself to do battle single-handed, with the hag. His friends are not there. No more assistance will come from outside. He has had plenty of that, however, to bring him up to this point. He has been helped by the dynamic-protecting force of his animal anima. Llamrei his mare, that essence of the maternal side of his archetypal nature, has been tamed and is now honoured by being used in this highly personal task: the final destruction of his own seventh point (see diagram), the hag. In this case this is the seventh point in a *negative* aspect. In order to acquire and absorb its positive aspect, the witch's blood must be taken. (This probably explains, incidentally, the seven pigs, brood of Twrch Trwyth. For everything on one side of the battle, or any problem, is mirrored on the other side. The five small pigs and two big ones of Twrch Trwyth's brood may be thought of as the four centre points and the 'seventh' in the middle and the two major figures at opposite ends of the diamond.)

Arthur is now at last complete within himself and so the hag is slain. "And then Arthur seized the entrance to the cave, and from the entrance he took aim at the hag with Carnwennan his knife, and struck her across the middle until she was as two tubs. And Cadw of Prydain took the witch's blood and kept it with him."

APPENDIX II: ANIMA AND ANIMUS

The deed of splitting open Zeus's head is sometimes attributed to Prometheus, but usually to Hephaestus. Both have the common characteristic of being sufferers at the hands of the gods. The story of Zeus and Hephaestus is the most illuminating. Hephaestus was born of Hera, but some say without Zeus's physical participation, that is to say parthenogenetically. Normally this would mean that Hephaestus would be a typical 'mother's son' proficient in bodily virtues but untransformed. But, unlike her other son, the war god Ares (with whom he is often coupled as the other of a pair of opposites), Hephaestus was born weak and a cripple. Crippledom we know to be a sign of change (it is the sign of many psychological as well as mythical 'heroes'). (A 'hero', which may come from 'Hera', was originally a sacred king who was ritually sacrificed to the fertility goddess. In Greek and Celtic myths, he used golden apples as passports to paradise. In later hero cults, he acted mainly as intermediary between men and gods.)

In this case we may surmise that, Hera being the great matriarch always jealous of her husband Zeus, Hephaestus was an animus figure symbolising what might have become a change in her towards acceptance of the male principle. He might have become for her, that is to say, a positive animus, as he did later indeed for the world of male gods and men for whom he became the great artificer and smith, making their armour and such notable symbols as Achilles' shield, as well as jewellery for women. But Hera could not accept this change, and with disgust threw him away. He fell into the sea, where he was rescued by two goddesses, Thetis and Eurynome, the latter the primal 'Goddess of All Things' who separated the sea from the sky. But the most important for our story is Thetis, for when, after they had set up Hephaestus as a smith under the sea, "Hera one day met Thetis, who happened to be wearing a brooch of his workmanship, and asked: 'My dear, where in the world did you find that wonderful jewel?'" When Hera learnt who it was, "she fetched Hephaestus back to Olympus, where she set him up in a much finer smithy... and arranged that he should marry Aphrodite."[1] In this story of the birth of Hephaestus we find the familiar motive of the 'two mothers', the 'natural' mother Hera who gives birth to him, and Thetis (doubled by Eurynome) who undertakes the work of transformation under the sea and gives birth to his soul (his power of workmanship and fashioning with iron). This 'indestructible' soul-substance can be likened in our Celtic myth to the boar's tusk.

Hera eventually accepted what she had first rejected, but before this had happened Zeus had become jealous of her having this man-child (formation of positive animus) without his help (even though it was abortive for her since she spurned it), and had taken a lover. Here again is the problem of the 'two women': the sister-wife Hera, and now, to balance the matriarchal son, the secret lover

211

Metis, daughter of Oceanus, god of that same watery element that had rescued the son. The name Metis is said to mean 'counsel' (which will remind us of Olwen, and the 'counsel' she gave to Culhwch as to how to deal with her father's jealousy). Her function is that of intermediary, substantiated by the fact that she is the female tutelary deity of the planet Mercury. Some of her attributes remind us of Themis, Zeus's wife before Hera (and his father's sister). She is called the Titaness of Wisdom. It was she who had helped Zeus as an infant when Cronus sought to swallow him up as he had swallowed his elder brothers, by making him vomit them up. (This swallowing of sons is a clear instance of the father taking over the role of the matriarchal Devouring Mother, resembling the Ysbaddaden of our Celtic myth.)[2] Metis was also identified with Protogonos Phaeton, "the first-born shining one", who was "double-sexed, being a woman before and a man behind", and "as Metis was 'Wise Counsel' — a deity who, to judge by the name, was female, but of whom it was said that she carried the semen of the gods", which we may interpret as their creative wisdom.[3]

It was said of her that she was fated to bear "exceedingly wise children".[4] Zeus "lusted after Metis the Titaness, who turned into many shapes to escape him until she was caught at last and got with child".[5] He thus lusts after wisdom. This shape-changing is due to her *mercurial* character and is a typical characteristic of the anima, standing as she does in the middle and facing all ways, uniting them. We have seen this with regard to Olwen in her understanding of the opposites, facing one way towards her father and another towards Culhwch. As to the child conceived by Zeus in Metis, "an oracle of Mother Earth then declared that this would be a girl-child, and that, if Metis conceived again, she would bear a son who was fated to depose Zeus",[6] just as Zeus had done to his father Cronus, and as Cronus had done to his father Uranus by cutting off his penis and throwing it into the sea. Zeus was happy enough to have thus castrated and deposed his father in this chain of sons castrating their fathers. On the surface this is a typical Oedipus myth but on a deeper level means the opposite: the son denying his own patrilineal origin and so his spiritual inheritance. In other words, on this level it is a matriarchal myth levelled against husbands.

Zeus, however, stricken with a sudden access of consciousness, bethought him that, if not put a stop to, the same would happen to himself, as Mother Earth had said (and obviously desired), and his son would depose him. So he resorted to trickery. We have seen that this is the only way to defeat the Great Mother, who is far too powerful to be defeated in open conflict. (Can anyone prevent the sperm from fertilising the ovum if it reaches it? Only by the trickery of artificially interfering with the course of nature can it be prevented from reaching it. If the sperm does reach it, it is 'swallowed up' in the moment of its entry, just as a man can lose his identity in a woman's embrace, and as the father loses his if he is castrated by his son.) Zeus, terrified of losing his individuality, turned the tables on the Great Mother by suddenly opening his mouth and swallowing Metis.

This action represents a reversal of the previous order. The man swallows the woman; this also means internalising what has been projected outwardly on to external women up to now. It is one of the turning points leading to the birth of the anima. Zeus could accept a girl-child. He did not want a son. The social and externally emotional attitude of that time had men wanting sons to carry on their line. As a spiritual phenomenon, the son represents the extension of a man's life into the future in the flesh, and this implies his father's death. Zeus, the supreme god, wanted to become immortal, retaining creative power that would go on and not be lost to him, as his father's had been and his father's father's. To do this — and this is a figure for man's immortality in the creation of a soul — he must at all costs curtail his own patricidal tendency (represented by the 'son') by preventing that son from being born, that is to say that physical extension into the future which would continue in a long line of endless births and deaths which Mother Nature decrees — but which the spiritual world abhors. The spirit wants to put a stop to this and to transform time into depth, a succession of events in time into a succession of psychic levels deepening the character, until it reaches the bisexual level in which a man is sufficient unto himself, having found his internal anima and so being capable of approaching the Self (of which Zeus is a symbol).

Nobility is not a quality of the Self if this means that the Self is *only* noble. (As noted elsewhere, the survival of the hero is not so much instigated by nobility as by sheer necessity.) The Self contains all things, from the highest to the meanest, in time order from the meanest to the most sublime. For life begins with 'meanness' — pure selfishness, without which no infant would survive. Nobility comes, paradoxically, from the perfection of selfishness in this sense of the word, that no man can give to others what he has not already got for himself. He should always 'come first' even in the most selfless of men, that is to say possess the ability to let his fancy roam untrammelled by conventionality or fear of what others might think. This goes some way towards elucidating the paradox of Zeus being at once the highest, serenest and all-wise Greek god while at the same time indulging in every kind of amorous adventure and change of mind, even to being a hen-pecked husband. Such concepts are foreign to Western minds, for so long dominated by one-sided thought.

In the instance now under review, Zeus acts with the utmost selfishness. Metis being already with a girl-child by him, he swallows her by trickery lest she bear him a boy-child. He also, be it noted, deprives her of what 'natural' mothers want, a son. This is moreover a sort of secret union with her, directed against his wife Hera. Yet what he has swallowed is 'Wisdom'. Wisdom also can only be taken unawares, since once wisdom is conscious it tends to become conceit. The only wisdom lies in denying it. Therefore it is that Metis takes on so many forms. When grasped in some aspect, wisdom may become just common sense, but there are always other aspects demanding more wisdom still. So she eludes capture until the trick is found to obliterate her existence. (Then she is 'caught'!) That is Wisdom: static wisdom is not to be found; it is a flow of imaginative under-standing to which no halt can be permanently assigned.

Now Zeus had in him Metis, pregnant with a girl-child. This double load was too great a thing to bear. Metis is said to have given counsel to him from inside his belly[7], but we are not told what this was. It may or may not have been to get the help of Hephaestus to deliver Zeus from what was now his own great double pregnancy. He was seized by a raging headache as he walked beside a peak (symbolising a head) on the shore of Lake Triton[8] (in North Africa; some say the River Triton — in Crete).

Meanwhile Hephaestus had a grudge against his father Zeus. He had on one occasion sought to aid Hera against Zeus, whereon Zeus had taken him by the heel and cast him for the second time from Olympus.[9] This naturally was not too pleasing to Hephaestus, providing him with a motive for revenge. So the two motives of Zeus's need to be delivered of his pregnancy and of Hephaestus's desire for revenge, coincided in a single act. Hermes (the male counterpart of 'mercurial' Metis), seeing Zeus's distress and immediately divining its cause, per-suaded Hephaestus to come to the rescue. Hephaestus, seeing his chance, took "wedge and beetle, and made a breach in Zeus's skull, from which sprang Athene, fully armed, with a mighty shout".[10]

The shout may be the child's first shout at birth, or the warrior's battle-cry on entering into the fight. Both symbols coincide in that the birth of the fully-armed Athene from her father's head was a 'new thing': it was the Virgin Anima fortifying a man against matriarchal possessiveness (Hera's nagging) and against the deeper meaning of this — man's boundness to his own mother-nature, to purely fleshly desires, and to the endless round of birth and death which it had been Zeus's purpose to put an end to in swallowing Metis. Hera represents not only the external matriarch psychically swallowing up her sons, but also Zeus's (any man's) own anger and opposition against this external figure. He had to 'swallow his rage' as well and, in doing so, encompass wisdom. Swallowing rage does not just mean biting the upper lip and putting up with it while still raging internally and so destroying oneself. It means the joy of battle joined with one's own sense of dependence, which implies one's own sense of possessiveness. It is no easy task, as Zeus's distress and headache showed.

I cannot here refrain from quoting a remark of Homer Lane's, that great 'nature' psychologist who knew nature so well that he forgot civilised man's oppo-sition to it and so got himself into trouble with the authorities. Once a certain client was in an acute stage of mother-bound breakdown in which almost all phys-ical as well as mental faculties were paralysed; the client accused him of giving him a headache by his psychological talking, whereas headaches had previously been to him a thing unknown. This proved, he said, how harmful Lane's treatment was. Lane replied: "Good. Now at last something is moving in you. The mental adhesions are beginning to break down. Naturally this hurts. But that is the beginning of consciousness." By 'mental adhesions' he meant psychic adhesions to the psychic mother's womb from which the young man had as yet hardly begun to be separated. Such a remark was traumatic in the positive sense, undoing the original trauma of boundness. It was a counterblow to the headache, releasing the beginning of wisdom in the sense of self-knowledge, and the future welcoming of headaches to find out what they might have to say, or to 'deliver up', since these also were found to be sent by the initiating Great Mother for a definite purpose. This is but a small instance of what is meant by Zeus being delivered of his headache through the attack of his mother's (symbolised by his wife Hera's) positive animus appearing as a negative one, releasing the treasure of wisdom. The same can be said of the splitting open of Ysgithyrwyn's head for the delivery of the tusk.

Athene's triumphal shout is also the shout of the released prisoner, the goddess rescued from imprisonment (as Olwen, in our myth, has been imprisoned by *her* father). It is also the cry of relief of Zeus himself at being delivered of the burden of internal rage, now turned (as with the release of aggression in psychotherapeutic treatment) into psychic power available for good. Naturally, Athene became Hera's greatest enemy, arousing Hera's jealousy because of her defence of men against the spiteful and negatively regressive forces in the unconscious, for which the possessive mother or wife largely stands. Hera therefore took her revenge. She had already produced a brother to Hephaestus, Ares the war god (she was a most militant woman) whose emblem was the wild boar. In revenge for Zeus giving birth to Athene without her help, she brings forth a yet more terrible son, Typhon. He was later identified by chroniclers with the Egyptian Set who also was a boar; in this form he slew his brother Osiris and 'crippled' him by cutting his body into pieces, to be reassembled again only by Isis his sister-wife (who at one time was symbolised by a white cow), that is to say was the 'white witch' or consciously initiating patriarchal woman *par excellence*.

Hera, however, did not mean any good by creating Typhon. His name means stupefying smoke, hot wind, hurricane. She did it "in wrath against her husband when he, Zeus, bore Pallas Athene. In anger spoke Hera to the assembled immortals: 'Hear me, all of you, gods and goddesses, how Zeus undertakes to bring shame upon me — how he is the first to do so, after taking me to wife. Without me he has born Athene, who is glorious among all the immortals, whilst my own son, whom I bore, Hephaestus, is the least of us all.' "[11] Note this in relation to all mystical concepts of the least becoming the greatest, applicable also to our Celtic myth, in which Culhwch 'born of a sow' becomes the hero. And, incidentally, some say (Apollodorus: i.1.5 and Hesiod: *Theogony* 453-67) that "Zeus was suckled by a sow, and rode on her back, and that he lost his navel-string at Omphalion near Cnossus"[12], in which case Zeus also has somewhat of a boar nature, so that the relation between him and Ysgithyrwyn, who also had his head split open to give birth to a gender-symbol, is not so distant. Zeus's sister, the Great Mother Demeter, was closely connected with the sow, which was her sacrificial animal, as was their daughter Persephone, the Core, whose rape by Pluto was observed by a swineherd and whose pigs were swallowed up by the earth along with her, so that young pigs were ritually cast into pits in honour of the two goddesses.

Hera goes on, referring to her scorn of Hephaestus, "I myself threw him into the sea; but Thetis, the daughter of Nereus, caught him up and cared for him with her sisters: she might well have done us another service! Thou deceitful monster! How hast thou dared to bear Athene? Could *I* not have born thee a child? Was I not thy wife? Now I shall see to it that I may have a son who shall be glorious amongst the gods! I shall do it without dishonouring thy bed and my bed, yet without coming to thee. I shall stay apart from thee...' Thereupon Hera went apart also from the other gods and prayed to Gaia and Uranos to 'give me a son who shall not be weaker than Zeus himself! As Zeus was mightier than Kronos, so let my son be mightier than he!' She struck the earth with powerful hand. Gaia, the source of life, quivered; and Hera rejoiced, for she guessed that she had had her will. Thenceforth for a full year she did not lie with Zeus... She abode in her temples and enjoyed the sacrifices. When a year later the time came, she gave birth to something that resembled neither gods nor men: Typhon, that terrible disaster for mortals."[13] Thus did Hera arouse the great Earth Mother, Gaia, to do her worst, conceiving this monster. It will be noted that Hera takes the male part, "striking the earth with powerful hand", an angry phallic gesture which evidently quickened her. Preferring her son to her husband, she thus sought to destroy the husband by giving birth, this time clearly parthenogenetically. Developing further away from the positive forward-looking animus Hephaestus, whom she had rejected, this regressive animus was no longer in human form; it is sometimes referred to as a dragon.

What was this 'dragon' and the outcome of his creation? Some say that Mother Earth conceived Typhon by lying with Tartarus in the Corycian Cave. He was "the largest monster ever born. From the thighs downwards he was nothing but coiled serpents, and his arms, which when he spread them out reached a hundred leagues in either direction, had countless serpents' heads instead of hands. His brutish ass-head touched the stars, his vast wings darkened the sun, fire flashed from his eyes, and flaming rocks hurtled from his mouth. When he came rushing towards Olympus, the gods fled in terror to Egypt, where they disguised themselves as animals... Athene alone stood her ground, and taunted Zeus with cowardice until, resuming his true form, he let fly a thunderbolt at Typhon, and followed this up with a sweep of the same flint sickle that had served to castrate his father Uranus....Typhon fled to Mount Casius, which looms over Syria from the north, and there the two grappled. Typhon twined his myriad coils about Zeus, disarmed him of his sickle and, after severing the sinews of his hands and feet with it, dragged him into the Corycian Cave....The news of Zeus's defeat spread dismay among the gods... "[14]

Having been rescued by Hermes and Pan "Zeus returned to Olympus and, mounted upon a chariot drawn by winged horses, once more pursued Typhon with thunderbolts. Typhon... reached Mount Haemos in Thrace and, picking up whole mountains, hurled them at Zeus, who interposed his thunderbolts, so that they rebounded on the monster, wounding him frightfully. The streams of Typhon's blood gave Mount Haemos its name. He fled towards Sicily, where Zeus ended the running fight by hurling Mount Aetna upon him, and fire belches from its cone to this day."

Different as this atmosphere is from that of our Celtic myth, essential features of the story are astonishingly similar. Typhon, the fantastic giant animal, is similar to the boar, who covered huge tracts of country as the ultimate carrier of the mother's negative animus, too powerful to be conceived of as a human. This symbolises the immense power of the unconscious, against which man alone is powerless unless he enlist the co-operation of something female, of the same nature as the Great Mother herself but operating with opposite intent. This is, in the Greek myth, Athene, who alone can stand fast and rally Zeus, and in the Celtic one Olwen, who alone knows the secret of how to counteract her father's deadly scheming. A second point of interest is that Typhon himself attacks Olympus, just as the boar finally pursues Arthur to his soul-stronghold of Celli Wig.

A third and most significant point is the two battles that Zeus has to fight, corresponding to the two boars. We have noted that in the Welsh myth the first encounter is with Ysgithyrwyn, the phallic one. Here in the Greek myth the first combat takes place in the north — where Arthur had caught Cyledyr the Wild, and where the hag is — and Zeus uses that same flint sickle with which he had castrated Uranus. The myths differ in that here Zeus is defeated, whereas in the Celtic one Arthur succeeds. But in both myths there is a second encounter ending with the flowing of blood. In the Greek case it is Typhon's own blood, since Typhon here has such obvious female characteristics in his coiled snake-likeness. The Celtic myth is more explicit, the second boar giving place finally to the hag whose blood is treasure. A fourth important point is the femaleness of the male dragon throughout, seen in his coiling around Zeus and so immobilising him. This is a frequent symbol for being constricted within the hostile animus-like womb. A fifth similarity is the cave in which Typhon is born of the Earth Mother and Tartarus, the dark nether region, and in which he confines Zeus, compared to the cave in which Arthur finally encounters and overcomes the hag.

Another aspect of Hera's speech brings out clearly the conflict between the 'two mothers'. These are Hera the matriarch, who rejects Hephaestus, and Thetis who rescues him and thus arouses her jealousy. The contrasting characters of the two can well be seen by the animus figures which they sponsor. Hephaestus's 'crippledom' connoted difference, with this special meaning: loss of arms or legs in dreams (therefore also in myth) means loss of 'projections', that is to say loss of those attitudes and assumptions belonging in this case to matriarchy, to the pre-eminence of women over their men. The 'cripple' is, through loss of these

217

limbs or projections, on the way to re-becoming a foetus, as it were, to being re-born without assumptions so that new attitudes may be acquired more in con-sonance with the future than with the past, with patriarchy and individuality instead of with matriarchy and undifferentiated collectiveness. As extravert, Hera saw only the weakness and crippledom and had no knowledge of what it meant. So, in rejecting the future because she was embarrassed and disgusted by it, she regressed on to a lower level still, to get the Earth Mother to produce for her a real monster.

But Thetis was an introvert. She lived in the sea, that is to say she knew her way about in the unconscious and what it was pregnant with, and served its purposes. She rescued this odd-man-out, nursing his individuality, and gave him other 'arms and legs' in the form of tools with which to beat the hard uncon-scious metal got out of the unconscious earth into weapons and armour for men and jewellery for women. She honoured his person, this rejected one, till he be-came the great artificer for the Greek world, as good as any other god and in some ways more powerful because subtler. And just as Olwen had a dual nature, so also had Athene. In this they both differ from Hera; she only had one, the extravert, and rejected the other. The point about this dual nature is that every-one has it, but that its use or misuse depends on consciousness. The woman not knowing hers acts as Hera, thinking herself loving but a victim of men's horrible wiles; whereon she proves herself a horror by the production of something like Typhon, who ravages even in the end the men she loves, and ultimately finds herself on the shelf because Typhon must in the end be slain. The woman know-ing her two natures, however, is like Thetis, who understands things from the inside (or from below — the sea with its life-giving fluidity). The greatest of all is Athene, modern up to her fingertips, and knowing men from the inside because she came from one, and therefore also herself. She can thus wield her power knowingly.

No one could possibly wield power as great as hers without having a back-ground of such duality, and knowing it. This takes in the mythology two forms: bisexual, and what psychologically would be called homosexual (not physical homosexuality but any kind of relationship between a woman and her other female side). Virginity implies this in a marked degree, whatever kind of virgin-ity this may be, a physical or a spiritual one. Virginity is in either sphere a mascu-line function. The quality of the rejected or absent male (whether a man, or a projection on to a man) is taken on internally, so that her animus function is always very marked. This reflects itself, so far as Athene is concerned, both linguistically and mythologically.

"The word *pallas* can be variously accented and inflected so as to have either a masculine or a feminine meaning. In the masculine it means a strong young man, in the feminine a strong virgin, a *virago*, as she would be called in Latin." According to one legend she had a father, a Giant called Pallas. "The male Pallas was always the same figure, although given various genealogies, a wilder and even more warlike male version of Pallas the goddess. It is said of Pallas, the father of Pallas Athene, that he sought to do violence to his own daughter. The goddess overcame him, took his skin as booty,... and herself wore the skin." [15] This is very relevant to the idea of the outraged female taking on the appearance of a man. In this case it is to defend her virginity. This must not, however, be taken only in a physical sense. "Pallas the father was winged, as also was Pallas the daughter in old portrayals of her." This means that both symbolise psychic functions. Both have, however, the same name Pallas. This is one of the tricks the psyche plays on the unwary, and also one of the revelations she makes to those who can understand her ambivalence and consequent extraordinary wisdom. It is connected with the fact in *Culhwch and Olwen* that the new always has to grow out of the old – the tusk has to be taken, Dillus's beard has to be plucked, the blood has to be caught, while their 'donors' still live. These are all used then with opposite intent from their original purpose.

In the myth, Pallas the father seeks to do violence to his own daughter, who refuses to be raped. That father and daughter bear the same name indicates that it is with the very strength and qualities derived from her father that she resists her father. This is so basic to psychology that it needs emphasising. It is the key by means of which such things as schizophrenia can be cured, and also the hysteria which underlies schizophrenia. In schizophrenia the two elements are so divided that neither recognises the other. In hysteria they are so intertwined that they cannot separate. It needs in each case an outsider with a clear view of the opposites to bring them together in the case of schizophrenia, and to separate them in the case of hysteria. In psychotherapy this outside influence is the analyst. In religious systems it is called God, who is at once all things in one, and all things separately. In Christianity it is that aspect of God which is called on the one hand the Holy Ghost who unites the opposites, and on the other Satan who performs the equally necessary task of dividing.

This is what shows Zeus's problem to have been a hysterical one, a double pregnancy (*hysteros* = the womb), an extreme identification with womanhood, cured only by 'splitting', that is to say separating the opposites. Thus a third thing can emerge as separated off from Zeus himself and so become objectified, the female Athene. Zeus now could see her, instead of being doubly burdened by the female element internally and so unconsciously. This is also the case in our Celtic myth. Culhwch was at first undivided – he saw himself simply as a whole undifferentiated being, a straightforward 'mother's son' without complexes of a patriarchal nature, that is to say a simple 'animal man' without a soul. The problem of the soul arose when his stepmother pronounced on him the 'destiny' that he must seek Olwen (in order, though this is just hinted at, eventually to marry the stepmother's daughter). His first glimpse of Olwen finds her identified with her father. But she, being 'wisdom' on the model of Metis and later of Athene, knows better. Before he can separate her from her father he has to separate himself, or suffer himself to 'be separated' through conflict. His calling

Arthur indicates his dawning knowledge that he is dual. The sequel shows a large number of further separations — all symbolising increase in consciousness — until finally he is fully split, so that he masters his spirit as well as his body. The spirit unites with Olwen, leaving the body free, since this is allegory, to make a differentiated human marriage, in which no mother-derived anima is projected on to the wife.

Thus, in the syndrome of Pallas the father being repelled by Pallas the daughter, the 'father' represents straightforward animal desire (not only sexual but of any kind), and the 'daughter' this same desire transformed from seeking its satisfaction outwardly to finding strength and satisfaction inwardly; having the quality of maleness derived from the father internalised, so as to make her unassailable by the very father (or untransformed desires) whose strength she now uses against himself. She thus becomes the Male Mother or Female Father of her devotees. As Male Mother she thus becomes a goddess of childbirth, taking the role here of 'godmother'. As Virgin Mother she cannot herself give birth to physical children; Nature looks after that in the form of all the ordinary mothers who give birth. The 'children' she assists into the world are, on the contrary, spiritual functions such as 'wisdom', with which she endows the physical children thus born in a natural way. 'Wisdom' implies a split, the conscious possession of soul as well as body. Athene thus gives birth to souls such as herself.

As Female Father she defends these souls, protecting and furthering their interests in every possible way: by wise counsel or by armed warlike action, when in a whirlwind of fury she descends to do battle against those who deny her transforming will. In this she acts quite independently of Zeus her father, who, as in the Trojan war, often so firmly sits on the fence and remains neutral, or changes his mind, at one time serving Hera's interests, at others Athene's. For Zeus, though god, is in his passionate nature only a man. It is the anima who in the end decides the issue in favour of souls, and has the power to implement it. The matriarch, who gave birth to and ruled the world at the beginning, still rules, but rules in a transformed state, having on her part, like Athene, in contrary direction, passed through the crucible of men.

Inwardly, for the modern matriarch, this crucible is the animus. 'Crucible' being allied to 'crucifixion', she has not only to be crucified (that is divided) by her animus, but also in the end has to crucify him. (Flesh must be nailed to the slower-growing tree of life, and thereby redeem itself.) We have already seen this process at work in Pallas by her refusal to allow herself any responsive basic desire towards her father Pallas. She separates out her own basic nature from his, and is rewarded by the 'trophy' of his name (represented by an animal skin). Her refusal symbolises both crucifixions simultaneously. In crucifying her own internal desire, she also saves him. Crucifixion means at one and the same time division (two shafts cutting across each other) and wholeness (held together by a central point). It means not the original wholeness of undifferentiated unconsciousness but what results from the agony of being divided up, what may be described as the state of schizophrenia imposed by life's conditions on everyone, particularly on 'unfortunates' with disturbed childhoods, divorced parents or quarrelling parents — parents, that is to say, who have not themselves accepted the split nature of life but like Oedipus and his mother/wife still hanker after the original unity that cannot be regained. On the contrary, it means an integrated wholeness arrived at after the manifold splits of life (beginning with the incest taboo) have been accepted and found to be creative challenges which, if welcomed instead of being rejected, create a larger wholeness which cannot be destroyed (as the original wholeness can). Like a good engineering structure, it is held together by innumerable tensions between opposites equally balanced and honoured. The better balanced and the more tempered the materials, the lighter and easier to carry the whole structure becomes.

Athene's own nature is thus achieved not without conflict, but as a result of it. In the story of her birth out of the head of Zeus the conflict was in the mind of Zeus. But other versions of the myth show it as taking place within herself. In one the 'nature' side of herself which she overcomes is symbolised by a girl roughly of her own age, named Pallas. Once again, Triton the river or lake god figures as a father figure by adoption, causing her to be given the surname of Tritogeneia, "the terrible, the awakener of the din of battle, the chieftainess of armies, who rejoices in tumults, in wars and affrays".[16] In this version Triton undertook the task of bringing her up. Pallas was then the name of Triton's own daughter, and the two girls were associates. According to Apollodorus, "Athene and Pallas played the war-game together. As Pallas was about to strike Athene with her javelin, Zeus feared for his daughter and held in front of her his fear-awakening goatskin, the Aegis. Pallas turned aside her gaze and was mortally hit by Athene."[17] It is said that this contest was a 'friendly' one with spear and shield, and that it was 'by accident' that Athene slew Pallas. Accidents are typical dream motifs indicating unconscious desire prompted by the autonomous psyche (in this case emanating from Zeus, a Self symbol). It was in token of her subsequent grief that Athene set Pallas's name before her own.

In this myth it is clear that, of the two girls (two aspects of Athene), Pallas, as daughter on the one hand of Triton the nature-god (as opposed to Zeus the cultural one) and on the other hand of Pallas the father who, as we have seen, tried to rape her, symbolises the 'nature' side of Athene's personality. This is the side Athene, as cultural (or individuational) anima issuing from Zeus's head, had to separate out from herself, as she had rejected unbridled nature in the form of Pallas the father. And it was Zeus himself who came to her assistance. Once more we see Mother Nature too strong to tackle direct, and her unconscious tricks only to be overcome by mankind's more conscious 'trickery': superior wisdom of what the ultimate purpose of life is about. It is the action of the positive anima backed by the Self. "I come not to bring peace, but a sword", the sword which divides, which makes the split conscious, and acceptable as being the gateway to new life.

NOTES

1. Robert Graves, *The Greek Myths*, Harmondsworth, Penguin Books, 1955, vol. I, p. 87.
2. *Ibid.*, pp. 27, 289, 40.
3. C. Kerényi, *The Gods of the Greeks*, London, Thames and Hudson, 1951, pp. 114, 118.
4. *Ibid.*, p. 114.
5. Graves, vol. I, p. 46.
6. *Ibid.*
7. *Ibid.*
8. Kerényi, p. 119.
9. *Ibid.*, p. 156.
10. Graves, vol. I, p. 46.
11. Kerényi, p. 181.
12. Graves, vol. I, pp. 39-40.
13. Kerényi, p. 152.
14. Graves, vol. I, pp. 133-4.
15. Kerényi, p. 121.
16. *Ibid.*, p. 119.
17. *Ibid.*, p. 122.

APPENDIX III: SPLITTING OPEN THE HEAD

The symbolism is on a par with that of the birth of Athene out of the head of Zeus split open by Hephaestus. The parallel passage in this myth is that Zeus, though married to his sister-wife Hera, had a secret lover named Metis, who "turned into many shapes to escape him until she was caught at last and got with child". For reasons we go into in Appendix I, he "suddenly opened his mouth and swallowed her... "[1] In due process of time, he was seized by a raging headache as he walked by the shores of Lake Triton, so that his skull seemed about to burst, and he howled for rage until the whole firmament echoed. Up ran Hermes (the Interpreter, knowledgeable of hidden things), who at once divined the cause of Zeus's discomfort. "He persuaded Hephaestus...to fetch his wedge and beetle and make a breech in Zeus's skull, from which Athene sprang, fully armed, with a mighty shout." Other versions attribute this deed to Prometheus, and say that the instrument with which Athene was delivered was a hammer or double-edged sword, but that just given is the more usual. The birth symbolism of this cannot be doubted.

The parallel is very apt — birth pangs in the midst of battle. This consideration may help us to appreciate the archetypal significance of both the better known Greek story and the Celtic one as well. To begin with, Athene, like Olwen, is a 'father's daughter', and Hephaestus, who acts as male midwife at the birth of Athene out of her father's head, is himself, like Culhwch (whose surrogate in the Celtic myth is Cadw), a 'mother's son'. He is by birth mainly matrilineal, since, according to several accounts regarding him, Hera conceived him parthenogenetically, without concourse with Zeus or any other male. Hera is known to have been a pre-Hellenic earth goddess, and her union with Zeus as chief goddess of Olympia is commonly held to symbolise the conquest of Greece by the Hellenes and the absorption by them of the pre-Hellenes. That does not, however, preclude interpretation on a psychological level also, since history and the development of consciousness go hand in hand; cultural and spiritual happenings are but two aspects of one another. Hera was matriarchal, if in no other way than by her constant nagging of Zeus, her obvious dislike of his patriarchal sway, and her jealousy of his many love affairs showing his independence of her. It is evident also by the sons she bore on her own account, without being impregnated by him. Some of these have fathers provided for them in some versions, but she had a marked tendency towards parthenogenesis. She is not said to have been a sow, although her contemporary Demeter's sacrificial animal was one. So although Hera herself was not a sow, one of her lover-sons, Ares the war god, had as his emblem the wild boar, and, when flying to Egypt from the giants, took the form of one, while Hera took that of a cow, thus identifying herself with Isis.[2] So she is not far off from boar mythology, and in her character as destructive matriarch reveals the reason for her spite; for it is said to have been Hera who, as Earth Mother, produced the horrible monster Typhon (later identified with the Egyptian Set who was the boar).[3]

This reveals the same problem of the 'two mothers' (the 'two-headed briar'): the frantic jealousy of the matriarchy when faced with the new phenomenon of men seeking to establish their own autonomy and its symbol, the anima figure Athene, a female figure sprung out of the male psyche and upholding 'chastity', that is to say independence from the possessive mother-image. It also reveals the destructive lengths to which the matriarchy will go to prevent this, and the 'male' form this matriarchal opposition takes, which is that of producing out of the mother only, unaided by man, a 'matriarchal son', Typhon, in opposition to the father: a son whom she can rely on to uphold the matriarchal position against the father since it is she who gave birth to him and suckled him out of her own untransformed fatherless and husbandless nature.

This is a form which the woman's negative animus often takes, even in our own society, valuing the son (who issued from her and is, to her, her own male image) more than the father; the latter represents the 'other' or patriarchal line, and relationship with him would demand an 'otherness' or spirituality in her which she is not prepared (or is not mature enough) to concede. The father succumbs (in jealousy or henpeckedness or general feebleness) unless he, like Zeus, has been able to engender within himself an anima figure such as Athene (or, in terms of our story, Culhwch can contact Olwen).

223

In terms of the Greek myth (as also in real life) the father cannot, however, do this without help from the matriarch herself. So, in this myth, help comes from another of Hera's sons, Hephaestus, whom (in contrast to Typhon), she valued so little that she threw him into the sea, because he was so weak when he was born. In this respect of being unusual, Hephaestus resembles Culhwch, who also was mythologically 'fatherless' in so far as he was born of a mother who shunned human habitation (that is, her husband's house) and went mad. The old matriarchal order always 'casts away' that which might lead on to the new, making it out to be ugly, deformed, or simply unwanted. Such misfits, precisely because they are so, tend all the more to be transition figures, forced by their situation to break new paths, carrying the virtues of the old order, without its vices, over into the new. Another such figure is the dwarf mentioned in task nineteen, who alone has the bottles in which the blood of the Black Witch can be kept warm, that is to say can carry over the life-blood of the matriarch into the patriarchy, since nothing can be founded on a vacuum and the old is the indispensable foundation for anything new. The transition process destroys nothing, but, in preserving, changes the relative positions of the constituents. Instead of the mother image being externally dominant, with the son under her control, the son acquires an internal anima, derived from the mother but free from her. These two opposite poles of femininity are symbolised in our myth by Culhwch's mother and his sister-anima Olwen, in the Greek myth by Hera and Athene.

Each of these anima figures has forerunners in the form of a 'second', 'patrilineal' mother who rescued him. For Culhwch it was the stepmother, and for Hephaestus it was two sea goddesses (Thetis and Eurynome) who rescued him when Hera had cast him into the sea, took him to their bosoms and kept him for nine years. This duality runs through the whole Hephaestus story, as it does through that of Culhwch. The very opposite to the jealous and enraged Hera, who creates the monster Typhon, is Metis, whom Zeus internalised and of whom it was said that she should bear 'exceedingly wise children'. It was she, a function of Zeus himself, who was the real 'mother' of Athene. Zeus "put her in his own belly", so that it was inside himself that Athene was nurtured to be "equal to Zeus in courage and wise counsel".[4] She was born out of his head, the seat of conscious understanding and the man's psychic 'womb'. Thus while Hephaestus was 'mother's son', Athene was 'father's daughter'. But, as with Culhwch, it needed the 'mother's son' to deliver the 'father's daughter'. This could not happen till Culhwch submitted to Arthur. In the more complex case of Hephaestus, however, there was much quarrelling between him and Zeus. On one occasion he sought to aid his mother against Zeus, but his father seized him by the heel and hurled him from Olympus for the second time, thus crippling him still further and bearing out this matriarchal tendency. On another occasion, he bound Hera until he had forced from her the confession that he had been born parthenogenetically. He was somewhat ambivalent: though a cripple, he also was the master craftsman and smith of classical Greek mythology. Thus, as mother's son and cripple, on entering the father world through the help of the sea goddesses, he became by way of complementary opposite the powerful artificer. It was in his patriarchal capacity of smith and craftsman that he smote Zeus's head and out of it sprang, fully armed, the all-wise Athene. One of these aspects of Athene was the 'natural daughter', the other, the transforming or transformed one, the anima.

Of the various 'fathers' attributed to her (which included Poseidon, but she preferred Zeus and asked him to adopt her), Athene did not have to defend herself from Zeus, because she issued forth from his own intelligence. But she did have to defend herself from the male Pallas, another parent attributed to her. Furthermore, in defending Athene from the female Pallas, daughter of Triton, Zeus was in fact implementing his fatherly jealousy, since 'Pallas' here symbolises almost certainly Triton's natural desire. ("First the natural man, then the spiritual man," says Paul.) In taking Pallas as her forename, Athene — that is to say those among whom the Athene-myth grew up — made due and public acknowledgement of the fact that, to whatever extent nature may and must be transformed, nature herself remains the inescapable basis of spiritual life. Athene's mourning for the lost Pallas is not at all unlike Demeter's mourning for the lost Persephone.

In another myth, Athene's father was one Itonus "whose daughter Iodama she killed by accidentally letting her see the Gorgon's head, and so changing her into a block of stone... "[5] This myth is similar to the last, and refers to the worship of the moon as a cow, the horned moon being connected with rain. This would indicate an ancient moon goddess's statue. Once more we have the motif of the accident. Athene also carried an image of the Gorgon's head as a clasp on her clothing as a sign that she had conquered the terrible earth mother and used her strength.

These myths, like many others, symbolise the creative tragedy of life, the fact that Nature must die, which we deplore, for something stronger and that does not die to grow up in its place, founded on nature but replacing it. "I could not love thee, dear, so much, loved I not honour more" (Richard Lovelace, "To Lucasta, Going to the Wars"). It is the eternal tragic love story of man torn from various loves to seek a wider life. The tearing of the umbilical cord with mother — or with self-regard — is never sought. It is imposed both from within and without through the inevitable working of the incest taboo, which acts on so many levels that we never get to the end of them. In the end we have to turn and seek the anima internally, who will do battle for our souls as no man can, since she derives her strength from the Earth Mother whom she has superseded.

. These myths also refer to the incest taboo regarding the father. They are all veiled as father-incest dreams are apt to be, since this involves a very deep psychic level. Less veiled is the problem of incest with Athene's 'brother' Hephaestus. These were not brother and sister physically even in the mythological sense, since Hephaestus was brought forth by Hera (with her parthenogenetic tendency), and Athene was born in opposite manner out of the head of Zeus. Theirs was therefore a relationship between opposites of spiritual or psychic brother-sisterhood. The following myth shows how Hephaestus tried to turn it into a physical one and how Athene parried this, with the result that what was actually born of their union was the *puer aeternus* or divine child of the Athenian Acropolis. "On one occasion, in the course of the Trojan war, not wishing to borrow arms from Zeus, who had declared himself neutral, she asked Hephaestus to make her a set of her own. Hephaestus refused payment saying coyly that he would undertake the work for love; and when, missing the implication of these words, she entered the smithy to watch him beat out the red-hot metal, he suddenly turned about and tried to outrage her [Poseidon having tricked him into expecting her consent]... As she tore herself away, Hephaestus ejaculated against her thigh, a little above the knee. She wiped off the seed with a handful of wool [Erichthonius signifies 'wool on the earth'], which she threw away in disgust; it fell to the ground near Athens, and accidentally fertilised Mother Earth, who was on a visit there. Revolted at the prospect of bearing a child which Hephaestus had tried to father on Athene, Mother Earth declared that she would accept no responsibility for its upbringing. 'Very well,' said Athene, 'I will take care of it myself.' So she took charge of the infant as soon as it was born, called him Erichthonius and, not wishing Poseidon to laugh at the success of his practical joke, hid him in a sacred basket; this she gave to Aglauros, eldest daughter of the Athenian king Cecrops, with orders to guard it carefully. Cecrops, a son of Mother Earth and, like Erichthonius...part man, part serpent, was the first king to recognise paternity... He also instituted monogamy."[6] Erichthonius was also king of Athens... Another myth has it that Hephaestus tried to ravish Athene on the plain of Marathon.

We can be sure that stories such as this reveal rather than conceal deep meanings. Erichthonius was the divine child of the Athenian Acropolis[7], and was the non-physical child (even in the myth) of Hephaestus by Athene, a sister-anima figure for him. The whole story is bound up on the one hand with the institution of patrilineal descent, and on the other with the attainment of individuality, of which 'monogamy' is a symbol, being, as we have seen, the sign of the anima-relationship. A man has only one anima or 'soul'.

Finally, Hephaestus brought into the world not only Athene. "He created young virgins made of gold, who moved as if they were alive, and thought and talked and worked,"[8] to help him in his smithy. He also fashioned the first woman, Pandora, the very antithesis of Athene, and yet Athene also had a hand in this. Hesiod gives two versions of it. In each version the cause of this disaster was Zeus's anger at Prometheus's theft of fire from the gods. "Anger filled Zeus's heart, when he beheld the light, visible from afar, of the fires kindled by men. He straightway prepared for men an evil thing that would weigh equal with the boon of fire. 'Son of Iapetos,' quoth Zeus, 'thou art wiser than all of us, thou hast rejoiced that thou hast stolen fire and hast deceived me. This shall work harm unto thyself and unto men yet to be. For they shall receive from me, in retaliation for the theft of fire, an evil thing in which they will all rejoice,

226

surrounding with love their own pain.' Thus spoke the Father of Gods and Men, and laughed aloud. He bade Hephaestus straightway to mix earth with water, to set in it a voice and strength, and to create a desire-awakening beautiful maiden, whose face should be like those of the immortal goddesses. Athene was ordered to teach her womanly crafts and weaving. Golden Aphrodite was ordered to encompass her head with the radiance of lovely charm and rending desires. Hermes had Zeus's command to fill the figure with bitchy shamelessness and treachery. They all did as the ruler had bidden. The famed master-craftsman fashioned from earth the likeness of a bashful maiden. Pallas Athene adorned it with girdle and raiment... The Messenger of the Gods furthermore gave her a voice, and named the woman Pandora, since all the Olympians had created her as a gift to the bane of men... "[9]

The name Pandora means " 'the rich in gifts', 'the all-giving': a name also of the Earth itself, of which she was made."[10] Yet what she gives is evil as well as good; from her box came all the spites. In pictures of her on vases, "she often appears only as a mighty and beautiful head of a woman" rising out of the earth in response to the hammer blows which created her — an interesting parallel to the hammer blow on Zeus's head that produced Athene. She may have let loose all passions, "yet primordial men...[who in the vase paintings are depicted as Silenoi or Satyrs] would never have received the gift of woman, rising like a full moon in their midst, beneath hammers and picks, had not Mother Earth been willing to bestow on them her own image". Kerényi says of her that "she came from earth and was associated with Earth by name as an *alter ego*".[11]

Let us examine the contrasexuality of the birth symbolism. Zeus, the man, gives birth, like a woman, to a full-grown female 'child' out of his male head. The woman thus born issues forth from it fully armed, as though she were a man, to defend her maidenhood, since she is the anima and belongs to no man but him whose anima she is and will remain. What in a physical birth would be a child's first cry in drawing its first breath is here replaced, in contrary motion, by a shout of triumph at the transformation that has thus taken place. The scene is pregnant with meaning, and this very phrase 'pregnant with meaning' symbolises the same thing; namely, that 'meaning' (wisdom which shows the other side of things) is female when it proceeds out of the masculine function of 'thinking', when this has already inwardly received and digested a sufficient degree of feminine perception originally entering it from the outside. This is what is conveyed by the myth of Zeus previously having 'swallowed' Metis, his secret Mistress. She and her offspring Athene seem to Hera to be utterly opposed to her own interests, and she vents her fury against her by producing (contrasexually again) the destructive monster Typhon. Only Zeus, that is to say the male perceptive intellect, knows, however, that Metis is the inner meaning of Hera, of which Hera, in her capacity of primitive matriarch uninfluenced by the male spirit (that is to say 'thinking'), is ignorant. She considers it hostile to her, as it is indeed hostile to 'mother nature' as yet untouched by man and not wanting to be. The female

227

function can only have its own inner meaning mediated to itself by means of the male function (and *vice versa*): we naturally think here of C.G. Jung, whose own male function was used to investigate these things. Zeus therefore internalises that part of the female function (Metis) which he can 'catch hold of' as the myth says, and by her becomes himself pregnant of Athene; but not without much mental upheaval symbolised by the headache — his mental labour pains. Athene (the man's anima, the 'patriarchal' and therefore 'virginal' woman) is the direct antithesis or complementary opposite to the matriarch Hera.

But Metis, the go-between, is still ambivalent, as shown by a further detail of the story. When Zeus got her with child, "an oracle of Mother Earth then declared that this would be a girl-child and that, if Metis conceived again, she would bear a son who was fated to depose Zeus, just as Zeus had deposed Cronus, and Cronus had deposed Uranus".[12] This, it will be remembered, was the sort of thing that Hera hoped for in giving birth to Typhon. But Zeus wanted no male rival (the girl was no rival but his own female complement), and it was for this reason that he had swallowed Metis, preventing her from producing a son. The contrasexuality and the duality go on. Hephaestus becomes a male midwife (with hammer blows of hard thinking) in two opposite ways, bringing to light Athene from the man's head, and her opposite Pandora from the earth.

A basic truth to be got out of all this is that, in so far as the whole body of a man symbolises a phallus and his head the glans penis, what is meant by this is that, in the transformation process which all these myths foreshadow, the phallus is transformed into its opposite, a male uterus. Its function is to produce the 'treasure', which may take any symbolic form, but which is ultimately the anima. It can, however, like everything, appear as good or evil. In the case of Athene the result was immediately good. In the case of both boars in the Celtic myth, the boar's head carries implements for trimming the hair, which we have seen to be a symbolic circumcision, head (beard) hair corresponding to the foreskin of the glans penis. The boar's head symbolises both phallus (in so far as the boar is physically male) and uterus (in so far as the boar represents the mother's attacking animus). The tusk would on the surface represent the father's hostile penis; in its more inner meaning it represents the mother's 'tooth', or teeth of the *vagina dentata*, by means of which women paralyse and castrate their men. In other words the mother sees to it that her son can serve no woman but herself. This imagery is clearer in the case of the Twrch Trwyth, the shears symbolising her two powerful sharp jaws, and the comb that which makes the hair (psychosexual libido) subservient to their malign action. Thus we have, in the boar, a hermaphrodite symbol standing for both parental images at once (as in the islands neighbouring on Malekula, actual hermaphrodite or intersex tusked pigs are reared as the supreme sacrificial animals).

Whether the tusk symbolises the father's hostile penis, or whether the shears symbolise the mother's *vagina dentata*, these things are 'treasures'; that is to say they are only hostile and deadly when possessed by the boar. When seized from him, they become precious. They then symbolise the hero's individuality rescued from the parental matrix, and so available to him as his own 'soul-substance', his guarantee of independent manhood and personal survival.

NOTES

1. Robert Graves, *The Greek Myths*, Harmondsworth, Penguin Books, vol. I, p. 46.

2. *Ibid.,* pp. 52, 134.

3. C. Kerényi, *The Gods of the Greeks*, London, Thames and Hudson, 1951, p. 151.

4. *Ibid.,* p. 119.

5. Graves, vol. I, p. 49.

6. *Ibid.,* pp. 96-7.

7. Kerényi, p. 123.

8. Graves, vol. I, p. 87.

9. Kerényi, pp. 71-2.

10. *Ibid.,* p. 219.

11. *Ibid.*

12. Graves, vol. I, p. 46.

APPENDIX IV: THE INCEST TABOO

As stated in Appendix III, these myths regarding the father and sister are all somewhat veiled, since the father-incest problem lies very far back in psychological development and psychic level, and the sister-problem belongs to a deep level also, since it is a purely internal one and ultimately has to do with the mother.

The problem of incest with Athene's 'brother' Hephaestus is less veiled partly, presumably, because the brother-sister relationship is on a more conscious level than that with either parent, and also because it has in it the germs of the future since they are age-mates and any progeny issuing from them would be the result of a relationship between equals. While incest between parents and children belongs to the 'cave period' of human psychology, that is to say it symbolises a complete return into the womb, brother-sister incest is that which carries with it the connotation of 'own anima' and 'own animus', capable of issuing outside the primitive cave of unconscious reactions. It is in its external manifestation the basic marriage relationship in the most ancient of royal families, and in its internal meaning it symbolises the *hieros gamos* or union with the soul. As mentioned in Appendix III, in this instance it produced a divine child who represented a spiritual entity.

229

There can be more than one kind of brother-sister relationship. The two can be full brother and sister by the same two parents, they can be children of the same mother by different fathers (the matrilineal line therefore being more important than the patrilineal), of the same father by different mothers (thus reckoned patrilineally). In no system of kinship based on strict bilateral exogamy can any of these marry. There is, however, a fourth kind of brother-sister relationship 'at one remove' which is at one and the same time the most primitive form of marriage in a rigidly organised mandala-like society, and is also found mythologically in the mystical association of such a pair as Athene and Hephaestus.

It is a matter of interest that this pair should be thought of in this order, with Athene named first, instead of Hephaestus. The natural order would be naming the husband before the wife, in a patrilineal society. This is a typical reversal of values belonging both to the highest and to the lowest forms of human development. And this in turn emphasizes the fact of how the highest and the lowest meet, such as we have already seen in the character of the 'hero' Culhwch, who is no hero in the ordinary sense of the word at all, that is to say one who carries all before him in an obvious and visible way. The hero is so often, on the contrary, an extremely 'poor fellow', complexed and twisted (like the cripple Hephaestus). He is forced to go abnormal ways because he is so different from the beginning — a prime sufferer — and is therefore impelled against his will and against everybody else's to go a highly individual way — often away from or 'above' the collective way. He finds internally those comforts and experiences and deep wells of forced insight that he is denied in external life on account of his very 'oddness'. That eventually he comes out on top is due only to his uncompromising search, which is not a matter of nobility but one of absolute necessity.

"Necessity is the mother of invention" is a good motto for this, and it is not chance that it is the 'mother' and not the 'father'. For, on the level of human society, mere survival is the most urgent matter for every primitive community. Primitive kinship, which is what knits human weaklings together (fantastically weak physically in face of the forces of nature which they are up against) into a force strong enough to conquer all nature, is always based on matrilineal descent, however patrilineal the external organisation of the tribe may be. So also the modern 'hero' is the world's greatest weakling, driven through utter necessity and despair to take the course prompted by his own weakness and its enormous need, the course his deeply repressed individuality demands. However masculine the body may be, this individuality is a female thing. It is the power of the Great Mother, concentrated in him for lack of ordinary warm human relationship with his actual human mother, who in hero myths has often deserted him. The father may have, and usually has, deserted him also, but this is concomitant on the mother's desertion of her son. The father may even be the prime mover, as in so many myths such as the Oedipus one, and, as Zeus in the Metis incident, refusing out of jealousy to have a son.

And so the lack of relationship with the actual mother builds up in the deserted son such an immense chaos of mother-seeking desire, which is a female thing, as to overwhelm him utterly, unless he can find some other outlet for it. This is the basis for schizophrenic or hysterical episodes on the one hand: the impetus behind the desire remains hidden and unknown. This leads to every kind of projection on to irrelevent objects, particularly on those who should be 'near and dear' to him, against whom his hatred most naturally concentrates itself as carrying the image of the rejecting and therefore rejected mother. For all such projections are ambivalent in the highest degree, representing the deepest need for the mother.

But this intense need and desire, once it is realised where it rightfully be-longs, can be given an altogether different channel. It can be directed inward, against itself, in order to fulfil itself. For the Great Mother is within, as well as without. Without, she may be impregnable. She is then represented by society, the wife, the husband, son, daughter, friend, business associate, any one in author-ity or having a claim on him. In cases of severe schizophrenia in which human relationships are almost entirely cut off, she is to be seen in chairs and tables, any-thing one may knock up against, the walls of a padded cell which confine and therefore have to be attacked, the wireless, waves of electric radiation of every kind tormenting one, voices 'out of the blue' (really out of the 'red' interior), and so on. In primitive society she manifests herself in animistic beliefs in the 'personality' of winds, trees, mountains, birds, animals both great and small. In more highly developed societies she appears as a devouring goddess with trains of lesser mythological beings fulfilling differing functions of her all-pervasive influence, many of which may be imagined as male gods doing her bidding or, in yet higher societies in which the male principle of transformed nature is beginning to show itself, as opposing her. In yet 'higher' forms of religion the female prin-ciple becomes more and more masked, gods replace goddesses, but the feminine principle still lies behind them all, namely that principle which 'has to be obeyed'.

In early infancy, externally it is the power of the mother that predominates. And that which 'has to be obeyed' internally by the infant is its own demanding desire, the fulfilment of which is quite literally a matter of life or death. This is the desire shown by Culhwch in his overweening imperiousness, not even fright-ened of Arthur, however dependent he is on him. For 'Arthur', in the depths of his being, though male, is that which will lead him to the anima, Olwen, the trans-formed mother image which, on the 'sister' level, and therefore the psycho-sexual one replacing the breast, will give him all the satisfaction he was deprived of by his sow-mother in the human and spiritual sphere.

Culhwch's imperiousness is not asking or begging for attention as an adult might, recognising that the other person has problems, but demanding it as right. It is fitting that the hero do this as a representative carrier of the future for the human race, and in particular for his own individuality. The mother is, for him, no human being, but the Great Mother who *must* instantly comply. For the infant he himself is the lord, the mother his slave. He himself is the only human, that is to say sentient thing existing, and the mother is the prime archetype — the Great Mother on whom absolutely everything depends to satisfy his sentient needs. Moreover she is a Great Mother, not to be prayed to but to be coerced, as Culhwch coerced Arthur (threatening to ruin his honour if he did not comply). Arthur as male mother consented willingly and with delight and reverence, calling him 'chieftain' as a mother regards her offspring as important. Arthur later coerced the boar, forcing it to yield up its treasure as a child forces its mother to yield up hers. Olwen refuses to be coerced by Culhwch, thus reversing the role of the Great Mother, who first gives and then withholds; the anima first refuses and then gives. The Great Mother gives natural satisfaction but withholds the spiritual part. The anima refuses natural satisfaction, but gives the spirit that frees and releases the spirit from its own trammels.

This is what Athene also does to Hephaestus. But let us examine the similarity between these two highly spiritual couples, its relation to primitive kinship, and how the very 'highest' and the very 'lowest', the most advanced and the most primitive, here meet.

Man is, for his size, physically the weakest and most defenceless of animals. But psychically he is the strongest. I want once more to emphasise the twin phenomena of weakness and strength in primitive communities. This is vital to our thesis of the 'hero' as being the weakest of the weak becoming the strongest of the strong. One of the sources of that strength is that extraordinary institution, the incest taboo. How could mother nature ever have thought of such restriction of her most vital activity and constant joy? The answer is that she did not, but that 'her husband' did; 'he' wanted to keep 'his wife' to himself. There is a great deal of evidence that it was originally the husband's jealousy in driving off his son that was the main factor bringing the incest taboo about. This is indeed a case of good coming out of evil. It gave rise to two factors that concern us here. It caused a split inside the family between what is *symbolically* the 'mother's son' (that is to say the mother's natural desire towards her son — her animus independent of the father), and on the other hand the 'father's daughter' (that is to say the father's desire towards his wife). Between the *actual* parents in the family, this brought about warfare; in so far as the father succeeded in pressing his claims, his jealousy was calmed; but the conflict was now in the mother's breast, between desire for her husband and her desire for her 'son'. If she continued to prefer the 'son' (for in primitive societies her son was her animus personified), there would be no society. The impetus for her to do so is strong, for her son issues from her and is of the same substance, though differing in sex. The father would remain an outsider (as he is in actual fact in extreme matriarchal societies) and there would be no real union between her family and his, that is to say the families would not be cross-fertilised in a cultural sense. Each would stagnate in its own lair. There would be no new blood. There would be no co-operation, and, for lack of it, each family unit could be easily mopped up by its enemies. Each nuclear unit would in fact be enemies of the next, since the mother's brother would tend to guard his own rights and those of his sister's son against those of the father, and there would be conflict without co-operation.

The essence of society is conflict *with* co-operation. Neither can be eliminated. Adjustments must be made if each party is not to perish. So, once the mother has acceded to her husband's rights over against those of her son, destructive conflict ends, and constructive conflict begins. This is the central theme of the myth of *Culhwch and Olwen*, as it is also of Hera and Zeus, and of Athene and Hephaestus. This constructive conflict has as its result (if not its purpose) the creation of 'spirit children' in the form of internalised psychic powers resulting from the self-assertion of the husband over against his fear of the wife's family, and the acceptance of this by both mother and son. The latter becomes thereby his 'father's son' as well as a 'mother's son'. The 'father's daughter' (the anima) remains in the background, as she does in many myths, having (symbolically as the father's desire) set the whole process going. He naturally tries to keep her to himself, 'eating his cake and having it' by claiming his rights over his wife without relinquishing those over his daughter. Just as his wife had, however, to yield up her rights over her son, so in the end (but only at the very end) does the husband have to yield up his rights over his daughter.

This argument can only be understood if we hold two thoughts in our mind at once. It has been stated more in terms of actual physical wife and husband, as well as to a certain extent physical son and daughter. Ultimately all these represent psychic functions, but for our purpose here we have regarded the wife and husband as being of the flesh. Son and daughter are 'spirit children' representing respectively the mother's animus and the father's anima. In a state of nature these four are inextricably intertwined, since neither the wife nor the husband are individuals in their own right. They are just tools used by unconscious forces intent on the propagation of the race, quite oblivious to the fate of any individuals concerned. The parents *are* primordially animus and anima, and it is as such that they mate. They are governed by instinctive drives, to which they are enslaved, and as such they cannot make individual relationships. They thus cannot co-operate for any purpose other than the propagation of children. Co-operation between individuals can be said to begin with conflict, when it is realised that the two have different aims, which have nevertheless to be reconciled.

The conflict was originally between rival males competing for women. This led not to the formation of society but to the negation of it: small family groups all living in isolation from one another, the males of which were mutually hostile. (In most animal species, even if the males band together as adolescents for co-operative hunting or on feeding grounds, they separate out hostilely in the rutting season. Such animals are a prey not only to those animals that are physically stronger or more cunning individually, but much more so to man.) Man, having faced not only external dangers but at least some of his conflicts internally, has released powers in himself capable of ruling not only the animal world, but conquering somewhat beyond as well.

This shift from animal-like conflict to a more cultural one, leading to society, has been achieved by means of the incest taboo: this changes the direction of the conflict from that of man with man to man with woman. This may sound odd to a generation brought up on the idea that love is simple and easy and 'natural'. Love, the love that makes marriage and gives rise to society, is not completely 'natural'. It is a highly complex artefact built out of conflict. We have only to observe the natural kingdom in which males never injure females but only other males, and then turn to contemplate the growth of civilisation: men beat their wives so frequently or nag them, and women nag their men and sometimes beat them or attack them with their nails. Love in this setting is not to be equated with straightforward desire as with the animals (it may or may not be joined to it). Love starts with conflict between men and women, not with desire between them, which can be quickly satisfied. Love, with love conflict, not only directs the conflict towards women; it also directs it inwardly. When a woman fights back, a man must regulate his own desires. This is a problem common to all mankind and so brings about fellow-sympathy among them, an understanding with all others inflicted with the same disability of basic frustration both inwardly and outwardly, and so tends to create friendship and co-operation.

In primitive societies this 'friendship' (the first outside the biological family group of blood-relatives) is, between men, first commonly directed towards the wife's brother, who, but for the incest taboo, would be a man's rival and enemy, since he would be the prime 'possessor' of the first man's wife, his own sister. Nothing could illustrate more clearly this change of direction of love and hostility. The male rival has become the friend, while the wife (so gently treated and respected if he were an animal) has become a subject whom the husband has the right to chastise. If he abuses this right too much so as to cause her brother to interfere, he will now do so only in cases of extreme mishandling; he recognises the husband's emotional need for frustrated outlet against the object he 'loves' (or is beginning to), together with society's upholding of it if it does not go too far. The amount of latitude varies immensely from tribe to tribe, but the conflict is always there — and is at its greatest in the early stages of patrilineality.

These are general considerations affecting all humanity. The problem has been further outlined in a short article entitled *The Incest Taboo and the Virgin Archetype* (the theme of which was taken up by C.G. Jung in *The Psychology of the Transference*). The thesis I advanced there was a preliminary answer to the self-imposed question of what was the purpose of the incest taboo, and what happened to the repressed libido formerly attached by any son to his mother and secondarily to his sister. The conclusion drawn was that, like all shadow phenomena (in this case phenomena due to repression or non-realisation of drives), this was split into two. One part went into sexual and emotional satisfaction with the nearest female object available — the wife — under the rule of endogamy. The other part, still deprived of its primary incestuous object, is forced to seek this object and, not finding it outwardly in the form of the external endogamous partner, is itself split into two. This double-bloomed shadow of the *satisfied* sexual and emotional drive we may call 'anger' and 'hope', or better 'aggression' and 'desire'. Each of these can be directed both outwardly towards the permitted external partner and inwardly towards the internal image of the mother or sister, with whom he is still emotionally involved. This image is still the old Earth Mother with all her ambivalence, of which his image is but a reflection, through his identification with her. If he can disidentify and so objectify her, that is to say observe dispassionately his own emotional attitudes towards his numerous problems, she can become his soul. Soul-making, in any case, is the job she relegates to him. She is, in a sense, the ultimate goal of all religious striving. But she appears bisexual. The 'good mother' in her appears female, the 'bad mother' male.

In our myth she is encountered direct only at the very end, when Arthur has eliminated the male boars. She first appears however as the 'sister' of equal age who, contrary to the Earth Mother who first gives and then refuses, at first is withheld, but when he has done battle with her father, the mother's negative animus, gives herself to him. What she 'gives' is his individuality. The 'mother's son' unites with the 'father's daughter'. She then, as his step-mother's daughter, leads him back to the Earth Mother in her beneficent aspect.

We must not, however, forget that the hero always starts as a forsaken waif, with megalomania to compensate himself for it. His life-story consists in the gradual acceptance of his forsakenness, which thereby changes from the weakness of waifdom into the self-reliance of finding an interior strength, that of the anima. The battles he has to wage are with his own indignation at being faced with this task, not knowing, or only gradually finding out, that they are his great opportunity, and sometimes having to have a helper, as Culhwch did with Arthur, to point this out.

This 'waifness' is common not only, at the beginning of their lives, to all heroes in the myths. It is also a situation in which primitive man finds himself. He does not know, any more than the waif does, what lies ahead. He has no part in any great civilisation to back him up, or to swim in, carried along on its strong tide. He is so weak and isolated, so small a thing in the world surrounding him, that his first task — man's first task everywhere — is to consolidate himself.

I have already pointed out how, in primitive society, what may here be called 'solidarity between weaklings' is the basis of strength in the battle for survival which every primitive community is engaged in. Without admission of weakness there could be no effort towards co-operation, and without co-operation there could be no society. Just as submission to weakness in the mother-child relationship (each being 'weak' towards the other according to the 'strength' of their mutual desire and need to satisfy it) is the foundation of its strength for the future, and for the very survival of the child, so also it is the admission of weakness that leads to strength. These tiny societies of 'weak ones co-operating', whom we now look on, where they survive, as being so 'backward', are the giants on whom our whole human development is based. They are, in mythological terms, the 'dwarfs' so apt to be despised, but who have in them the wisdom of the ages if we can but stoop to hear them murmur it. It is worth while therefore to examine briefly the foundation of this strength, which will be seen to be the same strength on which was founded the birth of Athene and the apotheosis of Olwen.

The relationship between Athene and Hephaestus consists of a 'mother's son' and 'father's daughter'. They are children respectively of a married sister and brother, though not visibly proceeding from their union but conceived of as having been given birth to separately by each parent parthenogenetically. In order to compare this with primitive kinship, this relationship may now be represented as follows:

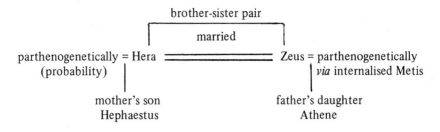

If we now turn to the most primitive kinship systems known to us, we find in many of them a similar pattern; the customary marriage is that between a pair of children whose parents are sister and brother in such a way that the 'mother's son' marries the 'father's daughter' not through the parents' own union:

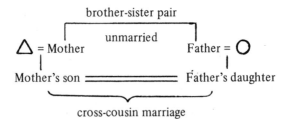

This may seem an unusual way of expressing the well-known institution of 'cross-cousin marriage', found throughout the world in many of the most primitive communities, in which every man marries his mother's brother's daughter. His wife's father is at the same time his mother's brother. I have expressed it in this way because, in this section of our account, we are working backwards against the stream of human development towards its origins, stripping off the disguises that

236

have accrued during that development in such a way that the character that originally was both mother's brother and wife's father has in mythology gradually
been deprived of its connotation as 'mother's brother' and appears starkly as only
the 'wife's father'. This progressive falsification of the issue is not only typical of
the prejudice of a predominantly patriarchal society. It is also due to an increas-
ing unconscious fear of the mother, and therefore relegation of her into the background of consciousness. The image of the 'bad mother' peeps out in children's
tales about witches, but is largely banished from the mind in adult life. Thus in
the earlier myth of Zeus and Hera there is no concealment of the fact (though it
is soft-pedalled and never mentioned as such) that Zeus is not only Athene's
father but is also Hephaestus's mother's brother. But in the later tale of Culhwch
and Olwen this fact has disappeared. Ysbaddaden Pencawr is referred to only as
Olwen's father. His *wife*, however, is a sort of double for Culhwch's mother: she
is her sister. The fact that he represented Culhwch's mother's negative animus
(which is the psychological equivalent to mother's brother, always negative from
the rival patriarchal point of view) was further deducible on general psychological
grounds backed up by his close association with the boar, the 'husband-brother'
of Culhwch's mother the sow.

Before we pass on to examine this more clearly in the light of yet more primitive kinship, another factor is due to be emphasised. However overtly patrilineal
primitive societies may be, kinship is always primarily reckoned through women,
that is to say through the female, ultimately the matrilineal line. Thus, in the kinship systems now being cited, it is the boy's father who seeks a bride for him, not
from among his patrilineal people, but from among the boy's mother's. The father
will go to the boy's mother's brother (his own wife's sister), and ask whether he
can provide his son with a bride. When the mother's brother consents, he gives
him either his own daughter or her equivalent in the kinship system. This is the
basic pattern. Two things thus follow the female track: kinship and spirituality,
not excluding organised religion. With regard to religion, I may cite Malekula,
where specially reared boars with artificially elongated tusks are sacrificed on a
stone platform representing the female (mother) principle, but before the sacrifi-
cer can approach the boar he has himself reared for sacrifice, he finds his way
barred by his mother's brothers who demand payment before letting him pass.
But it is these same mother's brothers who confer on him the titles and insignia
of his new birth arising from the sacrifice. This is an institutionalised proceeding
combining straightforward kinship ritual relationships with deep psychological
fact: the mother's brothers symbolise the mother's hostility to her son's liberation (the payment to them is an indemnification), after which they willingly yield
up the treasure of renewed life on a deeper plane — deeper psychologically, but at
the same time higher in hierarchical social and religious status. This is no isolated
phenomenon. It is basic to many religions, however concealed the function of the
'mother's brother' may be under the cloak of the priestly 'father'. So also the
anima comes basically through matrilineality in all its aspects since, though

237

mediated through the father (as primitive marriage is), her basic characteristic is that, like Athene, she is the hero's mother's brother's daughter. She is the internal *'alter ego'*, issuing from the aggressive aspect of a man's own ability for 'gestation'.

Closely connected with this is yet another fact. Although Athene and Hephaestus were born of a pair who were not only brother and sister but also married to one another, which might be thought to presuppose at least a common interest in their children, each was born more or less parthenogenetically in direct opposition to this union. It was as though Zeus and Hera were the most deadly enemies, and needed to eliminate one another's natures in their respective progenies. In point of fact, these natures were not eliminated, but simply reversed: Hephaestus was a cripple, the direct opposite of the glorious Zeus; Athene was a virgin, calm and serene in counsel but openly warlike against her enemies, the direct opposite of the matriarch Hera who was married, far from serene in her constant nagging of Zeus, and scheming rather than warlike. This has a psychological connotation as well as one in primitive kinship. Psychologically, brother and sister are so well known to one another from birth up and so used to one another's company that, while consciously thinking that they know all about each other they are, on account of this mutual projection, unconsciously most ignorant of one another and utterly different from their own views of each other. Thus from the viewpoint of Zeus and Hera, she, who thought of herself as being such a loving and faithful wife, produced a cripple as her animus (though she rejected the knowledge of it), indicating her own crippled attitude towards Zeus. Zeus, on the other hand, who in his life was so constantly unfaithful and so promiscuous in his loves, produced Athene the virgin, the constant and never unfaithful one. It will be noticed however that there is one great difference between the two: Hera the woman rejected her problem by throwing Hephaestus away, whereas Zeus managed to accept his, suffering labour pains in his head to bring it to consciousness. Allied to this difference in attitude between them is that Hera the matriarch hated her rival Athene, and did everything in her power to oppose her (though Athene always won in the end), while Zeus the patriarch, while having an up and down relationship with Hephaestus, did not oppose him to anything like the same extent.

This extreme opposition between a woman and her brother's daughter has a basic and institutionalised parallel to it in the most compact primitive kinship systems known in the world, founded on the opposition between two mutually hostile matrilineal moieties. ("The Incest Taboo and the Virgin Archetype" [1945] and "On Psychic Consciousness" [1959], John Layard, *Eranos Jahrbuch*, 12 and 28, Zurich, Rhein-Verlag. Reprinted by Spring Publications, 1972.) There the mother and her brother's daughter belong to opposite moieties and are thus traditionally and functionally opposed. These mutually hostile matrilineal moieties, which have not only cultural but also basic psychological significance, are also to be found reflected in the form of the 'two women', 'two wives', or 'two mothers' so constantly met with in our myth, balanced also by 'two fathers' — the son's own father and his mother's brother. The dual pattern is repeated with daughters in our myth in the case of the stepmother's daughter and Olwen herself, who are intertwined as worldly bride and anima. Culhwch also had two *sets* of 'fathers': firstly his own father, and by extension his stepmother's former husband; secondly there were on a much grander scale the negative father-figure Ysbaddaden and the positive one Arthur.

These all can be regarded as psychological functions of one another, but all these 'background' or 'shadow' figures in the myth as well as many other features of them have their counterparts in kinship systems. Both the kinship systems and the mythological accounts reflect the archetypal pattern behind both the physical entities of actual people, and the immaterial entities of their various spirit forms (for example, psychic functions). Both point towards a fuller realisation of the value of the feminine side for the male, as mediated through the actions of his older male counsellor or counsellors — the actual parent, or any of the father counterparts as exemplified in our myth — working through to a real relationship with the feminine side of his heritage. In the ancient heritage of mankind's imagination, Zeus and Hera were even closer than cousins — they were brother and sister (even referred to as twins); so also the lesser relatedness of Culhwch and Olwen, whose offspring we do not hear about. Our cross-cousin marriage system has loosened its hold: less is expected from the clan in man's struggle in life; more from his wife. This pattern is also reflected in his psychological development: his patrilineal representatives (knowledge, functions, or what-have-you) are called upon to serve as assistants in the effort to win through to his true marriage. This is represented in the flesh by a real relationship with his feminine partner, and spiritually, by a real relationship with his feminine soul.

LINGUISTIC NOTES

1. *Cilydd* means "friend, companion". *Celyddon* is most likely a Welsh rendering of *Caledonia*; if so, it would contribute to the importance of the North as a direction in the story. *Wledig* is a title variously translated as "emperor" or "governor": it implies a respected sovereign.

2. *Goleuddydd*, "light of day". Although the sun seems to be consistently masculine in known Celtic tradition (cf. *Belenus*, etc.), one would be tempted to see here a female sun-figure (as in Baltic or Germanic tradition), especially since she is contrasted with the lunar world of Olwen and the "second mother".

3. Anlawdd, who, as has been mentioned, is traditionally thought to be Arthur's maternal grandfather, seems to have been a historical ruler of Anglesey.

4. Doged was a historical king of the area around Denbigh, known for his tragic life. He was canonized as a saint.

5. *Ysbaddaden*, "hawthorn". The hawthorn is known to have been associated with a mother-goddess in antiquity (e.g., Cardea in Rome). Judging from a variety of European traditions, ancient and modern (unluckiness of the hawthorn month for marriage, burning of hawthorn-wood at weddings, etc.), one may conclude that this plant was symbolic of chastity in its terrible *vagina dentata* form (thorns around the white blossom). See also Note 31. *Pencawr = pen* "head", *cawr* "giant". The more obvious meaning is "Chief Giant", though it can also be understood as "giant head".

6. *Glewlwyd Gafaelfawr*: *glew* "brave", *llwyd* "grey"; *gafael* "grasp", *mawr* "great" — "Grey-Valour of the Mighty Grasp", a name well-suited to the gatekeeper as "Old Wise Man". Glewlwyd Gafaelfawr is a well-known figure in Welsh Arthurian tradition, and appears in other tales.

7. *Cei:* Caius, a Latin name. Probably from the memory of a figure associated with the historical Arthur. *Bedwyr* — the name of Cei's constant companion — is of obscure etymology.

8. *Gwenhwyfar*, "white phantom". The "three Guineveres" may originally have been a triad of goddesses, representing three complementary aspects of femininity. Such triads are well-known in Celtic tradition.

9. *Wrnach* (or *Gwrnach*, as it is also rendered) is certainly an Irish name, though its meaning is unclear. Perhaps it is an adjective *uirneach*, from *urna* "a hank of threads, flax, etc.", with some such meaning as "shaggy" (?).

10. Gwyddno Garanhir ("Long-crane" or "Long-legs") is famous as the Lord of a country which sank, Atlantis-like, beneath the waves. His hamper is one of the "thirteen magic treasures of Britain".

11. According to Lady Guest, there is a folk-tale in which this harp is stolen by a dwarf from a giant. In its magic properties it is clearly modelled on the Dagda's harp in Irish tradition.

240

12. *Diwrnach* is another Irish name of uncertain origin. The Celtic prefix *di-*, meaning "un-", may perhaps be intended here, to make of *di-wrnach* an opposite to *wrnach*. The meaning of the opposition remains unclear, but the two characters do form a symbolic pair: one owns a *sword* (male symbol), the other a *cauldron* (female symbol). These, incidentally, are two of the four great treasures which Celtic mythology attributes to the Tuatha Dé Danaan (the ancient Irish race endowed with godlike powers): the sword of Nuada and the spear of Lug (which can be considered male), the cauldron of the Dagda, and Lia Fail, the Kingstone (which can be considered female). These symbols appear to be very ancient and variants of them are known from as far away as Japan. They appear in medieval literature as "the Grail Hallows". They have also become the four suits of the Lesser Trumps in the Tarot, as well as, in a debased form, the four suits of our modern card pack. The allusion to the cauldron as being "filled with all the treasures of Ireland" makes it almost certain that the author was thinking of the Dagda's cauldron.

13. *Odgar* and *Aedd (Aodh)* are characters taken from Irish tradition.

14. *Ysgithyr* "tusk"; *wyn* "white"; *pen* "chief"; *baedd* "boar": White Tusk Chief Boar.

15. *Cadw of Prydain* (also rendered as Gado of [North] Britain): it is supposed that this Pictish character was once the central figure of a cycle of heroic myths now lost to us, but well-known to the author of our tale. The author is obviously well acquainted with all the branches of Celtic tradition, not only the Welsh, and intends to make a synthesis of them in this story. Having drawn from Irish myth by introducing Odgar son of Aedd and his cauldron, he now brings in the Pictish tradition with Cadw.

16. *Gwyddolwyn: gwydd* "knowledge, science", *gwyn* "white". Dwarfs are not necessarily earth-symbols in Celtic mythology. From the extant literature and iconography, they often seem to be associated with knowledge, inspiration, science (cf. the famous episode with the dwarf Gwion in the Taliesin story). Gwyddolwyn may have been a dwarf of this kind. He has a daughter named Eurolwen ("golden-white") who is mentioned in Arthur's long list of associates earlier in the tale. Perhaps there is a "hot", solar symbol here (cf. East-West).

17. There is some doubt as to whether this name should be read as *Rhin Farnod* "wonderful judgment" or *Rhyn Farfod* "frozen beard". [It has also been rendered *Rhin Barnawd*.] The derivation from *rhyn* "cold, frost" is more probable, especially as it would explain why the liquids never turn sour. Gwyddolwyn and Rhynnon may have been "hot-cold" opposites in a myth now lost to us.

18. *Drudwyn: drud* in one sense means "precious", in another "reckless"; *gwyn* "white".

19. *Greid* probably means "intense heat" (*greidio* "to scorch").

20. *Cors:* "reeds, bog".

241

21. *Canhastyr* or *Canastr* seems to mean "hundred bonds" or "hundred connexions"; as J. Loth comments, "quelquechose de très compliqué".

22. *Cilydd*, "companion, friend".

23. *Eiddoel*, if from *eidd-*, implies "zeal, ardour". *Aer* may refer to an old word for "fighting, war".

24. *Garselit* is the Welsh transliteration of an Irish name, possibly from *gar-* (prefix meaning "short, small") and *sealad* "while, period of time" – "the man of a short while" (?) or perhaps "the quick man".

25. The spelling of this name is uncertain; it also appears as *Dissull.* It must have puzzled the original copyist as much as the modern philologist.

26. Gwyn ("white") son of *Nudd* (the silver-handed god who, in Ireland, wields the Sword, one of the "four treasures") is, as King of Faerie, the traditional leader of the "wild hunt"; this is also called "King Arthur's hunt" in certain parts of Europe, which implies an ancient association between the two characters.

27. Dyfed being South Wales, the enumeration of Celtic regions recruited for the hunt is continued here.

28. *Aned* is unclear. *Aethlem* would be the feminine form of *aethlym*, "sharp-pointed". There is also a possibility that it might be an Irish name, from *aith-* (prefix indicating repeated action) and *léam* "jump, leap". Perhaps both names are from Irish sources.

29. *Bwlch* means "gap, notch". The names are probably just onomatopaeic, intended as a joke, as is indeed the whole passage.

30. *Llyn* "lake"; *llyw* "rudder", "ruler" (cf. French *gouverner*, from which we have both *gouvernail* and *gouverneur*): Lake of the Rudder, of the Ruler. (*Llyw* may have been *lliw* "colourful".)

31. Caer Loyw ("glossy castle") is Glastonbury, an important ritual centre in the ancient Celtic world. It also appears in the Mabinogi of *Peredur,* as the abode of the witches who initiate the young hero and must be overcome by him in the end. By being a "glass castle", it is a place of the great Mother-Goddess of life and death – the Celts often imagined the land of the dead as a spiralling castle of glass, presided over by a goddess (e.g. Caer Arianrhod), and sometimes equated with a constellation (Corona Borealis). It is also the home of the Glastonbury Thorn, a sacred hawthorn tree around which pagan ritual continued to be practised until the 17th century, when the Puritans destroyed it. This serves to reinforce our symbolic interpretation of *Ysbaddaden.*

32. *Gast Rhymhi*, "the bitch of Rhymhi". Rhymhi (or Rhymni) is a small town in Monmouthshire (now Gwent).

33. Celli Wig, Arthur's stronghold, is from *celli* "grove" and *gwig* "wood". This might suggest a *nemeton*, a ritual centre of some sort in the forest. The *Triads* reinforce this image by saying that Arthur held gatherings there on religious high holidays.

34. *Creiddylad* may be related to a word for "rowan".

35. *Gwythyr* may have some association with *gwyth* "anger, fury" and *Greidiol* (or *Greidawl*) may be from *Greid* with the same idea of heat. Since Gwyn ap Nudd is a subterranean, "cold" figure, an inhabitant of the Land of the Dead, Gwythyr ap Greidiol may be his opposite, and both may represent the waning and waxing halves of the year respectively (a Sun-Moon idea again). See Note 36. Greidiol, Gwythyr's father, may be the Greidiol or Greidawl Gallddofydd ("divine capacity") who is famous as a mythological architect of extraordinary talent.

36. *Nwython* is from the Pictish *Naithon*, corresponding to an Irish name *Neachtán*, which itself has a cognate in the Latin *Neptunus*. *Nodens (Nudd)* was identified with Neptune by classical writers. Perhaps the Welsh author, obviously a very erudite man, was jokingly aware that Lludd, Nudd, and Nwython could be interpreted as being all the same person.

37. The North, in Welsh, is *gogledd,* the "place of the left hand" (*cledd* "left hand", archaic). One could associate it with the "sinister" implications of the left-hand direction, the matriarchal, lunar "feeling" side as opposed to the patriarchal, solar "thinking" side.

38. May-calends *(Calan Mai)* correspond to the ancient Celtic feast of Bealtaine (May 1), which was one of the turning-points of the year, the first day of summer, as Samhain (November 1) was the equally important first day of winter. This fact would support the identification of Gwythyr and Gwyn with the waxing and waning halves of the year.

39. Llydaw is Brittany (Armorica). Another Celtic region is brought in to participate in this Pan-Celtic story.

40. Gware (or Gwri) Gwallt Euryn ("golden hair") is none other than Pryderi, the hero of the *Four Branches of the Mabinogi*. This is the name he bore when he was the fosterling of Teyrnon, not knowing his real parents. He himself thus appears in this tale as an "immature hero".

41. Glythfyr the Breton. The name is obscure: it seems to come from *glyth* "gluttonous" and *byr* "short".

42. Llamrei is from *llamu* "to leap", and means something like "gambolling".

43. *Menw* means "mind, sense, feeling, intelligence". He is a mythological figure associated with inspiration and imagination. *Teirgwaedd* would seem to mean "three shouts". A story well known to the author's contemporaries must have been associated with this name (as with many others in the tale), but it is now lost to us.

44. *Caledfwlch* ("hard notch") is Arthur's sword. It is fitting in this context that the sword (male symbol) should conquer the cauldron (female symbol).

45. The Summer Country (Gwlad-yr-Haf) refers to Somerset near the Severn. Its inhabitants, the *Galedin,* were considered a separate Celtic people.

46. *Llwyddog:* "successful".

47. Most of the piglets' names are various words for "pig". Two of them, Banw and Benwig, seem to correspond to the king's Ban (Lancelot's father) and Benwick of Arthurian literature – further evidence that the swine are indeed transformed men.

48. Osla Gyllellfawr: *Osla* is a non-Celtic name, probably Anglic in origin, related to *Offa* or *Oswald.*

49. This outlandish name is variously spelled *Kagymwri* (with the expected Brythonic sound-change), *Kachmwri,* and *Kacmwri.* It could hardly be a Welsh name. Lacking better evidence, it may be suggested that this is a "non-Celtic Pictish" name. The author might have had a special intention in coupling two non-Celts during the following episode.

50. *Gwyngelli:* "white grove".

51. The term used here is *uffern,* the Christian hell.

52. Hygwydd seems to mean "who knows well", from *hy-* (prefix indicating possibility or facility) and *gwydd* "knowledge".

53. *Amren* is obscure. *Eiddil* means "slender, thin, weak".

54. *Carnwennan* "white hilt". (Black is here killed with white.)

LIST OF PLACE AND PERSONAL NAMES by Ivor B. John
(From the Appendix in *The Mabinogion* by Lady Charlotte Guest, with notes by Alfred Nutt, Long Acre, 1904.) [N.B.: The spelling is frequently outdated.]

Aber Deu Gleddyf – mouth of two swords – two rivers merge at this point, both called *Cleddyf*

Aber Gwy – mouth of the Wye

Anlawdd – fame or riches

Banw – swine, barrow pig

Bedwyr – *bedw*, birch

Cachamwri – Cacamwci, the great burdock?

Caerlleon – Latin: Castra Legionum – camp of the legion

Camlan – Camelot

Ceredigiawn – Cardiganshire

Cilgwri – nook or retreat

Cwm Cawlwyd – *cwm* – dingle; *cawl* – cabbage; or *Caw-lwyd* – Caw the Grey

Din Tywi – hill fort of the Tywi

Drudwyn, drudwen – a starling

244

Dyffryn Llychwr — valley of the Loughor

Esgeir Oervel [Esgair Oerfel] — Sescenn Uairbeoil in Leinster. The Welsh meaning —
mountain spur of cold weather

Gelli Wic — perhaps the old camp now known as Kelly Rounds in Cornwall

Glwyddyn Saer — Glwyddyn the carpenter

Glyn Ystun — a farm near Carmarthen

Gwalchmai — the hawk of May (cf. Gwalhaved — the hawk of summer)

Gwern Abwy — carrion swamp

Gwrhyr — long man

Gwynn (son of Nudd) — white son of Nudd. Secondary meaning — famous or
illustrious

Henwas — old servant or hero

Hygwyd — he who falls easily (?)

Kynwas [Cynwas] — old servant or hero

Llwch Ewin — pool of Ewin, now a bog, on the southern slope of the Amman Valley

Llwch Tawy — the pool of the Tawe, near Ynispenllwch [Ynyspenllwch], Swansea
valley

Llwyr son of Llwyryon — *llwyr* — completely

Llyn Lliwan — probably Llyn Llu-wan, the lake of the weak army

Mabon — hero, youth [Latin: Maponus — associated with Apollo]

Menw ab Teirgwaedd — the little one son of three shouts

Pengwaed — chief shout, or headland of the shout(?), (attracted by the context);
the modern Penwith in Cornwall

Pen Nant Govid — Source of Stream of Sorrow [cf. head of the Valley of Grief]

Prydwen — fair aspect

Rhinnon Rhin Barnawd — *rhin* — secret; *barnawd* — judge

Taredd — prince

Tawy — the modern Tawe, on which Swansea (Abertawe) stands

Ystrad Tywi — the valley of the Towy, Carmarthenshire

Ystrad Yw — valley of the Yw, small Brecknockshire stream

BIBLIOGRAPHY

Ellis, T.P. and Lloyd, John, translators, *The Mabinogion*, 2 vol., Oxford, Clarendon Press, 1929.

Graves, Robert, *The Greek Myths*, 2 vol., Harmondsworth, Penguin Books, 1955.

Guest, Lady Charlotte, translator, *The Mabinogion*, London, Bernard Quaritch, 1877.
— *The Mabinogion*, Notes by Alfred Nutt, Long Acre, 1904.
— *The Mabinogion*, London, J.M. Dent and Sons, 1906.

Jones, Gwyn and Jones, Thomas, translators, *The Mabinogion*, London, J.M. Dent and Sons, 1949 and 1974.

Kerényi, C., *The Gods of the Greeks*, London, Thames and Hudson, 1951.

Layard, John, *Stone Men of Malekula*, London, Chatto and Windus, 1942.
— "The Role of the Sacrifice of Tusked Boars in Malekulan Religion and Social Organisation", *Actes du Congrès International des Sciences Anthropologiques et Ethnologiques*, 2, Vienna, 1952. Reprinted in *Harvest*, London, 1954.
— "Boar Sacrifice", *The Journal of Analytical Psychology*, Vol. I, No. 1, 1955.
— "The Incest Taboo and the Virgin Archetype", *Eranos-Jahrbuch*, 12. Reprinted by Spring Publications, Dunquin Series, No. 5, 1972.

Loth, J., translator, "Les Mabinogion", *Cours de littérature celtique*, Arbois De Jubainville, M. H. d', Vol. 3, 4, Paris, 1889.

Rees, Alwyn and Rees, Brinley, *Celtic Heritage: Ancient Tradition in Ireland and Wales*, London, Thames and Hudson, 1961.

250

253